BRAIN/MIND AND PARAPSYCHOLOGY

PROCEEDINGS OF AN INTERNATIONAL CONFERENCE

HELD IN MONTREAL, CANADA

AUGUST 24–25, 1978

BRAIN/MIND AND PARAPSYCHOLOGY

PROCEEDINGS OF AN INTERNATIONAL CONFERENCE

HELD IN MONTREAL, CANADA

AUGUST 24–25, 1978

Edited By

Betty Shapin and Lisette Coly

PARAPSYCHOLOGY FOUNDATION, INC.
NEW YORK, N.Y.

Published by Parapsychology Foundation, Inc.
29 West 57th Street, New York, N.Y. 10019

ISBN 0-912328-31-2
Library of Congress Catalog Number: 79-84820

Manufactured in the United States of America

PARTICIPANTS

John Beloff	University of Edinburgh Edinburgh, Scotland, U.K.
J. Bigu	Elliot Lake Laboratory Canada Centre for Mineral and Energy Technology Ontario, Canada
Thomas H. Budzynski	Biofeedback Institute of Denver and University of Colorado Medical Center Colorado, U.S.A.
Norman F. Dixon	University College London, England, U.K.
Jan Ehrenwald	Roosevelt Hospital New York, New York, U.S.A.
Charles Honorton	Division of Parapsychology and Psychophysics Maimonides Medical Center Brooklyn, New York, U.S.A.
Edward F. Kelly	Duke University Durham, North Carolina, U.S.A.
Karl H. Pribram	Stanford University Stanford, California, U.S.A.
Emilio Servadio	Psychoanalytic Center of Rome Rome, Italy
Charles T. Tart	University of California, Davis California, U.S.A.

OBSERVERS

Louis Belanger	University of Montreal, Canada
David Davies	Province of Quebec, Canada
Douglas Dean	Princeton, New Jersey, U.S.A.
Leopold Goegebeur	British Columbia, Canada
Bernard Grad	McGill University, Montreal, Canada
Michael Thorne Kelly	Brooklyn, New York, U.S.A.
John McAllister	Ottawa, Canada
Diane McGuinness	Stanford University, California, U.S.A.
Carmen Olmedo	Jamaica, New York, U.S.A.
Luther Rudolph	Syracuse University, New York, U.S.A.
Charles Small	Montreal, Canada
Edward Storm	Syracuse University, New York, U.S.A.

CONTENTS

INTRODUCTION

ANGOFF: Good morning . . . I am Allan Angoff of the Parapsychology Foundation. For the trustees, I am glad to call to order and open this Twenty-Seventh Annual International Conference of the Foundation.

This conference series was begun, as many of you know, almost three decades ago, shortly after the Foundation was organized by Eileen J. Garrett and Frances P. Bolton, two remarkable friends of science and learning. They recognized in those pioneering days of parapsychology the importance of bringing together from all over the world some of the men and women working in isolation in a field regarded by so many of their academic colleagues as too remote for respectable research. Let us recall here again that even the daring Thomas Henry Huxley called it "twaddle" and that Hermann Von Helmholtz said telepathic communication "is clearly impossible." He would not believe it even if it were endorsed by the Fellows of the Royal Society itself.

In the midst of such negativism pervading the academic world—as it still does, albeit to a lesser degree—Eileen Garrett inaugurated these conferences to encourage those early parapsychologists "to advance beyond an easy orthodoxy of thought and technique into the broader aspect of physics, chemistry, and biology, and to relate these fields of research to the human personality and the largely unknown extrasensory capacities it contains."

Our conference sessions today and tomorrow are addressed to the theme: "Brain/Mind and Parapsychology," and the distinguished scientists it has brought together are, I think, eloquent testimony to the vision of Eileen Garrett and to what she so well termed—again, to use her precise words, "the advance beyond easy orthodoxy." A pause now for a moment, ladies and gentlemen, to introduce Eileen Garrett's successor—the second president of the Parapsychology Foundation —Mrs. Eileen Coly.

EILEEN COLY: I have already had the pleasure of greeting all the participants. Now I would like to welcome the observers, as well as the participants, to this conference. And let us start immediately.

CONVERGING LINES OF EVIDENCE ON MIND/BRAIN RELATIONS

EDWARD F. KELLY

Like most other working scientists, I find it altogether too easy to become completely absorbed in the endless details of ongoing research. For me, this conference therefore represents an exceptional opportunity to escape this mole-like everyday perspective and hopefully to acquire some renewed sense of location and direction within a larger intellectual context.

The central problem before us is whether the properties of minds are reducible to—or identifiable with—those of brains. I will assume without further discussion that this is largely, if not wholly, an empirical problem and not "just" a metaphysical or linguistic one. I further believe that the empirical status of the problem has shifted considerably within the last several decades. Certainly one of the perennial obstacles in approaching the relation of mind and brain has been the scarcity of detailed information about either term. Without exaggerating the volume of knowledge we now possess, I believe it is still fair to say this ignorance has been substantially reduced and is being further reduced at an accelerating rate.

The main contention of this paper is, therefore, that we may be approaching the point where converging lines of evidence from several sources can intersect to produce a decisive resolution of the mind-body riddle. In developing this theme, I will draw principally upon the three disciplines which have engaged me professionally, namely, cognitive psychology and computer modeling of human cognitive capacities, psychophysiology and contemporary neuroscience, and parapsychology. I certainly do not mean to imply that these supply the only relevant considerations—they simply represent relevant scientific areas with which I feel I have sufficient direct acquaintance to make realistic judgments. I particularly regret my scant acquaintance with the pertinent technical literature of philosophy. In what follows, I hope I do not commit too many philosophical *faux pas*, but perhaps my fellow participants will be able to correct or at least identify such defects as shall undoubtedly creep into the presentation.

An essential aspect of my thesis is that the complementary perspectives provided by these various disciplines can and must be brought to bear simultaneously. Historically, there have been relatively few discussions of these problems which successfully crossed traditional disciplinary lines, and none to my knowledge which has brought all the parties together with a realistic appraisal of the possible contribution of each. Many contemporary discussions continue to be infected either by an appalling ignorance and even disregard of neighboring disciplines, or by naive over-valuation of their results.

In this paper, therefore, I hope to take a small step in the proposed direction, by describing the framework of ideas within which I perceive this convergence of perspectives to be developing. Because of the large amount of ground to be covered, the presentation will necessarily be a bit telegraphic—really more of an outline than a finished presentation. However, with the exception of the fragmentary and speculative lattermost parts of the discussion (section 5), I feel confident that the framework is basically sound and that in a more detailed treatment the remaining gaps could, in principle, be filled.

1. Background-the biological perspective

Any contemporary discussion of the mind-body problem must take into account the enormous advances made during this century in our understanding of the brain. New manifestations of mind appear everywhere to be closely associated with modifications of structure or process in brains. In phylogeny, for example, we see the gross correlation across species between behavioral complexity and the level of organization of the nervous system. The rapid post-natal mental evolution of the human infant likewise is associated with massive structural and functional changes in the developing brain. And as human adults we are all presumably familiar with numerous facts—such as the normal diurnal fluctuations of consciousness and the effects of mild cerebral trauma induced by fatigue, alcohol and other substances, thumps on the head and so on—which reflect in a general way the dependence of mind on brain. But what about the details? In recent decades, freed at last from the rigid behaviorist prohibitions of an earlier era, brain researchers have begun to "open up the black box," using a vast variety of clinical, pharmacological, surgical, electrophysiological and behavioral approaches in increasingly successful efforts to understand what brains can do and how they do it.

Scientists and philosophers confronting the mind-body problem even as recently as a century ago knew only that the brain was in some gross undifferentiated way the organ of mind. Today we know a great deal more, although our knowledge undoubtedly remains in many respects extremely primitive relative to the virtually unimaginable complexity which the human brain presents. We know a lot about the structure and operation of neurons and even lower-level constituents. We also know something about the basic structural organization of the brain and, most important of all, we have begun to learn a fair amount about its functional organization, the contributions that different components of brain structure make to the overall content and organization of behavior.

Correlates of mind have spatial distribution inside the brain. In particular, the kinds of performances that we regard as most characteristic of human mental functioning are known to require specific, coordinated patterns of activity of a multiplicity of identifiable brain regions (particularly regions of the cerebral cortex), patterns which differ systematically from function to function (Luria, 1973). Similarly, one of the most conspicuous trends characterizing recent work in the psychology of perception is its increasingly physiological cast. In vision research, particularly, theory has become steadily more deeply anchored in increasingly detailed knowledge of structural and functional characteristics of the physiological pathways from eye to brain. Indeed, a variety of subtle phenomenological aspects of human vision such as color, brightness and numerous contrast effects have even been directly linked to identifiable physiological mechanisms, some as far out in the periphery as the retina (e.g., Lindsay and Norman, 1972; Uttal, 1973 and, for some especially elegant examples, Julesz, 1971 and Ratliff, 1965).

In short, the connection between mind and brain so far appears to grow ever tighter and more detailed as scientific understanding of the brain advances. Certainly, it is not unreasonable, particularly in light of these successes, to assume as a working hypothesis that this process can continue indefinitely without encountering any insuperable obstacles, and that properties of minds can ultimately be explained entirely by those of brains. For most scientists, however, this useful working principle appears to have become more like an established fact, or even an unquestionable axiom. Whereas the plain man, confronted by the phenomenological duality of private conscious experience and the public physical world, opts for interactive dualism in the tradition of Descartes, current opinion among brain scientists on the mind/body question—if they stop to think about it at all—strongly gravitates toward one or the other of the theories that assume a strict one-to-one relationship between mental events and physical events in the brain.

Epiphenomenalism, the old favorite, acknowledges mental events as a separate category of existents, but denies that they have causal efficacy; conscious experience is merely a passive by-product of causal processes occurring wholly within the brain. Identity theory and its variants, the current favorite, asserts that the duality exists in terminology only, and that mental events (should they ever need to be referred to) are in some difficult-to-analyze sense "identical" to certain subclasses of physical events occurring in the brain (Beloff, 1965; Shaffer, 1968). The identity theory in particular thus attempts to provide an intellectually respectable theoretical foundation for what everyone would presumably agree is currently sound scientific practice. Let us call this majority theoretical viewpoint and its relatives collectively "the official brain doctrine."

2. Heresy in the temple of neuroscience—some opponents of the official brain doctrine

In light of the above, it is of particular interest to study the opinions of those few eminent brain scientists who have publicly repudiated the official doctrine in favor of more or less explicitly interactionist positions. The principal examples I have in mind are Charles Sherrington (1955), Wilder Penfield (1975), and J. C. Eccles (Popper and Eccles, 1977), although there may well be others. I will not attempt to review their arguments here in any detail, but will focus chiefly on Eccles as the most contemporary and radical representative of the group. In no case do I think the arguments succeed.

For Eccles as well as the others, the bottom line of the argument is clearly the difficulty one intuitively feels in reconciling the unity of conscious experience—and especially self-consciousness—with spatially and temporally diverse physical processes in the brain. This feeling by itself, however, is certainly insufficient to establish interactionism. Therefore, it is of much greater importance to examine Eccles' more substantive arguments, in which he attempts to supply positive evidence of aspects of human activity that, in his view, resist explanation in terms of brain function alone.

For concreteness, let me give a few examples. First, he cites phenomena which suggest to him that the relation between neural events and conscious experience may not be 1:1 in the manner required by the official doctrine. In particular, he cites the work of Libet on "antedating." The idea may be expressed as follows:[1] The elaboration of conscious experience following stimulation takes time;

in particular, suppose that it takes longer to hear an isolated *soft* drum-beat than an isolated *loud* drum-beat. Yet, if loud and soft beats are interspersed in a sequence of equal short intervals, we hear them in their proper temporal relations—hence the experience of the soft beats is somehow referred backward in time. Eccles doubts that brain mechanisms alone can account for such effects (Chapter E-2, Section 9.2; Chapter E-7).

Second, he reviews some of the modern work on sensory coding in mammalian nervous systems. For example, while giving due credit to the impressive results on hierarchies of feature-extraction mechanisms and the like in the visual system, he correctly points out that the known processes provide only a fragmentary analysis of the optically available information, and do not yet come anywhere close to explaining the overall visual synthesis which ultimately emerges. A fortiori, we cannot at present explain the larger synthesis of perceptual experience over multiple sensory modalities. Although Eccles does not explicitly argue or even claim that this synthetic activity could not in principle be carried out by the brain itself, it is evident that this is what he in fact thinks (Chapter E-2, Section 10.3; Chapter E-7, especially p. 358).

Similarly, he describes work by Kornhuber on elementary voluntary movements (Chapter E-3, Section 19). The critical finding is the gradual development of a surface-negative potential in the cerebral cortex preceding simple movements such as a self-initiated finger-tap. This "readiness potential" takes surprisingly long to develop (almost a full second), and is distributed surprisingly widely over the cortex (p. 285). Eccles argues that this is best explained as the effect of a weak influence cumulatively exerted upon the ongoing activity of the cortex at critically poised "liaison" regions by an independent entity which he terms "the self-conscious mind," and which he feels must be responsible for all the "higher" mental phenomena, including the integration of both perceptual experience and voluntary motor activity.

In this last example, we are shading over into the sort of higher-level argument that is really central to Eccles' presentation. I think he sees the power of his theory as residing not so much in an incontrovertibly superior ability to explain *particular* phenomena as in the ease with which it can assimilate a wide *variety* of phenomena. Other things being more or less equal, this would certainly be a defensible attitude. In this case, however, I fear other things are far from equal. None of the individual examples given is remotely persuasive as an argument against the possibility that brain processes might in principle account for everything. Even in the antedating experiments, the information about the presence of the weak stimulus is already available at the cortex in the required time frame; the fact that we do not know at present how to account for the antedating phenomenon in terms of brain processes, therefore, by no means constitutes a demonstration that in principle we never will.

The theory is central, an imaginative construction that goes very far beyond presently available data. In fact, I think it is fair to say that Eccles uses his neurophysiology, in essence, to rationalize or interpret a pre-existing theory whose real intellectual origins lie elsewhere. He has been a declared dualist for many years; his dualism is apparently founded chiefly upon the Sherringtonian intuition that the phenomena of brain and mind are irreducibly incommensurate (*cf.* Sherrington, 1955, pp. 205, 218, 244, 252), but is also appears to have sources in his Catholicism, in a powerful experience (on OBE?) he had as a teenager (Popper and Eccles, 1977, p. 357), and in a naive belief that only dualism can "restore to the human person the senses of wonder, of mystery and of value" (p. 374). In the present exposition, he has updated his familiar dualistic theory considerably in light of recent neurophysiological discoveries. In particular, his hypothesis that the self-conscious mind interacts with critically-poised regions of the brain is now greatly refined. The critical regions of the brain where interactions with the self-conscious mind can occur now seem to him most likely to involve the upper layers of vertically oriented cortical modules recently revealed by Szentagothai's microstructural investigations. Moreover, on the basis of Sperry's split-brain studies and related clinical investigations he further believes the relevant modules to be confined exclusively, or at least primarily, to the dominant hemisphere, in particular to areas concerned with language comprehension (Wernicke's area, Brodman areas 39, 40) and to the prefrontal cortex (p. 363).

While the increasing specificity of the theory is welcome and good, the theory itself remains, in my view, highly premature. The phenomena adduced in its support, while perhaps consistent with a dualistic interpretation, cannot possibly serve to establish it since alternative possibilities of explanation based on brain processes alone are nowhere decisively excluded. Moreover, and more seriously, the Popper/Eccles theory seems to me to exemplify conspicuously what I take to be the central scientific problems confronting any dualism:[2]

1) First there are the diachronic questions: Where does immaterial mind first appear in the phylogenetic spectrum, and at what point in the course of ontogeny? Closely related to these (but more interesting to me) is the synchronic or functional question: How shall we

determine which human functions are mediated entirely by mechanical processes in the brain, and which functions require
intervention of the immaterial mind? There are many complex
regulative and goal-directed processes going on which never require
conscious attention (indeed may well require the *absence* of such
attention), or which once did but no longer do. Some of these, such as
driving a car, clearly entail complex perceptual and judgmental
processes of a rather sophisticated sort quite impossible for lesser
brains. In perception, thinking and the rest, where do brain-processes
end and mind-processes begin?

2) Supposing that we feel compelled to admit such a division of labor
among two or more irreducible parts, what account can we provide of
the relations among them? In this respect, Eccles' account is hardly
more satisfactory than the crude instrumental analogies of earlier
times. Instead of an immaterial pianist playing the bodily piano, we are
offered a self-conscious mind which scans, interprets and reciprocally
influences the activity of "open" cortical modules. This is surely
unsatisfactory. Except by way of very indirect technical arrangements,
we have absolutely no acquaintance with events taking place in our
brains.[3] Moreover, this and all similar metaphoric accounts seem to me
implicitly to confer upon the mind an entirely unrealistic degree of
independence of the body. Although as a parapsychologist I am well
aware that many transient experiences of such separability have been
reported, these experiences so far remain open to alternative
explanations, and in no way alter the fact that the vast bulk of every
individual's mental life appears to go forward in strict conjunction
with, and dependence upon, a *particular*, *intact* and *functioning* brain.

3) Finally, what really is gained by ascribing complex mental
functions of whatever sort to an entity of the type Eccles proposes? We
are still faced with exactly the same problems we might have hoped to
solve in terms of observable or inferable brain mechanisms; the
problems simply recur in a relatively inaccessible domain. William
James (1909) identified this problem with characteristic precision:

"You see no deeper into the fact that a hundred sensations get
compounded or known together by thinking that a 'soul' does the
compounding than you see into a man's living eighty years by thinking
of him as an octogenarian, or into our having five fingers by calling us
pendactyls. Souls have worn out both themselves and their welcome,
that is the plain truth. Philosophy ought to get the manifolds of
experience unified on principles less empty. Like the word 'cause,' the
word 'soul' is but a theoretic stop-gap—it marks a place and claims it
for a future explanation to occupy." (p. 209)[4]

Problems of this magnitude should certainly make us tremble before the prospect of embracing interactionism. At least, we should certainly demand much more compelling evidence than Eccles has so far been able to offer. I think he is entirely correct in stressing how little we really know, as against the hubris of many contemporary brain scientists, and indeed, his theory or something like it might ultimately prove to be correct. On the other hand, he displays a large amount of hubris himself, by dismissing, in effect, any possibility that mechanistic models will ever come significantly closer to explaining the central capacities of the human mind.

The dismissal takes two forms, really. On the one hand, Eccles seems strangely reluctant to entertain the possibility that future discoveries about the brain itself might run counter to his hypothesis and strengthen the official doctrine. Much more damaging—and indeed this seems to me the most fundamental flaw in the book—neither Popper nor Eccles seems to have any appreciation of the fundamental developments that have transformed cognitive science in recent decades. For example, particularly in their "Dialogues" it becomes clear that one of the central facts driving them toward dualism is the *activity* of the mind as against what they seem to believe is the necessary passivity of a mechanical apparatus based on brain processes alone. Related to this, they point to a number of phenomena—such as incorrigible illusions, reversing figures, recognition of accuracy of memory retrieval, awareness of awareness, etc.—which suggest a kind of hierarchical organization of levels of integration of conscious experience; although no compelling arguments are provided to show that any portion of any such hierarchy necessarily lies outside the brain itself, they seem to believe that the phenomena cited can in principle only be explained by a dualistic theory of the sort they propose. In a particularly revealing example which exemplifies both of these attitudes, Popper rails at length against the old linear associationist theory of thinking, correctly describing it as a transposition of earlier and outmoded philosophical doctrines into an artifically simplified conception of conditioning processes in the brain. He and Eccles both seem to believe that simplistic theories of this sort are the inevitable outcome of mechanistic theorizing and that, in demolishing them, they are *ipso facto* establishing interactionism.

In this expectation, they are without doubt gravely mistaken. The image of the brain that appears implicitly to guide and limit their assessment of the capacities of mechanism—as it had Sherrington's decades previously—is essentially that of a gigantically complicated automatic telephone switchboard, a network of passive relays. But, since Sherrington's time, a vastly more powerful mechanistic technology has come into being, one which is certainly capable of capturing many more of the properties—such as activity and hierarchical structure—that Popper and Eccles correctly view as fundamental to human mental processes, and that in fact have long since become cornerstones of modern cognitive theory. Let me briefly review these developments.

3. The analysis of mind as an information-processing system—cybernetics, artificial intelligence, and cognitive psychology

The old concept of "machine"—and no doubt for most of us still the everyday concept—is that of a physical contraption which transforms energy by means of pushes and pulls involving gears, pulleys, shafts and so on. The fundamental insight underlying the modern developments is the recognition that these physical arrangements are quite secondary. The essential attribute of the machine is rather that its normal behavior is *bound by rule*.

This insight opened the way to an enormous enrichment of our concept of mechanism, beginning with the contributions of logicians and mathematicians in the 30's and 40's and continuing into the present day. These developments, furthermore, immediately began to have profound impact on the questions we are addressing in this conference.

For example, it was quickly recognized that machines could transform information as well as energy, and that a machine could in principle utilize information about its performance to regulate its own behavior. These ideas had immediate and urgent practical application in the construction of servocontrolled antiaircraft systems during the second World War, but their general theoretical implications for the understanding of behavior were no less apparent. Rosenblueth, Wiener and Bigelow (1943) showed that, from the point of view of an external observer, a device constructed on this principle of "negative feedback" behaved purposively, i.e., as a teleological mechanism. Thus, mechanism penetrated one of the last strongholds of vitalist thinking.[5]

These analogies were developed much more systematically by Wiener in his influential 1948 book *Cybernetics* (significantly subtitled *Control and Communication in the Animal and the Machine*). In addition to providing a general analytic theory of feedback control processes, Wiener gave a number of concrete examples of physiological phenomena that seemed to fall within the province of the theory.

Nevertheless, the direct applications of cybernetic theory at this level have remained relatively limited. The real power of the ideas emerged in conjunction with the extremely flexible applications technology provided by the digital computer.

To appreciate the full significance of these developments, it is necessary to follow the generalization of the concept of "machine" to its ultimate development in the hands of the English logician A. M. Turing and several others.[6] Turing devised an abstract representation which formalized his intuition of the core meaning of the concept of mechanism, as applied to the theory of computable functions. Any computation can be regarded as the transformation of a string of input symbols by a sequence of rule-governed steps into a string of output symbols. A procedure which is guaranteed to lead to the desired output in a finite sequence of steps is called an "algorithm" or "effective procedure." Turing envisioned a machine consisting simply of a read/write head operating on an infinite tape ruled off into squares. The behavior of the machine is governed by a set of rules organized as quintuples; given the machine's current state and the input symbol written in the current square, these rules instruct the machine to change state, write a new symbol on the tape and move one square left or right. By altering the number of states, the size of the vocabulary and the behavioral rules, an immense variety of behaviors can be realized by such devices. In fact, Turing argued persuasively that *anything* that would naturally qualify as an algorithm can be represented by a suitably constructed machine of this sort. He further showed that he could construct a "universal" Turing machine which would simulate the behavior of any other Turing machine. The intuitive notion of "effective procedure" was thus explicated in terms of the formal notion of "realizable by a Turing machine." That this is not an arbitrary result, but, in a fundamental sense, exhausts the possible meaning of the term is strongly suggested by the fact that several other workers arrived at provably identical results from widely different starting points.

Because of their utter simplicity, Turing machines do even very simple things, such as adding two numbers, in extremely cumbersome ways. Their direct significance is theoretical, not practical. But the link to a vast field of applications was made when it was demonstrated that any digital computer is also in effect a universal Turing machine. McCulloch and Pitts (1943) further showed that networks suitably constructed from artifically idealized neurons could realize the elementary logical functions of computers, and other workers promptly demonstrated that the same capacities could be realized using richer elements that more nearly approximated the characteristics of real neurons. Thus, it became apparent that brains in principle have access to the capacities of Turing machines. They may conceivably have additional capacities as well, but if so—and this is the essential point—these capacities probably lie beyond the reach of understanding based on mechanistic principles alone. To the extent that mind and brain are governed by formalizable rule, their activities can in principle be modeled on a suitably programmed general-purpose digital computer. Indeed, to those who are sufficiently committed *a priori* to mechanistic principles, the very existence of a given class of behavior virtually *entails* the possibility of such formalization.

There were other more specific theoretical results that further strengthened this point of view. Consider, for example, some of the early results in theoretical linguistics. The skills underlying use of language, certainly one of the central manifestations of human mentality, defied explanation in terms of simple conditioning and S/R models (although many were offered). Chomsky (1963) and others showed that the possible classes of formal models of these skills (generative grammars) formed a hierarchy, in which the weakest or most highly constrained class (finite-state grammars) was obtained from the strongest or least constrained class (unrestricted rewriting systems) by the application of progressively severe constraints on the form of the permissible rules of the grammar. Furthermore, the hierarchy of grammars corresponds to a hierarchy of classes of automata derived from Turing machines in parallel fashion. Formal results from automata studies thus transferred to the analysis of candidate grammatical theories. Chomsky (1957) was able to show that the existing psychological and linguistic proposals for theories of language, when formalized, corresponded to the weakest members of the hierarachy of grammars, and that these grammars were in principle too weak to account for systematic structural properties of many kinds of sentences in natural languages such as English. He was thus led to his famous theory of transformational grammar as the weakest class of theory which is still strong enough to account for the known grammatical facts of language. The result that the corresponding automata are weaker than Turing machines greatly strengthened the presumption that linguistic behavior might be formalizable for computer modeling.[7]

The central idea that computers and brains could fruitfully be regarded as two varieties of a more general class of information-processing mechanisms quickly took root. The ground was very well prepared. Indeed, these developments seem to me an inevitable outcome of our western scientific tradition. This is not meant disparagingly, however; I have stressed these results about Turing machines and so on precisely to underscore the impressive depth of the theoretical foundation on which the ensuing applications rest, a foundation which I feel has not been adequately appreciated by many critics of this kind of work.

In practice, the applications came a bit slowly at first. In part this was due to purely technical factors. The early computers were small, slow and highly prone to malfunction. More important, in the early days programming a computer was an exasperating business requiring detailed familiarity with the lowest-level details of its hardware organization. The primitives of the available languages referred to data structures and operations virtually at the hardware level. As the technology advanced, however, machines grew larger, faster and more reliable, and so-called "higher-order" languages (such as FORTRAN) were created whose primitives refer to data structures and operations at a level which is relatively natural for human problem-solvers. Programs written in the higher order language congenial to the user are then translated by special programs into the internal language of the computer for subsequent execution by the hardware.

I mention these details because they relate to the other main reason for the delay, which is more theoretical in nature and involves a basic question of strategy. The fantastic complexities of the brain can obviously be studied at many different levels from the molecular or even sub-molecular on up. At what level shall we seek scientific explanations of human mental activity? Many scientists, particularly those working at lower levels of the hierarchy of approaches, assume that events at the higher levels are in principle reducible to events at lower levels, and that reductive explanations employing the concepts of the lower levels are necessarily superior or more fundamental. Like many other psychologists, I strongly disagree with this view. Furthermore, I believe it is easily shown to be false (or at best inefficient), even without appeal to the (controversial) notion that higher levels may display "emergent" properties not predictable from those of lower levels.

Consider, for example, the problem of understanding the behavior of a computer playing chess under the control of a stored program. It seems obvious that we might observe the behavior of its flip-flops forever without gaining the slightest real understanding of the principles that govern its behavior. Similarly, one of the essential characteristics of both human and animal behavior is that functional invariance at a higher level may be coupled with extreme diversity at lower levels. Thus, the rats whose cortex Lashley surgically disturbed in efforts to locate the engram could wobble, roll or swim to the food box, and I can write a given message with either hand or even with my feet if necessary. Attempted explanations based on activities of the participating muscle-groups, neurons, and so on would probably never get to the essential feature which is the invariance.

Thus, it seems appropriate in general to seek a distinctively "psychological" level of explanation of mental processes. For the computer simulation approach in particular this entails identifying an appropriate set of elementary information structures and processes which seem powerful enough to account for the relevant behavior. [Strictly speaking, for a consistent mechanist and identity theorist there is another requirement. The hypothesized information structures and processes should conceivably be physically realizable in the brain given the known properties of neurons or, at least, should not be demonstrably inconsistent with those properties. However, it is important to recognize that successful use of the computer as a tool of psychological understanding does not require the (obviously false) presumption of literal identity of computers and brains.][8]

By the late 1950's and early 1960's, a number of higher-order languages had been created which emphasized the capacities of computers as general-purpose information-transforming devices, rather than their algebraic and "number-crunching" capacities. These languages (such as IPL-V, SLIP, LISP, etc.) provided facilities for creating and manipulating complex tree-like data structures consisting of hierarchically ordered and cross-referenced lists of symbols. Structures of this sort played a central role in theoretical linguistics, and in this and other ways the new languages seemed to many workers to fall at about the right level of abstraction to support realistic efforts to model many aspects of human cognition.

Previous generations of workers had been obliged either to try to force mental processes to conform to artificially simple but relatively rigorous behavioristic models, or to lapse into the uncontrolled introspection and mentalistic speculations of an earlier era. Now, suddenly, we were provided with a conceptual and technical apparatus sufficiently rich to express much of the necessary complexity without loss of rigor. The black box could be stuffed at will with whatever mechanism seemed necessary to account for a given behavior. A complicated theory could be empirically tested by implementing it in the form of a computer program and verifying its ability to generate the behavior, or to simulate a record of the behavior. The seminal ideas of Craik (1943) could at last be put into practice.

Enthusiasm for the information-processing approach to human

cognition fairly crackles through the pages of influential early books such as Miller, Galanter and Pribram (1960). Their enthusiasm has been amply justified in the ensuing flood of theoretical and experimental work based on these ideas. In addition to the specific efforts at computer modeling of cognitive functions that is our main concern here, the rise of information-processing psychology has also brought in its train a healthy reawakening of broader interests in many of the old central concerns of psychology, such as mental imagery, thinking and consciousness.

The depth to which the metaphor of the human mind as an information-processing machine has penetrated cognitive psychology can, perhaps, best be appreciated by referring to recent introductory books such as Arbib (1972), Lindsay and Norman (1972), Oatley (1972) and many others. There can be no doubt that this metaphor has been and will continue to be enormously productive scientifically. However, it currently appears well on the way toward hardening into literal dogma, a companion to the official brain doctrine. I wish now to examine some indications that as dogma it is false.

4. Some difficulties in the mechanical concept of mind

A convincing demonstration that the essential capacities of the human mind can be embodied in technical artifacts would, in practice, presumably be fatal to an interactionist theory such as proposed by Eccles. Although it would not be strictly disproven—since the mind or "parts" thereof might conceivably be immaterial, but still governed by mechanist principles—it would certainly seem rather superfluous. On the other hand, a convincing demonstration that *any* capacity of the human mind can in principle *not* be embodied in such artifacts refutes mechanism and opens the way to various alternative possibilities.

In the following discussion, I wish to maintain a behaviorist perspective on the concept of "mental capacities" in order to avoid being immediately drawn into first-person questions about whether robots could be conscious, have feelings and so on (cf. Anderson, 1964). This is not because I think that consciousness is not important, or irrelevant, but because I think I can establish the point I wish to make without becoming entangled in these very difficult and quite possibly inconclusive arguments. Similarly, I follow Turing (1950) in excluding as inessential various matters pertaining to the physical embodiment of the artifactual intelligence—its sensory and motor appendages and so on. By "essential capacities," therefore, I shall mean rather the kinds of general behavioral skills that ordinary persons display in perceiving, thinking, producing and understanding language and so on. I am also willing to relax the requirements still further by allowing that a demonstration of such skills could be convincing even if not terribly general, provided that the principles embodied in the machine were convincingly generalizable. This loose characterization will suffice for present purposes.[9]

In his justly famous 1950 article, Turing himself expressed the expectation that by the end of this century machines will have advanced to the point where ". . . the use of words and general educated opinion will have altered so much that one will be able to speak of machines thinking without expecting to be contradicted" (Anderson, 1964, p. 14). Although this remark is perhaps a bit guarded, it is clear from other parts of his discussion that he fully expects machines to display what any reasonable person would be obliged to regard as general intelligence. Indeed, the major part of the article is devoted to clearing away various kinds of possible *a priori* objections to this thesis. Of course, as Turing acknowledges, this is still all theory. How far has this work progressed?

With the appearance of suitable higher-order languages in the late 50's and early 60's, numerous research groups set to work to endow computers with capacities for varied kinds of skilled performance, including game-playing (especially complex games such as checkers and chess), problem-solving (for example, proving theorems in the propositional calculus), pattern-recognition (such as recognizing sloppy hand-written characters), question-answering (in restricted domains such as baseball) and natural language translation.

An important strategic difference quickly appeared, separating these efforts roughly into two streams, often called computer simulation (CS) and artificial intelligence (AI) respectively. Workers in CS remain faithful to the aim of increasing psychological understanding, in that they seek to reproduce not only particular kinds of human performance, but also possible models of the mechanisms by which humans achieve those performances. AI workers, by contrast, disavow any direct interest in psychology and seek rather to achieve high-level performance by whatever means possible. Although a powerful simulation might seem rather more interesting to us than an AI result of equal power (in the unlikely sense that each reproduces the same range of skilled behavior), I think it is reasonable to admit that results of either type would in practice have substantially the same impact on our central question; and hence I will discuss the two streams of work together.

I will not attempt to review the substantive accomplishments here.

Persons interested in following the history of such work can refer to landmark publications such as Feigenbaum and Feldman (1963), Minsky (1968), Schank and Colby (1973), Winograd (1972) and Winston (1975). Suffice it to say that many of the individual pieces of work represent considerable intellectual and technical achievements. Computers have already done a number of quite remarkable things and there can be no doubt that in the future they will do many more.

However, without intending to disparage these attainments of digital computers, I must add that so far they still fall very far short of what anyone could plausibly describe as general intelligence. I would not even bother to mention this were it not for the extremely inflated image many people have of the progress of this work, an image which in large part has been promoted by the research workers themselves. Many extraordinarily grandiose prognostications have been made on the basis of relatively modest concrete accomplishments.

Of course, these predictions might conceivably some day prove correct. The theoretical foundation is deep and after all the work is still in its infancy. Might we not simply be in the early stages of an evolutionary process in which machines will inevitably attain at least the equivalent of human cognitive abilities?

Recently, an important book has appeared which profoundly challenges this vision of the future of mechanical intelligence. Hubert Dreyfus (1972) systematically attacks both the progress and the prospects of CS and AI. He begins by reviewing early work in game playing, problem-solving, language translation and pattern recognition. Work in each domain was characterized by a common pattern of early success, followed by steadily diminishing returns. Subsequent work in artificial intelligence, according to Dreyfus, has fared little better, achieving its limited successes only by operating in artificially constrained environments that do not exemplify basic difficulties handled with conspicuous ease by everyday human intelligence. Dreyfus argues that the extreme efficiency of human intelligence, which becomes progressively more apparent as we move toward problem domains more typical of its ordinary application, rests on a complex of related abilities which he terms fringe consciousness, ambiguity tolerance based on efficient use of context, essential-inessential distinctions and perspicuous grouping. Human performance is characteristically guided by an overall grasp of the problem situation, with essential aspects at the foreground of attention set against an organizing but implicit background. Phenomenologically, the *situation* is primary. Specific facts or features of the situation may only become evident by a deliberate attentive effort of a quite secondary sort. By contrast, Dreyfus argues, for the computer all facts must be specified in advance as explicit bits of atomic data; whatever crude representation of the situation the computer can achieve is necessarily constructed by explicit calculation upon these situation-independent facts. Building upon these and related observations, Dreyfus attempts to establish his thesis that central human mental skills are *in principle* not reproducible on digital computers.[10]

I will not attempt to develop Dreyfus' thesis here in further detail. Suffice it to say I have no doubt whatsoever that he has identified a cluster of problems which at the very least constitute extremely difficult problems of practice. My confidence in this view arises in large part from extensive and sobering experience of my own in attempting to fathom what might be involved in enabling computers to understand and use common words in English (Kelly and Stone, 1975, Chapter 4). Our group was principally concerned with the applied technical problem of reducing lexical ambiguity in keypunched English text, the practical aim being increased precision and power of automated content analysis procedures. In approaching this problem, we constructed a concordance of some half-million words of "typical" behavioral science text. This concordance identified the frequently-occurring words and supplied information about their typical ranges of use. Although our main concern was to build computer routines to recognize pre-established word senses with a useful degree of accuracy, we also went to some pains to determine whether the brute facts of everyday language as we are seeing them could successfully be captured by existing theories of semantic representation.[11] In a word, they could not. I argued that all of the existing schemes utterly failed to capture what to me had become the most characteristic property of word-meaning, namely, a felt Gestalt quality or wholeness, at a level of generality which naturally supports extensions of usage to novel but appropriate contexts. The available proposals could only represent the content of a general term by some sample of its possible particularizations; thus, no computer system in existence then or now could distinguish systematically between metaphorical truth and literal falsehood. For details, see Kelly and Stone (1975). Clearly we were approaching from a different angle a domain of problems strongly overlapping those identified by Dreyfus. Although we acknowledged that the properties we stressed appeared likely to be very difficult to capture in a digital representation, it is only candid to admit that, at the time, it was quite unthinkable to me that they might be not merely difficult but *impossible* to capture.

Since that time such a notion has become thinkable, but I remain unconvinced that it is correct. I cannot go into details here, but I do not find Dreyfus' theoretical arguments convincing, and I fear that his polemical fervor occasionally blinds him to the merits of the views he attacks. I will content myself with two main points of rebuttal.

First, it strikes me as significant that the difficulties primarily revolve around "Gestalty" phenomena with a distinctly analog flavor. It still seems at least vaguely conceivable that these difficult but fundamental qualities of embodied cognition might be deeply rooted in the special properties of the nervous system as a particular kind of computing machine. Whereas early discussions focused on the all-or-nothing neuronal spike discharge as the equivalent of a digital relay, in more recent times we have become increasingly sensitized to the complex analog processes of spatial and temporal summation occurring prior to the axon hillock. Workers in CS and AI have rather cavalierly assumed that they could safely disregard these low-level structural and functional properties of neurons and pitch their efforts at a level of abstraction which happens to be congenial both to them and to present-day machines. However, what we may be seeing is that these low-level properties enter into the overall computational possibilities of the brain in a much more fundamental way than we have heretofore suspected. Perhaps the "missing" cognitive attributes are reducible to such low-level characteristics. It is at least suggestive that the relevant phenomena appear continuous with phenomena that are both ontogenetically and phylogenetically of lower order (see Kelly and Stone, loc. cit.). Also relevant here are the facts that, in humans particularly, the cerebral hemispheres tend to show considerable differential specialization, and that in right-handed adults the right hemisphere displays more prominently, though certainly not exclusively, various kinds of Gestalty skills, particularly in relation to visual synthesis. Thus, one is led to imagine the possibility of hybrid devices with a mixture of digital and analog components. Alternatively, schemes might be invented for capturing analog properties with a digital representation, and even if that representation were so clumsy as to render implementation as a broad scale transcomputable in the sense of Bremermann (1977), enough might be accomplished to convince us of the generality of the underlying principles.[12]

Second, it seems likely that computers can in fact progress a good deal further toward grasping situations than they so far have. It is particularly interesting that in recent years workers in AI have showed increased appreciation of the fact that the only *general* intelligence we know is that associated with the human body and brain. Thus, intelligence artificers now show great interest in studying human cognitive development, and there are many interesting signs of convergence between researchers in cognitive psychology and in AI. In particular, both groups have now clearly recognized (apparently quite independent of Dreyfus) the critical role played by our overall sense of the situation in guiding various forms of intelligent behavior. Thus, several proposals have recently emerged for representational schemes by which computers might be enabled to construct and manipulate more global understandings of this sort (see for example Neisser, 1976; Schank and Colby, 1973 and especially Minsky, 1975). The basic notion is to have the computer store "frames" representing typical situations at varying levels of generality. In a given situation, the appropriate frames are then to be extended or specialized in a manner appropriate to that particular case. It should be stated, however, that efforts in this direction so far remain largely programmatic, with relatively primitive concrete accomplishments. I would also argue that the notion of general *frames* harbors severe difficulties quite analogous to those which I earlier argued arise in the case of general *terms*, and hence that these too may be intimately bound up with specialized analog properties of neural computation. The two classes of problems thus seem to me strongly interdependent.

To sum up, although there appear to be major difficulties ahead, I nevertheless think that the kinds of problems noted so far might not prove fatal for the mechanistic approach, and that on these fronts we have to remain agnostic for the present. I concur with Weizenbaum's (1976) judgment that we cannot at this point reliably predict the possible progress of computer mentality. We must wait and see what can be accomplished. Meanwhile, we should strongly support further efforts along these lines, for as CS and AI evolve they are constantly sharpening our understanding not only of what computers can do, but of what we ourselves do in a broad range of cognitive activities. Even apart from its ultimate success or failure, each new attempt to extend computer mentality into a novel area of human performance forces us in the first instance to try to understand in detail what capacities are presupposed by that performance. As our understanding of the capacities of minds deepens and becomes more detailed, it thus should become increasingly possible to judge to what degree those capacities may be explainable in terms of the properties of brains.

There remains, however, one area of human capacities regarding which I think we can conclude immediately that present day mechanistic principles must necessarily fail. I am referring, of course, to parapsychological abilities. Taking advantage of the theoretical equivalence of brains and computers under the mechanistic theory, we can simply ask what it would take to endow a computer with psi ability. Although there are some slight complications that I will not go into here, it seems quite clear that generalized psi ability, and particularly psychokinetic ability, could not conceivably arise from any kind or degree of complication of the basic capacities presently available to machines. It is certainly not a matter of developing more complex or subtle algorithms, data structures, or the like, but of providing one or more *extra capacities* of a fundamentally novel sort.

I was astonished to discover, upon re-reading his 1950 article, that Turing himself had anticipated this argument. Indeed, he evidently took it quite seriously, since it appears last in his list of *a priori* objections to the possibility of mechanizing human abilities, a list which appears to be presented, at least roughly, in order of increasing difficulty. His attempted solution to the problem, moreover is patently defective — as he probably knew, since it requires a telepathy-proof room(!) — and seems to me to reflect little more than his ardent and freely expressed wish that the phenomena should simply go away. In this he was of course adopting a strategy that has been widely practiced by contemporary philosophers and scientists.

I believe that this argument shows clearly that mechanism is false, or at least incomplete. It succeeds without appeal to consciousness, by displaying a behavioral capacity of the human mind that lies entirely beyond the reach of mechanistic principles as currently understood. Although psi phenomena thus play a pivotal role in the argument, I want to stress that they seem to me only the leading edge of a pattern of connected developments, other elements of which might well eventually point to similar conclusions, and all of which merit continuing study by those of us interested in the mind-body problem. Let me explore this pattern a bit further.

5. Beyond mechanism-what?

First to review: I began by characterizing identity theory and its variants as the official brain doctrine, to which most contemporary scientists subscribe, at least in their more philosophical moments. Subsequently, I introduced the mechanistic theory of mind as a companion doctrine which is (or should be) accepted by a consistent materialist as the framework within which the explanation of cognitive capacities in terms of brain processes must develop.[13]

We saw that Eccles and a few others have repudiated the official doctrines, on grounds that there seem to remain large gaps between the properties of brains and those of minds, gaps which they believe can only be filled by postulating interaction between brain processes and the activities of an immaterial mind. However, I rejected these skeptical conclusions as premature. The experimental evidence presented was insufficient to refute the official doctrine, and the theoretical position seemed to raise at least as many fundamental difficulties as it resolved (or perhaps dissolved). Furthermore, Eccles and the others have not adequately appreciated the full possibilities of the mechanistic approach, nor the depth of the theoretical foundation upon which it rests.

However, precisely because of the depth of that foundation, we were able to pierce through the official doctrines at one small but significant point, based on the inability of mechanistic principles to account for the human capacity for psi performance. I further suggested that psi abilities may represent just the sharp corner of the wedge, and that broader kinds of mental capacity may subsequently turn out, as both neuroscience and the cognitive sciences advance, to be likewise irreducible to mechanical brain activity.

These latter possibilities so far remain to my mind uncertain, but even the one small definite result already in hand opens the way to a wide spectrum of theoretical positions lying beyond the currently orthodox doctrines. I wish now to outline very briefly where things seem to me to be headed.

Some extension or modification of prevailing views is clearly going to be required, but just how drastic need these revisions be? I believe that fundamental considerations of scientific policy enjoin us to confine the damage as much as possible, and to accept only such minimal revisions as we can judge are absolutely necessary to repair the limitations of our present outlook. In this way, we shall also minimize the risk of running afoul of the powerful empirical and theoretical considerations raised in the first two sections of this paper.

Although my ideas are not definite and clear enough to spell out in any detail, the minimum scenario, which represents my current position, would seem to go something as follows: Practically all of the behavioral aspects of human mentality may be accounted for by brain processes alone. It may subsequently prove necessary to refer to consciousness to fill a few small but irreducible gaps in our understanding of the synthesis of perception and voluntary motor action, as well as memory, thought and so on; but perhaps consciousness somehow "emerges" in physical systems that reach a certain threshold of complexity. (Indeed, some have suggested that machines themselves might become conscious, and it certainly would be very difficult to *prove* that they are *not* conscious even now, however unlikely that may seem). The difficulty with psi phenomena, however, seems to require some more radical kind of emergentism, which might or might not be associated with the appearance of consciousness itself. Nevertheless, the kind of theory I am pointing toward could conceivably remain very close to present orthodoxy. Taking advantage of the greatly expanded horizons of modern physics, as opposed to the old-style materialism, it might remain a physicalist theory, and I think in the same way it could still be an identity theory, although perhaps of a sort somewhat different from what most current proponents have in mind. Let me denote theories of this type collectively by the term "augmented official brain doctrine."

I would be very happy to leave the story here, in hope that these vague outlines and obscure concepts will take definite and intelligible form with the steady progress of future scientific research. Such a story is, to me, intellectually and temperamentally congenial in a general way, and it is specifically congenial to the sort of research program on possible physiological correlates of psi processes in which our group at Duke is making such a heavy investment.[14]

It is with considerable reluctance, therefore, that I acknowledge increasing discomfort with the kind of picture I just sketched, and several variants of it. I fear that the gaps may ultimately prove substantially larger than I have so far indicated. Although I and (I presume) most other scientists would be willing to tolerate a good deal of straining of the minimum scenario to accommodate new difficulties, at some point one reaches one's elastic limit. That will occur in different places for different persons, of course, depending on complex temperamental factors and the range of evidence they are willing to consider seriously. Although I emphatically do not feel compelled to abandon the augmented brain doctrine, I do feel considerable, though still ill-defined, strains in maintaining it.

My thinking is really just beginning to take shape in these areas, so again I will not try to go into details at this time, but I would like to mention just briefly, some of the points at which I sense, with varying degrees of clarity, *possible* conflicts emerging between properties of human cognition and the physical capacities of the brain. Please note carefully the emphasis on the word "possible"; I am not claiming that any of the phenomena to be noted currently provide a compelling argument for abandoning the augmented brain doctrine, but only that they reveal points of strain that may merit further investigation in this light. I simply wish to convey in rough-and-ready fashion my overall "sense of the situation."

Some of these phenomena involve "normal" behavioral functions, and can thus be added to the kinds of problems raised in the previous section. For example, consider human long-term memory. It is really an astonishing system, and one about which stunningly little is known even at this late date. There does exist a consensus that possible physiological mechanisms exist in the brain sufficient to account for the required volume of storage capacity. (These might involve, for example, macromolecular configurations and/or structural changes of neural junctions that affect overall patterns of functional activity of the brain.) But there are scarcely any remotely realistic proposals describing details of mechanisms both for storage and especially for *retrieval*. Meanwhile, recent experience with computer systems has cast the situation in an interesting new light. The largest computer memories are still orders of magnitude smaller than a typical human memory, by anybody's way of counting. They are, of course, also physically relatively enormous and functionally very different. The structural elements of machines are individually exceedingly much faster and more reliable than their neural counterparts. Nevertheless, computer "knowledge-bases" of even relatively modest size already present formidable problems of organization and access. Experience with such systems is rapidly sharpening our appreciation of the extreme flexibility and efficiency of human memory processes (e.g., Norman et al., 1975; Anderson, 1976). At the very least it is clear that we need drastically more powerful concepts of data representation and retrieval; hence the increasing efforts to develop so-called "associative memories," which, although so far rather unsuccessful, at least seem to be going in the right direction (Kohonen, 1977).

The memory problem is a good one because it is now widely recognized by both psychologists and intelligence artificers to lie at the very core of generalized intelligence. Whereas earlier workers tried to approach functions such as pattern recognition, thinking and sentence understanding in a relatively piecemeal and isolated way, it has become increasingly apparent that all human skills, and particularly our central everyday skills, are embedded in a continuous interplay between present performance and stored information. While recognizing that fundamental new discoveries in this area may arise both from neuroscience and from research with computers, I think it is appropriate to entertain the question whether the informational characteristics of human memory might not prove inconsistent with the physical characteristics of the brain. This question has, of course, been raised previously, both by persons interested in parapsychology such as Bergson (1911) and Driesch (1935) and, in a curiously fence-straddling way, by the physicist Elsasser (1958), but as our knowledge advances it may eventually become possible to pose it in a sharply quantitative way.

Other phenomena that make me uncomfortable are phenomena that suggest degrees of precision and reliability in at least some mental processes that seem intuitively hard to reconcile with what we might hope to extract from a fundamentally analog device working in a statistical way with components of low precision and reliability (cf. von Neumann, 1956, 1958). For example, the kind of "complete" memory-record phenomenon suggested by certain hypnotic states and by Penfield's cortical stimulation studies with epileptic patients undergoing brain surgery might, if better established, fall in this area. A related phenomenon is that of so-called "eidetic" imagery, as best exemplified to my knowledge in the extraordinary experiments of Stromeyer (1970). It must be pointed out, however, that many psychologists—perhaps because they feel similar discomforts—simply refuse to believe any of these memory results. A further and related phenomenon which certainly occurs, however (although it remains to my knowledge very poorly studied), is that of calculation prodigies. I find it quite astonishing that there have existed people capable of multiplying together two arbitrary thirty-digit numbers, or taking the 23rd root of a 201-digit number, all in their heads, often in very short times and sometimes in the absence of any conscious effort. For an entertaining account see Barlow (1961); F.W.H. Myers (1961), with characteristic prescience, also sensed the possible significance of these phenomena.

Other phenomena more directly involve consciousness and alterations of consciousness, and shade over toward the realm of the paranormal. Another oddity pointed out by Myers concerns so-called "glove anesthesias" and kindred phenomena, in which hysterically induced paralyses or anesthesias may correspond to a "psychological" unit of the body, in apparent disregard of the underlying physiological organization. Another possibly important behavioral manifestation, if genuine, is the concurrent multiple use of a single basic set of skills. Although psychologists are beginning to think that, with suitable training, people can probably do more things at once than we customarily suppose, this generalization seems to apply only to relatively divergent things, and conspicuously fails as the simultaneous tasks become more alike (Neisser, 1976). Although I do not have a reference for this at the moment, I remember reading with considerable sense of alarm that Mrs. Piper would occasionally communicate while in trance with as many as three separate sitters at once, writing with both hands and speaking to the third sitter, all apparently simultaneously. Observations of this sort if firmly established are at the very least of great psychological interest and would pose severe difficulties for prevailing notions of mind-brain relations. A further set of phenomena occurs in conjunction with clinical cases of the "multiple personality" type. The particular occurrence that interests me most in this connection is the phenomenon of co-consciousness, in which the sphere of awareness of one personality may entirely include that available to one or more others. Some interesting physiological observations supportive of clinical descriptions of this phenomenon have been published by Ludwig et al. (1972). Finally, I have read a large number of accounts of transcendental or mystical experiences, and talked with several individuals who have themselves had such experiences. Although better documentation is certainly required, I think we must reckon with a substantial probability that such experiences may often result at least temporarily in marked changes in overall pattern and level of cognitive functioning, at least occasionally including an influx of paranormal capacities. Suggestions of this sort are certainly potentially open to empirical investigation.

In addition, we have not yet exhausted the catalog of paranormal phenomena. In particular, I have so far not mentioned any of the kinds of work falling under the general heading of survival research. A potentially very important transitional class of cases involves so-called near-death experiences. Although to my knowledge no case has yet been reported with sufficiently detailed physiological records corresponding to extended episodes of veridical experience, it already seems likely that at least some such cases confront us with the prospect of elaborate perceptual and cognitive activity apparently taking place under physiological conditions we would have expected to be insufficient to support it. It remains to be seen just how sharply this apparent conflict can be drawn, but it seems virtually certain, given the increasing interest of medical personnel and the increasing availability of facilities for detailed physiological monitoring in hospital environments, that more information will be forthcoming in this area in the near future (Sabom and Kreutziger, 1977).

The more general survival literature of course confronts us still more starkly with evidence suggestive of mental activity occurring without its normal physiological accompaniments. Obviously I cannot discuss that evidence here, nor is my familiarity with it sufficient to qualify me to do so. On the other hand, I have made moderate efforts to acquaint myself with it, and I feel obligated to acknowledge that, on the basis of my studies so far, the weight of the evidence seems to me to tilt slightly in favor of survival of something undeniably mental. Along with most other parapsychologists, I do not find the evidence anywhere near sufficient to exclude decisively alternative explanations based on "ordinary" psi abilities of the living, but, despite its *a priori* repugnance, I feel that the survival hypothesis must be taken quite seriously.

Survival in any form, and reincarnation in particular, would appear to entail some kind of extracerebral representation of memory. Establishment of such phenomena would thus certainly overthrow even the augmented official doctrines, completely and decisively, and very likely precipitate us into some kind of pluralism with all the attendant difficulties. Despite its notorious problems survival research therefore clearly bears on the issues at hand in the most direct way imaginable, and for this reason it seems to me to merit intensive further effort.

I think I shall end my catalog here, for now. I repeat that my purpose has been only to draw attention to a number of areas that all of us interested in the mind-body problem—parapsychologists and non-parapsychologists alike—might do well to keep under surveillance. I will be very interested to hear from other members of this group, and from subsequent readers, both comments on these topics and suggestions of possible further topics for the catalog. For now let me quickly bring this long paper to a close.

6. Conclusions

I am impressed on re-reading this how little of it is genuinely new. Whatever virtue it has lies, I think, primarily in the organization of the material. Let me summarize the main themes.

The lines of evidence reviewed here are converging, but not yet convergent. Part of the difficult lies simply in getting the different intellectual disciplines to acknowledge each other's existence. I have tried to promote this kind of synoptic view by displaying the conflict between parapsychological findings and current doctrine in an unusually well-defined context, one which in addition brings into sharp focus some basic relationships between what parapsychologists are doing and various other contemporary approaches to the study of mind/body relations.

We parapsychologists have a tendency to feel victimized by lack of attention from neighboring disciplines. While agreeing that our findings deserve more consideration from others than they presently receive, I also feel that we have been almost equally culpable in our historical tendency toward professional isolation. I hope this essay will help contribute to the rapid demise of this kind of suffocating academic parochialism, on all the converging fronts.

Meanwhile, we can already see that mechanistic materialism of the currently fashionable sort is surely false or at least incomplete, as demonstrated by its inability to account for psi phenomena and possibly various others. Exactly what will take its place will depend, in a way I believe is currently not predictable, on future results turned up by the approaches reviewed here and perhaps others as well. For the present, something quite close to our present views seems to me to remain provisionally tenable, with significant, but still relatively minor, adjustments needed to patch up the presently identifiable shortcomings of current doctrine. At the same time, there are ominous signs of more fundamental difficulties ahead that may ultimately shatter even this extended picture and drive us on toward much more radical revisions of our basic ideas on the mind-body problem.

FOOTNOTES

1. This analogy was used by Eccles in his invited address to the 1976 P.A. convention, where he also very inappropriately characterized the antedating phenomeon as "precognition" (Eccles, 1977).

2. Here I omit mention of further difficulties of a more narrowly philosophical sort, such as the problems of *individuation* and *identification* of immaterial minds; see for example, Shaffer (1968). I also find it difficult to imagine conditions under which Eccles would *abandon* his theory, and quite surprising that Popper does not press him on this!

3. Popper is aware of this difficulty, and proposes a slightly better analogy: Just as in efficient reading we sometimes seem to grasp meanings directly, without conscious experience of individual letters or even words, so "In perception we read the meaning of the neuronal firing pattern of the brain and the meaning of the neuronal firing pattern is, as it were, the situation in the outside world which we try to perceive." (p. 418). Although this analogy helps, it is still radically insufficient. In particular, we are entirely unable to perform any kind of redirection of attention to neural processes, analogous to our ability to become aware of letters, words, and so on.

4. In light of the foregoing remarks it is particularly astonishing to find Eccles claiming (e.g. p. 366, 512) that his theory, unlike the official brain-process theories, does not require recourse to a homunculus which embodies most of the original problems!

5. Even as recently as McDougall (1911), it had still been intellectually possible to think of embryological development as lying outside the scope of materialistic theories. But, by the time Sherrington delivered his Gifford Lectures in 1937-38, it had already become clear that these tremendously complex and goal-directed events are at least very largely matters of physics and chemistry. Defenders of vitalist theories had thus been forced to retreat again, and the apparent purposiveness of human and animal behavior had become more than ever a cornerstone of their defense.

6. What follows is a brief heuristic introduction to a very complicated subject. For further detail, see, in ascending order of difficulty, Weizenbaum (1976), Trakhtenbrot (1963), or Davis (1958).

7. I am deliberately ignoring, for present purposes, the important (and controversial) distinction Chomsky makes between *competence*, as a formal representation of the skills underlying language use, and *performance*, or the exercise of those skills in speaking and understanding. Also irrelevant to the point I am making is the fact that the currently

most successful efforts at computer modeling of language do not explicitly incorporate transformational grammars.

8. Some of the early workers chose to attempt understanding the brain at a very basic level, by using the computer to model neurons and networks of neurons. Others carried out theoretical studies of so-called "self-organizing systems" (aggregates of simplified neuron-analogs modifiable through experience by elementary principles of conditioning and the like), which, it was hoped, could gradually come to display complex activities. These approaches have never yet come anywhere close to supporting interesting behavior, however, and although work still continues along such lines we will not be concerned with it here.

9. To the degree that machine intelligence begins to approximate our own, the problem of precise specification of adequate criteria will no doubt increasingly call for careful philosophical analysis as foreshadowed—quite prematurely, I think—in Anderson (1964) and numerous other discussions. My general impression is that many philosophers have been too easily influenced by pronouncements issuing from the mechanist camp. In what follows, I am displaying the progress of this work in the most favorable possible context, by restricting discussion to everyday cognitive phenomena which take place on what William James liked to call the "sunlit terrace" of the mind. Even there, I will argue, ultimate triumph of the mechanist approach is by no means assured.

10. Several of Dreyfus' arguments appear in less developed form in various chapters of a much earlier book by Sayre and Crosson (1963). Of particular interest are some remarks by Wittgenstein on mechanical mathematics. More recently, another critical attack on artificial intelligence has appeared, this time from an insider, a computer specialist from MIT (Weizenbaum, 1976). Weizenbaum is entirely conscious of the theoretical underpinnings of AI, and consequently much more reluctant than Dreyfus to argue the nonreproducibility thesis (although he verges on it in numerous places). His central argument is rather a moral one; that because it cannot emerge from a fully human situation, one which takes into account our biological uniqueness among other things, whatever understanding computers may ultimately develop will necessarily be in fundamental respects alien to human understanding; and, therefore, that there are many kinds of tasks—such as psychotherapy—which computers should never be permitted to perform.

11. The main such theory, that of Katz and Fodor (1964), built upon the central notions of Chomsky's transformational linguistics. It is particularly congenial to potential formalization, in that it depicts the representation of the meaning of a sentence as resulting from a rule-bound calculation operating upon semantic representations of the individual words in the sentence; furthermore, the meanings of the words themselves are claimed to be analyzable into an underlying universal set of discrete, atomic features or logical structures built out of such features.

12. The model described by Pribram at this conference and elsewhere is perhaps one concrete example of this sort.

13. Of course, strictly mechanistic theories no longer hold sway even in physics proper, and it is appropriate to ask what implications quantum-theoretic ideas may have for our understanding of brain activity. I am not qualified to discuss the subject in any detail, but I should like to indicate the main possibilities that seem to be open. On the one hand, the micro-structure of the brain certainly offers ample scope for quantum-level effects to take place, such as electron tunneling through synaptic clefts and the like. More broadly (and as noted previously at least as early as von Neumann, 1958) even at higher levels the actual operation of the brain is very unlike that of a deterministic machine, but rather saturated with probabilistic or statistical properties. None of this automatically has any bearing on the conclusions so far drawn, since effects of the sort mentioned might in principle be handled by extending the class of machines to include stochastic machines, i.e., machines which incorporate random elements. On the other hand, it also appears that quantum theory in one or another interpretation might be enlisted in support of a wide variety of much more radical departures from current notions. Certainly it forces us at the very least to acknowledge characteristics of physical systems that go far beyond

those contemplated by Newtonian physics, and in this negative sense has considerably softened the artificially sharp traditional dichotomy between matter and mind. Recent discussions by physicists such as Wigner and Walker further suggest the possibility of much more direct and positive contributions of physical theory to the mind-body problem, but I am unable at present to judge how far these discussions have actually progressed, and how they might supplement the framework outlined in this paper.

14. I should make clear at this point that *failure* to discover any physiological correlates of psi would not for me constitute independent evidence supporting interactionism. Although such failure might well be consistent with that interpretation, it could also readily be understood in terms of currently available neuroscience. It is entirely conceivable that psi processes may indeed have a physiological representation, but one which for any of several reasons would elude detection by present or future technology. For arguments suggesting a more hopeful view of the research prospects in this area, see Kelly, 1977.

BIBLIOGRAPHY

Anderson, A. R., (ed.) *Minds and Machines*, Englewood Cliffs, N.J.: Prentice-Hall, 1964.

Anderson, John R., *Language, Memory and Thought*, Hillside, N.J.: L. Erlbaum Associates, 1976.

Arbib, M. A., *The Metaphorical Brain-An Introduction to Cybernetics as Artificial Intelligence and Brain Theory*, New York: Wiley-Interscience, 1972.

Barlow, F., *Mental Prodigies*, New York: Greenwood, 1969.

Beloff, J., "The identity hypothesis: A critique," in Smythies, J. R. (ed.) *Brain and Mind*, London: Routledge and Kegan Paul, 1965, 35–61.

Bergson, H., *Matter and Memory*, New York: MacMillan, 1911.

Bremermann, H. J., "Complexity and transcomputability," in Duncan, R. and Weston-Smith, M., (eds.) *The Encylopedia of Ignorance*, Oxford: Pergamon Press, 1977, 167–174.

Chomsky, N., *Syntactic Structures*, The Hague: Mouton, 1957.

Chomsky, N., "Formal properties of grammars," in Luce, R. D., Bush, R. R., and Galanter, E., *Handbook of Mathematical Psychology*, vol. 2, chapter 12, 323–418, New York: John Wiley, 1963.

Craik, K. J. W., *The Nature of Explanation*, Cambridge U. Press, 1943.

Davis, M., *Computability and Unsolvability*, New York: McGraw-Hill, 1958.

Dreyfus, H. L., *What Computers Can't Do-A Critique of Artificial Reason*, New York: Harper and Row, 1972.

Driesch, H., "Memory in its relation to psychical research," *Proceedings of the Society for Psychical Research, 43*, 1935, 1–14.

Eccles, J. C., "The human person in its two-way relationship to the brain," In Morris, J. O., Roll, W. G., and Morris, R. L. (eds.) *Research in Parapsychology 1976*, Metuchen, N. J.: Scarecrow Press, 1977, 251–262.

Elasasser, W. M., *The Physical Foundation of Biology-An Analytical Study*, London: Pergamon Press, 1958.

Feigenbaum, E. A., and Feldman, J., *Computers and Thought*, New York: McGraw-Hill, 1963.

James, W., *A Pluralistic Universe*, New York: Longmans, Green & Co., 1909.

Julesz, B., *Foundations of Cyclopean Perception*, Chicago: University of Chicago Press, 1971.

Katz, J. J., and Fodor, J., "The structure of a sematic theory," in Fodor, J. and Katz, J. J., *The Structure of Language*, New York: Prentice-Hall, 1964, 479–518.

Kelly, E. F., and Stone, P. J., *Computer Recognition of English Word Senses*, Amsterdam: North-Holland, 1975.

Kelly, E. F., Physiological correlates of psi processes. *Parapsychology Review* **8**, 1977, 1–9.

Kohonen, T., *Associative Memory: A System-Theoretical Approach*, Berlin: Springer-Verlag, 1977.

Lindsay, P. H., and Norman, D. A., *Human Information Processing. An Introduction to Psychology*, New York: Academic Press, 1972.

Ludwig, A. M., Brandsma, C. B., Wilbur, C. B., Bendfeldt, F. and Jameson, D. H., "The objective study of multiple personality," *Archives of General Psychiatry*, 26, 1972, 298–310.

Luria, A. R., *The Working Brain-An Introduction to Neuropsychology*, New York: Basic Books, 1973.

McCulloch, W. S., and Pitts, W., "A logical calculus of the ideas immanent in nervous activity," *Bull. Math. Biophys.*, 5, 1943.

McDougall, W., *Body and Mind: A History and a Defense of Animism*, London: Methuen, 1911.

Miller, G. A., Galanter, E. and Pribram, K. H., *Plans and the Structure of Behavior*, New York: Henry Holt, 1960.

Minsky, M., (ed.) *Semantic Information Processing*, Cambridge, Mass.: MIT Press, 1968.

Minsky, M., "A framework for representing knowledge," in Winston, P. H., *The Psychology of Computer Vision*, New York: McGraw-Hill, 1975.

Myers, F. W. H., *Human Personality and Its Survival of Bodily Death*, Abridged edition, edited by Susy Smith, New Hyde Park, N.Y.: University Books, 1961.

Neisser, U., *Cognition and Reality-Principles and Implications of Cognitive Psychology*, San Francisco: W. H. Freeman, 1976.

von Neumann, J., "Probabilistic logics and the synthesis of reliable organisms from unreliable components," in Shannon, C. E. and McCarthy, J., (eds.) *Automata Studies*, Princeton, N.J.: Princeton University Press, 1956.

von Neumann, J., *The Computer and the Brain*, New Haven: Yale University Press, 1958.

Newell, A., Shaw, J. and Simon, H., "Elements of a theory of human problem-solving" *Psych. Review*, 65, 1958, 151–166.

Norman, D. A., Rumelhert, D. E. and LNR Group, *Explorations in Cognition*, San Francisco: W. H. Freeman, 1975.

Oatley, K., *Brain Mechanisms and Mind*, New York: E. P. Dutton & Co., 1972.

Penfield, W., *The Mystery of the Mind*, Princeton, N. J.: Princeton University Press, 1975.

Popper, K. R. and Eccles, J. C., *The Self and Its Brain: An Argument for Interactionism*, Berlin: Springer-Verlag, 1977.

Ratliff, F. *Mach Bands: Quantitative Studies on Neural Networks in the Retina*, San Francisco: Holden-Day, 1965.

Rose, S. R., *The Conscious Brain*, New York: Vintage Books, 1976.

Rosenblueth, A., Wiener, N. and Bigelow, J., "Behavior, purpose and teleology," *Philosophy and Science*, 10, 1943, 18–24.

Sabom, M. B. and Kreutziger, S., "Near-death experiences," *Journal of the Florida Medical Association*, 64, 1977, 648–650.

Sayre, K. M. and Crosson, F. J., *The Modeling of Mind-Computers and Intelligence*, Notre Dame: University of Notre Dame Press, 1963.

Schank, R. C. and Colby, K. M., (eds.) *Computer Models of Thought and Language*, San Francisco: W. H. Freeman, 1973.

Shaffer, J. A., *Philosophy of Mind*, Englewood Cliffs, N. J.: Prentice-Hall, 1968.

Sherrington, C., *Man on His Nature*, Garden City, N. Y.: Doubleday Anchor, 2nd edition, 1955.

Smythies, J. R., (ed.) *Brain and Mind-Modern Concepts of the Nature of Mind*, London: Routledge and Kegan Paul, 1965. (esp. essays by Beloff, Brain.)

Stromeyer, C. F. and Psotka, J., "The detailed texture of eidetic images," *Nature*, 225, 1970, 346–349.

Trakhtenbrot, B. A., *Algorithms and Automatic Computing Machines*, Health, 1963.

Turing, A. M., "Computing machinery and intelligence," *Mind*, 59, 1950. (Reprinted in Anderson (1964)).

Uttal, W. R., *The Psychobiology of Sensory Coding*, New York: Harper & Row, 1973.

Weizenbaum, J., *Computer Power and Human Reason-From Calculation to Judgment*, San Francisco: W. H. Freeman, 1976.

Wiener, N., *Cybernetics-Control and Communication in the Animal and the Machine*, 2nd ed., New York: John Wiley, 1961.
Winograd, T., "Understanding natural language," *Cognitive Psychology*, 3, 1972, 1–191.
Winston, P. H., (ed.) *The Psychology of Computer Vision*, New York: McGraw-Hill, 1975.

DISCUSSION

PRIBRAM: I have some comments to make—two minor and three major ones. I think you can believe Strohmeyer. There's just no way that one can fake the Julez patterns. He presented one pattern to one eye and then five days later the other patterns to the other eye. There is no way that one can cheat on that particular test. The second thing—about hysterical or hypnotic anesthesia—it is neurologically reasonable to think of the phenomenon as being thalamocortical since it is at the cortex that the whole body representation comes together. All of the various senses come together at the thalamocortical level.

Now, the major things that I want to discuss are the meanings of three words that you used: *mechanism, material* and *memory*. I think they may have different definitions for different people in the audience, and I think we should be very clear that they're used differently by different disciplines. Take "mechanism," for instance. If I use the word with my friends in physics, they say, "Well, nobody believes in mechanism any more." What they mean is Newtonian mechanism. When *you* talk about mechanism are you talking about Newtonian mechanism? It must be very clear that mechanistic analysis is a prevailing way for psychologists and physiologists to be thinking; but this approach is different from that of modern physics.

Thus, my second point—regarding "material." Modern physicists don't believe in a material world any more than they believe in a "mechanistic" world. The term "material" is at the same level of discourse as is Euclidean geometry and Newtonian physics. In that realm, things look hard and time and space are stable coordinates. But problems arise in this realm: For instance, light is transmitted from, let's say, a star to us through *nothing*. That's a funny kind of macro-universe. Further, in the quantum and nuclear micro-universe, the materiality of material disappears entirely.

Now thirdly, the problem of "memory." There is no reason why we can't imagine a brain process that operates in the same way that Turing's process works—a brain process that stores an unlimited amount of information which can be retrieved. We simulated a content addressable memory back in the 1960s in our laboratory. Furthermore, we've shown that the frontal lobes have an "execute" function and the posterior convexal cortex functions as a "fetch" mechanism to a content addressable memory. The brain's memory operation is not like that of current computers, that's all.

KELLY: I accept particularly the first of your major points, and if I'd had more time for oral presentation I would have, I think, made similar remarks myself. In a narrow way I don't think that the presence of quantum effects on the brain necessarily changes anything. In a deeper sense, it well might, but unfortunately I'm not qualified to comment on that. I do think, however, that quantum theory, as we've seen recently in parapsychology, might well be compatible with any of the wide spectrum of alternatives lying beyond the majority viewpoints as I characterize them. I also agree about the dematerialization of matter and its potential implication that the traditional hard and sharp outline between the material world of billiard balls and the mental world has softened considerably in the present century. That's an important point. As to the memory part, I look forward with great interest to what you have to say.

STORM: With respect to the analogy with computers, a Turing machine, and this is the case in approximately any other formulation, requires the notion of a fetch-execute cycle to drive the activity of the machine and make it anything other than a static device that might do something. Do you think that it is important or unimportant to look for the real equivalent of the fetch-execute cycle in the human mind or brain and, if you do, do you have any ideas about how we're going to identify it?

KELLY: I certainly have no ideas about how we might identify it. The success of work on computer simulation of psychological processes does not require any assumption of literal identity between the brain and machines, which is obviously false, anyhow. What it does require is that there is some level where things are *similar enough* that structures and processes in the brain can be usefully represented by structures and processes in the computer. The difficulty has been in providing such a level. Now, I do think, that people working in these areas have underestimated the degree to which properties of human cognition are dependent on these low level structural properties—brains—and it may be their inability to provide, say, analogies of the sort you would like to hear about, which may be part of the difficulty.

EHRENWALD: I was much impressed with Dr. Kelly's brief summary and criticism of the Eccles/Popper book and I would like to take issue with the point which he raised when he said, "Psi cannot be embodied in the mechanistic scheme." This is, of course, a statement describing the Popper and Eccles' observations. But the fact is that psi or "heteropsychic" experiences or ordinary perceptions and volitions cannot be embodied in a mechanistic scheme. There is an ultimate gap in our ability to account for such transactions in both parapsychology and psychology. Popper and Eccles have tried to fill this gap with a theory which invokes a kind of homunculus, as the last resort. Still, ultimately there remains an epistemological gap. Even if we are dealing with such a homunculus, the next question is: who begot the homunculus?

We are arriving at an infinite regress taking us from the homunculus to the son of homunculus, and so on. Nevertheless, I feel that we parapsychologists can live quite comfortably with this gap as long as we realize that we are not worse off than psychologists or philosophers at large. We can do our experiments and we can make our clinical observations even without being able to account for the very last step in the personal experience or the volitional act. We can do that without suffering from an epistemological hernia, so to speak. Now, you mentioned that certain death-bed experiences could be used as an example for a non-mechanistic event associated with personality or the brain. I pointed out in my book, *The ESP Experience: A Psychiatric Validation*, that all these death-bed observations published by Kübler-Ross, Moody and others are subject to very serious objections. I believe that those people who have reached the threshold of death and come back have never been dead. What they experience is the result of anoxia in the brain and the return of circulation to the damaged brain. When their circulation comes back it produces a sense of euphoria. There are all sorts of visual experiences which have something to do with what happens to the brain as a result of anoxia or recovery from it; for instance the seeing of lights, auras, or the like. You even have it after a migraine attack. So all these very important observations have to be taken with a grain of salt. While the observations are valid, the survival interpretations are, in my view, premature, if not out-right wrong.

KELLY: I certainly agree with you that there appear at present to be gaps even in our accounts of ordinary cognitive functions, but I do feel that Eccles and Popper are jumping the gun on that. I don't think we really know yet how large those gaps are. I don't think I conveyed this sufficiently strongly, but I think we have to welcome the advance of knowledge in both brain science and artificial intelligence and related fields because no matter what happens, they're going to illuminate us. Either the gaps will become steadily smaller and eventually disappear, or in time we'll become clearer about just where the irreducible gaps are. I personally don't feel that we can guess with any confidence where it's going to come out right now. That was the first point. Second point, about near-death experiences, I should perhaps have made more clear exactly what kind of an experience it is that I think is relevant. At the recent Parapsychological Association Convention in St. Louis, we heard a seven-minute tape from an interview with a patient who had undergone cardiac arrest while in the hospital, who described in considerable and unpleasant detail various kinds of resuscitation procedures that were attempted even though he had no direct medical knowledge of such things, at a time when by current doctrine he should not have been in any shape to attain that information by the usual means. Now, I agree with you that both the facts and their interpretation remain controversial at this point, but I indicate it as an area in which we can hope to see this potential conflict made much sharper by increasing information in next few years.

HONORTON: Ed, I agree with you about the need to push the mechanistic explanations as far as they will go and with the general loose and speculative nature of Eccles' proposals, but I think you're asking too much of Eccles at this stage to criticize his dualistic formulation because he hasn't shown where in biological development mind arises, or how mind and brain interact. These are questions that are unsettled by any theoretical account of relationship between mind and brain at the present time.

KELLY: I may have belabored poor Eccles a bit too hard. My point is really to stress the potential difficulties with that kind of argument. In fact, a good illustration of their difficulties is provided by the book itself, you know, the dialogues between Popper and Eccles, where they really go on and on about this question as to where in the phylogenetic spectrum different mental properties arise, quite inconclusively, I think. But I'm not averse to proposing theories that go well in advance of data. I just want to make clear that this is not one that is actually compelled by data. It's a story that's told about certain kinds of phenomena on the basis of what's really a pre-existing theory that develops, I think, out of other sources.

PRIBRAM: Eccles and Popper don't present a unified dualism in their book. There are really two theories that are proposed, one by Popper, which is an emergent property theory similar to your own, and the other is Eccles; which relies on a universal mind operating on the association cortex. These are opposite ideas of how the mind-brain interaction takes place.

A PARAPSYCHOLOGICAL TEST OF ECCLES' "NEUROPHYSIOLOGICAL HYPOTHESIS" OF PSYCHOPHYSICAL INTERACTION

CHARLES HONORTON

1. The Problem of Psychophysical Interaction

How are we to account for the reality of our own self-conscious experience? Does mind "emerge" out of or represent some "inner" aspect of physical states? Or is mind an independent entity that interacts with but is not reducible to physical states? Is the brain a generator or a transmitter of mind? If the former, what is the alchemical algorithm through which this remarkable transformation takes place? If the latter, what is the mode of interaction between mind and brain? Is it one-way or two-way: are mental states always effects and never causes of brain states, or are brain states sometimes effects as well as causes of mental states?

The problem of psychophysical interaction has traditionally been relegated to speculative philosophy because it has been empirically inaccessible. In this paper, I will suggest some ways in which psi research may contribute to the development of an empirical approach to this ancient and fundamental problem. My contention is that the methods and findings of psi research provide science with a unique opportunity to bring this problem into empirical focus. As an illustrative exercise, I will focus on one aspect of dualistic interaction theories that is central to the viability of such theories: the concept of two-way interaction between mind and brain. I will suggest that this concept has, as a direct consequence of psi research methodology, become amenable to experimental study, and I will offer some crude beginning thoughts on how these methods may be extended to enable us to ask more penetrating questions about the nature of psychophysical interaction.

2. *Physical Detection of Mind Influence*

Theories of dualistic interaction can be brought into empirical focus if—and only if—the hypothesized mind influence can be physically detected under conditions that render explanation through physiological reductionism untenable. It is here, I believe, that psi research methodology can make a unique and important contribution.

2.1. *Random Generator PK Studies*

Psychokinesis experiments with quantum mechanical random generators provide one such method. This line of research is now sufficiently extensive to warrant at least tentative support for the hypothesis that goal-directed mental activity can serve to induce small but measurable changes in the normal operation of remote physical devices.

These devices use fundamentally random processes such as radioactive decay or thermal noise in semiconductors to provide an electronic analog of "coin-flipping."[10] In a typical device of this type, electrons emitted by Sr-90 trigger a Geiger counter and the momentary position of a high-speed binary counter at the time of the electron registration determines whether a "head" or a "tail" has been generated. This output is latched to a target bit and if they match (e.g., both are "heads"), the trial is a hit, otherwise it is a miss. The target bit may be constrained to remain constant (e.g., "heads") over a series of trials, or it may be complemented (i.e., alternated between "heads" and "tails") on every trial. The latter strategy provides a built-in control to cancel out any side bias favoring one of the two output channels. The expected probability of a hit under these conditions is, of course, 0.5 and this may be routinely verified through control calibration tests run without observers attempting to influence the device.

These devices offer a number of advantages including imperviousness to outside ("nonpsi") influence, a high data rate (up to approx. 10^3 samples/sec., currently), automatic data recording and analysis, and sensitive feedback to the observer of the momentary internal state ("heads"/"tails") of the device.

Subject/observers monitor the current physical state of the device through a feedback signal that occurs whenever the device is in, say, the "heads" state, with no—or different—feedback when it is in the "tails" state. The range of feedback displays currently in use includes simple digital readouts, light and tone displays and computer graphics displays. One such computer display in use in our laboratory, e.g., involves a race car simulation. The subject/observer sees two cars racing up a TV screen. One car is "live," i.e., is driven by a quantum mechanical random source. This is the target car. The other car is driven by a deterministic pseudorandom source. This is the control car. Each car advances up the screen, one step at a time, as a function of the number of hits (target-source matches). The subject's goal is to make the target car "run faster" than the control car.

Superficially at least, these experiments are similar to biofeedback procedures. The subject/observer's task is to monitor the feedback display and to enforce the presence of a given feedback contingency, according to preset experimental instructions. Unlike biofeedback, the only direct physical connection between the subject and the physical system he attempts to influence is the feedback signal itself. The only apparent instrumentality available to the subject consists of his cognitive dispositions and strategies. If successful, properly controlled experiments of this type would seem to indicate that purely subjective states are capable of interacting with remote physical systems so as to directly influence the selection of values permitted by the probability distribution of the physical state.

Since this line of research was inaugurated in 1970 by the physicist Helmut Schmidt,[11] approximately five dozen experiments of this type have been reported by investigators in eight different laboratories. I have surveyed these studies elsewhere.[6] Approximately 65 percent of these studies yielded independently significant evidence of direct observer-instrument interaction, compared to the expected chance rate of 5 percent. None of these studies show similarly significant results in control calibration tests with the equipment run without observers or intended influence.

Given some of the more interesting potential implications, these findings must be treated with great caution. Considering especially the relatively high data rate, there is no way to determine with certainty how many nonsignificant experiments may have been conducted and not reported. We know that in the behavioral sciences generally, there is a pronounced and well-documented bias against the publication of nonsignificant findings.[1,13]

There are, however, several considerations that militate against the hypothesis that these findings are due to the selective reporting of "positive" studies. First, because of the controversy surrounding psi research, workers in this area tend to be more sensitive to the need for replication and unbiased reporting of *both* positive and negative findings than are scientists working in more conventional problem-areas. The Parapsychological Association is, to the best of my knowledge, the only professional scientific society that has an official policy against the selective reporting of positive results. Second, the fact that 35 percent of these experiments represent negative outcomes shows that *in practice* failures *are* reported. Third, even if we assume, as a worst case estimate, that for each of the significant experiments reported to date, there are 10 unreported and nonsignificant studies (i.e., over 350 unreported failures), the observed results would still be significant. Finally, this estimate is actually quite conservative since it is based on a 5 percent criterion of significance: 35 percent of these experiments are significant at the more stringent 1 percent level and 20 percent of them are significant at the 0.1 percent level.

Thus, these studies of observer influence on physically-remote random devices show a healthy level of replicability by any reasonable standard of behavioral science experimentation. Before proceeding to discuss how this methodology might be profitably extended to more directly address the mind-brain relation, it will be useful to briefly review some of the secondary findings that have emerged thus far through this line of research.

2.2. Goal-directedness and the Role of Feedback

These effects, like those studied in biofeedback, appear to be "goal-directed." The observer's task is to increase the frequency of a feedback signal. He need not know or be concerned with what is "inside the box," i.e., the internal mechanism of the random generator, in order to influence its output. This is indicated by studies in which physical parameters of the device have been systematically varied.[12]

For example, several studies in my laboratory have used a random generator that automatically complements the target *1 microsecond* prior to each trial. This feature was incorporated into our design as a control to cancel out any possible side bias in the output of the device. It serves this function quite adequately: in 7 million control trials, we have observed a total excess of 37 "heads" (observed mean = 50.00053 percent, or 0.027 standard deviations from the expected mean). Some of our experiments explored the role of device feedback in guiding these observer effects. In several studies,[7,15] subject/observers received tone feedback over headphones while relaxing in a room adjacent to the random generator. Their task was to keep the tone ON as much as possible. Unknown to the subjects, the feedback tone was sometimes contingent upon above chance scoring (hits) and sometimes upon below chance scoring (misses). The subjects' goal was to keep the tone ON and they did so to a statistically significant degree, regardless of the feedback contingency. The fact that in these experiments the target was defined *1 microsecond* in advance of the trial would seem to rule out any mechanistic "push-pull" interpretation of these effects, since this operation is approx. *3 orders of magnitude* faster than the speed of human neural transmission, which operates on the order of *milliseconds*.

Successful subjects often describe their state in these experiments as being characterized by passive intention or "wishing," as contrasted with effortful striving, and several experimental studies have shown superior performance with goal-directed as contrasted to process-oriented subject strategies.[9]

While in most of these studies subjects have received feedback to the momentary state of the random device, such feedback does not appear to be necessary in order for these effects to occur. In an experiment with Ingo Swann,[8] we found that his scoring rate improved and was independently significant in part of the experiment in which we increased his distance from the random generator and gave him only total score feedback at the end of each 500 sample run. Swann was separated from the instrument during this phase of the experiment by two 4-inch thick steel walls and a distance of approx. 4 m. Braud and Braud[2] have similarly reported significant random generator effects with subjects who received only delayed and partial feedback. The specificity of these effects is presently unknown. If two independent random sources are run simultaneously such that one drives a subject-monitored feedback display while the other is "silent" (i.e., unobserved), does the effect occur only on the displayed source or does it generalize to the "silent" source? We are currently in the design phase of an experiment to address this question. Needless to say, systematic research on the role of feedback is just beginning in this area. The current "best guess" is probably that momentary device feedback, while not necessary for these effects to occur, does facilitate directional outcomes.

3. Psi Correlates of Volition: A Feasibility Study

To what extent can this methodology be extended to apply more directly to the study of mind-brain interaction? If we provisionally accept the validity of this work, there are several important consequences for further research, the most interesting of which, it seems to me, are these: 1) The findings constitute *prima facie* evidence for two-way interaction between mind and brain, since it would seem most unlikely that mind could directly influence external physical systems and not be able to influence its own brain; 2) it suggests a plausible mechanism of interaction and accounts for the apparent elusiveness of exosomatic psi interactions and 3) it provides a methodological base from which to launch more intensive studies.

What follows is a feasibility exercise. It is loosely based on the speculations of the neurophysiologist J. C. Eccles. Eccles has long argued for a dualistic solution to the problem of psychophysical interaction.[3–5] The brain, according to Eccles, is a *detector* rather than a *generator* of mind. He suggests that "weak mind influences" psychokinetically modify the pattern of discharge of large neural networks.[4] ". . . the neurophysiological hypothesis," says Eccles, "is that the 'will' modifies the spatio-temporal activity of the neuronal network by exerting . . . 'fields of influence' that become affected through this unique detector function of the active cerebral cortex."

This hypothesis suggests that a primary function of psi phenomena is mind-brain communication. This idea is not new with Eccles. It has been proposed in various forms by psi researchers from F. W. H. Myers to J. B. Rhine. The most detailed formulation, prior to that of Eccles, was the "Shin" theory of Thouless and Wiesner.[14]

3.1. General Design

In a preliminary attempt to empirically formulate and test the hypothesis that there is a measurable psi component to volition, we have conducted two pilot studies. This work was carried out primarily by Lawrence Tremmel and myself. In these studies, a noise-driven random generator was used to detect PK activity in relation to subjects' volitional efforts to influence their ongoing EEG activity through biofeedback. Random generator output was sampled and gated ("triggered") by the subjects' success/failure in meeting preset EEG feedback conditions. If Eccles' hypothesis is correct, significant PK effects (i.e., deviations from randomness) should coincide with periods in which the subjects are volitionally active, i.e., when they meet the specified EEG feedback conditions. This was our only prediction in Experiment 1.

3.2. Description of Experiment 1

Ten volunteer subjects each contributed a single session. The subject was seated in a reclining chair in an Industrial Acoustics Corp. 1205A Sound-Isolation Room and was set up for ganzfeld stimulation. EEG recording was monopolar with the active electrode on the left occipital area, referenced to the opposite earlobe. Electrode impedance was 7 Kohms or lower. The subject was informed that the presence of EEG alpha rhythm activity (8-13 Hz) would be associated with an audible tone. The subjects' volitional task during the session was to keep the tone ON as much as possible.

EEG activity was recorded on a Beckman Type R Dynograph. Alpha detection and feedback was via a digital frequency discriminator requiring two alpha waves with a minimal amplitude of 10 uV (peak-to-peak). The random generator was run at 10 trials/sec., with the target bit logically complemented on each trial. Each run consisted of 100 EEG alpha gated trials. Ten runs were taken in each session.

Since no random generator feedback was given, we had no a priori reason to predict directional PK outcomes. PK scores were obtained by squaring the z-scores for each run and summing across runs to obtain a chi-square value with 10 df. The overall PK results were significant, with $\chi^2(100) = 145.7$ and $p = 0.002$ (2-tailed). Independently significant ($P_{0.05}$) random generator results were obtained in three of the 10 experimental sessions.

The results of this experiment, while demonstrating a significant PK effect, are ambiguous with regard to Eccles' hypothesis. Since we did not monitor ungated random generator output (i.e., when subject's EEG was outside the feedback range), it is possible that the observed PK effect was unrelated to subjects' EEG. Even had we monitored ungated random generator output and found the PK effect to be isolated to the gated EEG feedback condition, the results would still be ambiguous with respect to Eccles' hypothesis, since such a result might indicate an intrinsic EEG-PK relationship rather than a psi correlate of volition.

3.3. Description of Experiment 2

We addressed these issues in our second experiment. We monitored both gated (alpha) and ungated (nonalpha) random generator output and added a no-feedback "baseline" condition. The "baseline" condition was identical to the EEG feedback condition except that subjects were asked to simply relax and were not given EEG feedback or volitional instructions. This provided a basis for discriminating between the intrinsic alpha-PK hypothesis and the hypothesis that there is a psi component to volition.

Several procedural changes were made in Experiment 2: 1) EEG electrode placement was C_z to linked earlobes; 2) EEG recording and feedback was via an Autogenic Systems 120a EEG Analyzer; 3) the total number of random generator trials per run (gated + ungated) was increased to 500; 4) soft music was provided subjects over headphones with EEG feedback superimposed over the music during EEG

TABLE 1

Experiment 2: Mean Chi-squares/Run by Condition

Condition	Gated RNG	Ungated RNG	$t(16)$	P(t)
EEG Feedback	1.33 ± 0.47	0.80 ± 0.31	2.58	<0.01
Baseline (No Fbk)	0.97 ± 0.22	1.01 ± 0.35	<1	n.s.
$t(16)$	1.95	<1		
P(t)	<0.034	n.s.		

feedback periods and 5) subjects' EEG feedback was shaped by the experimenter by increasing the minimal amplitude threshold so as to maintain EEG alpha feedback approx. 20–30 percent-time during the feedback runs.

We tested the following predictions in Experiment 2: 1) the significant PK effect of Experiment 1 would be replicated in the gated feedback condition; 2) gated feedback PK scores would be significantly larger than ungated feedback scores; 3) gated feedback PK scores would be significantly larger than gated baseline PK scores and 4) for the gated feedback condition, there would be a significant relationship between EEG frequency and amplitude changes within the session and overall PK scores.

Seven subjects each contributed a single session. One subject contributed two sessions and another contributed three. Thus, 12 sessions were completed altogether under these conditions. In each session, the subject completed 10 runs of 500 random generator trials in both the "baseline" and EEG feedback conditions.

Results by condition are shown in Table 1. For the gated feedback condition, the PK results are significant, with $\chi^2(120 \ df) = 159.2$, and $p = 0.005$ (1-tailed). Thus, the alpha gated PK results of the first experiment are replicated, confirming our first prediction. PK results for the remaining three conditions (feedback ungated, baseline gated, ungated) are nonsignificant.

Predictions 2 and 3 were examined by t tests for uncorrelated means. The PK scores for gated EEG feedback trials are significantly higher ($p = 0.01$, 1-tailed) than the ungated feedback PK scores. This result indicates that the PK effect is related to subjects' EEG alpha activity, confirming our second prediction. Moreover, and very important considering Eccles' hypothesis, the gated EEG feedback PK scores are significantly higher ($p = 0.034$, 1-tailed) than the gated baseline PK scores, suggesting a relationship between PK and EEG feedback rather than an intrinsic relationship between PK and EEG alpha activity (prediction 3). These latter two findings isolate the PK effect in this experiment to the gated EEG feedback condition. Prediction 4 was not confirmed. Although in the anticipated direction, degree of change in EEG frequency and amplitude parameters were not significantly related to PK scores. Pooling the PK results of Experiment 1 with the comparable gated feedback condition in Experiment 2, we find $z' = 4.04$, and $p = 2.56 \times 10^{-5}$.

As I stated earlier, this work constitutes no more than a crude feasibility study. We are now in the process of designing an extensive replication of the second experiment. We are aware that there are many conceptual and methodological problems to be overcome. I welcome your criticisms and suggestions.

BIBLIOGRAPHY

1. Bozarth, J. D. and Roberts, R. R., *American Psychologist*, 1972(27), 774.
2. Braud, L. W. and Braud, W. G., *Research in Parapsychology 1977*.
3. Eccles, J. C., *The Neurophysiological Basis of Mind*, Oxford University Press, 1953.
4. Eccles, J. C., *Research in Parapsychology 1976*. 151–162.
5. Eccles, J. C., In Popper, K. and Eccles, J. C., *The Self and its Brain*, New York, Springer International, 1977.
6. Honorton, C., "Replicability, Experimenter Influence, and Parapsychology: An Empirical Context for the Study of Mind," Paper presented at the annual meeting of the American Association for the Advancement of Science, Washington, D.C., February, 1978.
7. Honorton, C., *Research in Parapsychology 1976*, 95–97.
8. May, E. C. and Honorton, C., *Bulletin of the American Physical Society*, 1976(21), 43.
9. Morris, R. L., Nanko, M. and Phillips, D., *Research in Parapsychology 1978*, in press.
10. Schmidt, H., *J. Applied Physics*, 1970(41), 462.
11. Schmidt, H., *Journal of Parapsychology*, 1970(34), 175.
12. Schmidt, H. and Pantas, L., *Journal of Parapsychology*, 1972(36), 222.
13. Sterling, T. C., *Journal of the American Statistical Association*, 1959(54), 30.
14. Thouless, R. H. and Wiesner, B. P., *Journal of Parapsychology*, 1948(12), 192.
15. Winnett, R. and Honorton, C., *Research in Parapsychology 1976*, 97.

DISCUSSION

TART: I'd like to make two brief comments. One is supporting Chuck's comment that he doesn't think these PK results might be a sample of only the successful experiments, the ones that happen to get selectively published. In a general survey of the field some years ago, I did a questionnaire survey of members of the Parapsychological Association and asked them how many experiments they had done *altogether* in the field, as well as how many they had published. In general, I found that something like one out of every three experiments is published, rather than the approximately one out of every twenty you'd expect if only positive results were getting published.

Secondly, I think there's a methodological point you made that's really very important and I just want to emphasize it. That is that results of PK tests on generators that are running several orders of magnitude faster than we can imagine neurological processes to run are specially important in arguing for some kind of dualistic interpretation of the results. That's really an exceptionally important point.

DIXON: I hestitate to ask this question as a non-parapsychologist, but it seems to me there is a philosophical problem here and also a methodological one—you can have an animate system that is affecting an inanimate one—the PK effect. You can have an inanimate affecting an animate system—the clairvoyance situation. You can also of course, have two animate systems affecting each other at a distance. It follows, therefore, that it would seem logical to expect that two inanimate systems could affect each other, but if they can, then this disposes of the parapsychological hypothesis entirely, *unless* you postulate, and you may have evidence of this, I don't know, that the presence somewhere of an animate system is somehow a catalyst for relationships between two inanimate systems. I don't know if this experiment has ever been done, but it seems to me it's one that should be done.

HONORTON: The problem with your proposals, it seems to me, is that so far (at least) no one has come up with a way in which you could test a synchronistic correspondence, let's say, between two computers, that could not be explained in terms of the final observation by some experimenter. There is a great deal of discussion among the physicists who are entering this area now as to the role of the observer. If momentary feedback to the temporary state of the device is not necessary, then maybe the end result is. What I didn't mention is that when we do the control tests, where we're looking at the "normal" operation of the machine, there's a lot of superstitious behavior that goes on. My standard procedure is to cross my fingers, hope it will come out very close to chance and leave the room. And I suspect, for me as a PK subject, my motivation is probably much higher in the control test than it would be in the experimental one, because if that machine is not behaving normally, then that casts doubt on any of the experimental results. I don't see how you could do that experiment to get the observer out of it. At some point somebody is going to come and look at the results, and that may be all that's necessary. I wouldn't know how to get the observer, who is going to come and look at the results at some point, out of it, so that we could isolate the effects to the inanimate systems rather than to the experimenter, who has needs or motivations in relation to the outcome of the experiment that might be satisfied in this way. The same problem occurs in animal research in this field. Some years ago there were some studies between a human and a paramecium, making a paramecium move to one side of the Petri dish. What was going on there? Was that the paramecium having the effect or was it the experimenter? There really is no clear way of resolving that. Over the last few years we've become very self-conscious over our inability to get the experimenter out of it and I've come to at least a temporary conclusion that it may be impossible in a fundamental sense to isolate the psi effects to a specific organism. It's quite clear that we can demonstrate that there is an interaction going on, but to say conclusively that it's the subject rather than the experimenter who goes through a randomization procedure or some other aspect of the experiment that could provide the basis for the result, there's really no clear-cut way of doing that, at least at present.

KELLY: Departing from what you just said, Chuck, I would reinforce that by saying to the non-parapsychologists particularly, that once one begins to take these things seriously, they intrude upon one's life as an experimenter in the most unexpected and horrible ways; and in this experiment I think we have a clear case of this kind of thing. It's impossible to resolve on any clear-cut and decisive logical grounds what the true source of the effects of this experiment are. I must say that I personally feel an almost overpowering compulsion to suppose that it's you, Chuck. One reason is that it seems to me entirely implausible that mind influence could be distributed in this kind of spatial way. For example, let us suppose that I were talking to Dr. Bigu; as I approach him might my mental processes begin to interact with his in such a way as to confuse their normal operation? Or, for example, in the kind of experiments that Graham Watkins did with anesthetized mice, where the mice were lying side by side on a platform—why should the intentions of the subject not have affected both mice equally? It just seems to me implausible that an intentional effect of this sort could be distributed spatially. I would much rather see you as the subject.

Also, I think it's implausible in more specific ways. For example, in your experiment, the suggestion is made that when a person is successfully willing something, he's more likely to have this kind of a field effect in the neighborhood. If there were to be any such effects, I would almost have expected exactly the opposite. It seems more likely that, if a subject is successful, he is affecting the particular system that he's trying to affect, whereas, if he's not successful, he may be just missing in a physically adjacent way. On that basis one might have expected the scoring on the generator to occur when he's *failing* at the task.

HONORTON: Well, I certainly cannot deny the possibility that I might be a major source, or Tremmel, who was the other experimenter, but why should either of us have that effect? It's not a clear choice between a plausible and an implausible explanation. It's really a choice between several implausible possibilities and it seems to me that it's much too early, given the small amount of systematic research that's been done in this area, to suggest one or the other interpretation with regard to specificity here. There haven't been any studies to my knowledge. Maybe you know of some in which two independent generators are being monitored simultaneously, where one is being observed and the other isn't. I would say that such a study could be crucial to the interpretation of this kind of study. If there's a generalized effect, then that, I think, would tend to support the idea that we have in these random generator studies a crude detector of, for lack of a better term right now, mind influence. As far as the Watkins studies are concerned, why didn't the subjects affect both mice equally? I don't think we can say that they didn't. At least some of that work seemed to involve a differential effect where the results weren't clearly significant on the target mouse, but it was a difference between the target mouse and the control mouse that was significant.

BELOFF: I cannot let the occasion pass without wanting to congratulate Chuck Honorton on being the very first parapsychologist who has attempted experimentally to test what I would still like to call the Thouless/Wiesner theory, although he's related it much more to Eccles' recent speculations. This theory was put forward twenty years ago, but, so far as I know, no one has ever seen a way to try and test it experimentally. But I am still a bit worried about the point Ed Kelly raised and which I don't think you've quite met yet, which is why—and I'm sure Eccles would have difficulty seeing this sort of inference drawn from his theory—if we are successfully controlling our brain rhythms, we should or should need to influence some external physical system. I can't quite see how you make this deduction from the theory. Perhaps you could elaborate on this more clearly.

HONORTON: I don't have a good answer to that. The best that I have at the moment is that the random source is in circuit here. It's been gated by the subject's meeting or not meeting the EEG conditions and may therefore be more likely to show some peripheral influence than it would otherwise. What I'm trying to do here, and it's admittedly very crude, is simply to start seeing how we might apply some of the psi research methodology to this question and begin some empirical work where previously it has been entirely speculative. I don't have any tremendous investment in the Eccles' type of interpretation of these effects, and it could be just as valuable or important if it turned out to be an intrinsic relationship between psi and EEG activity. In the second experiment, the effect is isolated very clearly to the condition in which the subjects are given feedback and are successful in meeting the feedback conditions. So there seems to be something about feedback which is not contingent on the random source here that is important.

PRIBRAM: You said the first experiment, suggested a plausible mechanism of interaction and I wondered what that plausible mechanism is.

HONORTON: Well, maybe it's plausible only to me. I think that for all its vagueness and speculative quality, what intrigues me about Eccles' speculation is that he's suggesting here a way in which the phenomena that we in parapsychology are studying might have a natural home. That is, psi phenomena are characterized in the way that we've been studying them, by their sporadic nature, and if it were to turn out that a primary function of psi phenomena is to provide a means of communicating back and forth between brain and mind—whatever mind is—that would provide a plausible explanation, from the parapsychological end, at least, in terms of making psi phenomena fit in.

PRIBRAM: That's not a plausible mechanism.

HONORTON: No, it's not a mechanism.

PRIBRAM: You said plausible mechanism.

HONORTON: I will take that back.

PRIBRAM: Or even a possible explanation, if you will. What's the explanation? You're simply saying Eccles has "mind" wandering about the association cortex and this somehow relates to what you're saying. I don't see the connection. By the way, that's the only thing concerning what you said today about which I have some reservations. I think there is an explanation which I'll present tomorrow.

HONORTON: What are you asking for in terms of explanation?

PRIBRAM: Well, an explanation of synchronicity; an explanation in terms of reasons.

HONORTON; Perhaps explanation is too strong. It seems to me to be a plausible possibility given the fact that we do have good evidence that human beings are able in some anomalous way to interact with remote physical devices.

PRIBRAM: We know that we can interact with physical devices. I can write a computer program, and that computer program can then manipulate the switches in the machine. That isn't the problem. The problem is that in your experiments we don't know the "connection" between the events. Somehow the connection seems mysterious and unexplained. This, not the fact the events occurred, is what produces doubt in the scientific community. Thus, I repeat—it's the "connection" between events that remains mysterious.

HONORTON: It clearly is at this point.

PRIBRAM: Then you don't have a plausible explanation.

HONORTON: O.K., I don't have a plausible explanation.

EHRENWALD: Thank you. I think we have now witnessed the enormous philosophical or epistemological difficulties into which we are running when we try to account for certain parapsychological phenomena. I advisedly say "account," because I get cold feet at the thought of "explanations." I think we can find a way out of this if we try to make, first of all, two propositions. One proposition would be (and this is perhaps in response to Dr. Dixon's remark) that psi does not happen between two machines—it cannot, because unless there is, sooner or later, a human observer to register the fact that something happened which was not just random, independent of any human being, no statement can be made. When psi happens, it invariably is predicated on the involvement of the human factor. Now this leads to a nearly unmanageable source of error in every parapsychological experiment. I called attention to it many years ago when I talked about para-experimental telepathy, telepathic leakage, para-experimental PK or doctrinal compliance. This was later on taken up by Robert Rosenthal's description of observer bias influencing even normal psychological experiments. We know today in the parapsychological setting, the experimenter's expectations invariably have an effect. It is one of our main concerns to find out how much the observed effect is due to experimenter expectations and how much is due to other intrinsic factors which are independent of the observer. As far as the continuity or the connection between my ability to influence my EEG pattern and influencing an object "out there" is concerned, I have tried to make allowance for this fact by proposing my Extension Hypothesis, leaning closely on the theories of Thouless and Wiesner. I submit that we have gotten so used to the fact that my "selfconscious mind" can influence my body and my brain that we have stopped wondering about it. Honorton's experiments redirect our attention to it. They are striking illustrations of the extension hypothesis. Unfortunately, we cannot account for them in strictly mechanistic terms. Nor can Karl Popper's reference to what he calls "promissory materialism."

TART: First, there is the point raised by Dr. Kelly about the specificity of psi. I think that we should remember that, when we ask someone to do a psi task, we're asking someone to basically do a "miracle" that he's had no practice on, and he doesn't really know what to do, so it shouldn't be surprising if the result comes out rather non-specifically. If we look at an infant first attempting to move something, we get a lot of crude movements rather than the controlled motor skill we're used to later. I think there's a lot of evidence that indicates that psi is often used in a way that's poorly focused, that's not very controlled.

Second, I think Chuck should use PK even more strongly as an *explanation*, and not simply as a paradoxical thing we can observe. I think saying that we use PK to influence brain mechanisms is not really a different order of statement than saying the reason we have light coming out of these ceiling fixtures is because we have "electricity." In either case we have an invisible something that we never observe directly. We see effects and we postulate something behind them. I'll go out on a limb tomorrow when I give my paper and use PK in a much more positive sense rather than simply as experimental anomalies.

Third, on Dr. Dixon's question about whether two inanimate systems might use something equivalent to psi. I've been associating with a lot of physicists lately and their world view is so totally weird and unusual that parapsychological phenomena seem much more commonplace to me! One effect that has intrigued me very much lately that sounds exactly like psychic effects between two inanimate systems is an experiment based on the Einstein-Podolsky-Rosen paradox. As I understand it, you generate two particles that move apart at the speed of light and have absolutely no connection; you perturb one and the perturbation affects the other one. Now, that sounds to me like a classic PK experiment where you totally isolate two physical systems and then show an effect that's non-explainable in terms of current explanatory systems. My physicist friends assure me this is not hypothetical; the experiment has been done, and works this way. Naturally, they simply now try to modify the explanatory system, but it sounds very much like a classical PK experiment, ignoring the later effect of the experimenter in making the experiment happen. Of course, the very fact that we, as animate systems, ask the question, immediately involves us in it.

SMALL: To go back to the specific experimental design that you were talking about, if I understand you correctly, it seems to me that there are two things involved. One would be the direct application of Eccles' hypothesis and a question of volition—in other words, the intention of the subject to create that effect. The other thing would be feedback, and I'm not sure whether that's clearly distinguished here. The test of whether the feedback is necessary seems to me to relate to Helmut Schmidt's idea that in order to get psi, there has to be feedback involved. On the other hand, it seems to me Eccles' idea would have implied that only intention was necessary without necessarily the feedback. Can you comment on that?

HONORTON: I think Schmidt has either severely modified or has abandoned his feedback postulate because there have been a number of studies in which there is no momentary feedback to the random source. That's the kind of feedback Schmidt is talking about. The kind of feedback that was given in these experiments was to the subject's EEG activity, not to the random source. The random source was being gated on the basis of whether or not the subject was meeting the prescribed EEG conditions, but there was no feedback from the random source except, of course, to the experimenter who took down the data, and is an alternate possible psi source here. I said that there are many methodological problems here defining volition in a way that is empirically useful. That is a very big problem. If anybody has any suggestions on how to do that better, I'd appreciate hearing about it. The subjects' task was to keep the tone on and to the extent that they kept the tone on we defined that as satisfying the volitional condition of the experiment.

KELLY: Despite my earlier critical remarks, I fundamentally admire these experiments, and just wanted to raise a question about their interpretation. I think, particularly, it's encouraging the way you're going about developing it. Clearly you're focusing in on the relevant aspects of the proposal, but I'd also like to suggest there might be other ways to go about the same kind of thing. It seems to me, for example, to flow much more directly from the theory, that there would be certain kinds of systems that should be much easier to affect. In particular, systems that become more neural-like in their structure might be easier to affect. Majority vote systems, for example, have a distant connection to neural networks. You can think of a majority vote as a particular kind of decision structure. You can also loosen the requirements on that structure to have more neural-like patterns of connectivity among the elements that you're deciding with, and, of course, the ultimate generalization of that would be to work on brains themselves. It might be by doing allo-biofeedback experiments such as William Braud has done, but doing them with EEGs or something of that sort. I also believe it's now technically possible to maintain fairly sizeable clumps of neural tissue *ex vitro*, as it were, and have them functioning. That might constitute a particularly interesting system to try a PK experiment with. Of course Eccles himself might counter negative results by retreating further into his notion of "openness" to liaison.

HONORTON: Yes, we're also thinking about a possible parapsychological version of the Kornhuber experiment where the subject, at his own discretion, just wiggling his finger, gates the random generator, to see whether there is a specific PK effect associated with that kind of volitional act. In closing, my own enthusiasm here, which is quite strong, is not toward any data that we have, but the potential of some of our psi research methodology for making a positive contribution to help develop an empirical approach to some of these problems. I believe that had Eccles and Popper in their book and Penfield in his made use of parapsychological data, they would have a much stronger case.

A BIOPHYSICAL APPROACH TO PARANORMAL PHENOMENA

J. Bigu

Introduction

Countless attempts made in the past have been aimed at explaining certain kinds of phenomena which, because of their peculiarity, have come to be known as paranormal or psi phenomena. All psi phenomena share a commonly intriguing although disturbing feature: their occurrence cannot be accounted for or predicted by any conventional prevailing scientific ideas. This fact has prompted a number of researchers to advance a variety of theories ranging from those based on rather unorthodox physicalistic concepts to theories rooted in psychological, neurophysiological and spiritualistic arguments. However, it is only fair to say that while a great majority of these theories have met with little success when put to experimental test, others, by virtue of their very foundation, are virtually untestable and, therefore, non-falsifiable.

This paper is aimed at developing a physicalistic approach to psi phenomena based on biophysical and psychophysiological arguments. Because main emphasis for the basis of this theory is placed on the interaction of environmental stimuli and biological systems, biophysical mechanisms thus playing a fundamental role, the theory presented in this paper will be referred to as a biophysical theory of psi phenomena. This paper is an extension of an earlier one published by the author elsewhere.[1]

This paper will first review several physicalistic theories of psi phenomena put forward in the last few decades. A brief discussion of the significance and limitations of these theories will be made, and the need for a different approach will be indicated. Next, a description of various naturally occurring and man-made sources of different stimuli will be followed by a brief discussion of the different interactions of these stimuli with living organisms. Finally, a possible theory based on multiple stimuli-multiple biological response relationships, derived from the above biointeractions, will be tentatively formulated.

Some Physicalistic Theories of PSI

Theories of psi phenomena can be broadly classified into physicalistic, non-physicalistic and hybrid, i.e. those containing both physicalistic and non-physicalistic arguments. Non-physicalistic theories argue that ESP and PK, and other related psi phenomena, are mediated by unknown *non-physical* fields of force, forms of energy, or other *non-physical* agents. Spiritualistic theories fall in this category. In contrast, physicalistic theories postulate physical fields of force, forms of energy, or other physical agents, although perhaps as yet unknown or undiscovered, as the sole effective sources of psi. Finally, models of psi phenomena have been suggested which integrate some aspects of both physicalistic and non-physicalistic arguments.

This section will examine some of the most advanced physicalistic theories of telepathy and precognition. Only brief comments will be made in reference to non-physicalistic and other theories. The present review on theoretical models of psi, which does not pretend to be exhaustive, is aimed at indicating some advantages and some weaknesses inherent in these theories. It is also intended to serve as an introduction, and as a platform, to a tentative formulation of a *biophysical theory of psi* (which will be undertaken in a subsequent section) which in the author's mind seems more promising in the context of psi phenomena, than other existing theories.

Although reasons of space prevent discussion at a reasonable length, a few introductory remarks will be in order with regard to the possible role of the unconscious and of different states of consciousness in psi phenomena.

It has frequently been argued that paranormal experiences strongly depend on several parameters such as: 1) the psychological "state" of the subject (e.g. expectation, beliefs, interest), 2) the subject's attitude toward psi phenomena, 3) the emotional content of the psi message relative to the subject and 4) the state of consciousness of the subject (e.g. "trance," meditation, hypnotic states, sleep, dreaming, drug-induced states).

The importance of the unconscious in parapsychological experiences has often been indicated. The dream telepathy experiments conducted by Ullman et al.[2] and the telepathy experiments carried out by Vasiliev[3] using subjects under hypnotic states, provide clear evidence in favor of this contention. Other equally relevant research such as that conducted by Targ and Puthoff[4] on "remote viewing," and by Schmidt[5] on precognition using a random number generator (RNG), do not provide clear or direct evidence for the role of the unconscious in these phenomena. The results obtained by the above authors can only be interpreted if the psi message 1) is received and/or conveyed via the unconscious, or subliminally, emerging somehow into consciousness (in the case of telepathy) by so far unknown mechanisms; or 2) is conveyed at a conscious level; or a combination of 1) and 2). Relevant to item 2) is a quantum mechanical theory of consciousness developed by Walker[6] to provide a foundation theory for psi phenomena. Equally relevant to items 1) and 2) is a neurophysiological theory put forward by Ehrenwald[7]. A mathematical theory has been proposed by Schmidt[8] which contains "psi sources," the properties of which are axiomatically specified in mathematical form with no attempt to reduce these properties to some underlying mechanisms. Chari[9], after a review of the attempts at a physical theory of psi, has called for an unprecedented revaluation of psi physics. An excellent review of psi theories has been given by Rao.[10]

A. Theories of Telepathy

1. Electromagnetic Theories

It has been known for a long time that the brain is a source of low frequency electromagnetic (EM) activity. Also, there is overwhelming experimental evidence suggesting the brain as the center of consciousness and of the unconscious "mind" to which psi phenomena are closely related. Consequently, these arguments combined led some researchers to formulate an EM theory of psi phenomena. Chronologically speaking, theories of telepathy based on electromagnetic considerations were the first to be considered.

One of the initial attempts to account for telepathy, mental suggestion (hypnosis) and the like was based on the electrical activity of the brain's cortex. The cortex activity gives rise to the brain rhythms which are known to bear a close relationship to the mental and health states of the individual. The activity of the cortex extends from approximately 0 to 50 Hz in frequency. The alpha-rhythm ($\sim$ 10 Hz) was first measured on the human scalp by Berger.[11] After the initial attempt, a theory of telepathy based on brain-rhythm activity was abandoned because of 1) the minute amount of energy available from the brain at these frequencies and 2) inverse-square law considerations.

Bechterev considered mental suggestions to be affected by high frequency (HF) EM waves, and several theories were put forward to explain the existence of these HF components. The HF EM theory of mental suggestion and telepathy seemed to be confirmed by the work of Cazzamalli[12] conducted through the years 1925–1933. Experiments carried out by Vasiliev[3] indicated, as expected from EM theory, that such a HF component could not penetrate metal shielding, i.e. a Faraday cage, where the subjects were located. Vasiliev's results suggest that the notion of a HF component associated with telepathy is no longer tenable, and hence that Cazzamalli's contentions were in error. Bigu[13] conducted some radiometric measurements, based on the solid-state properties of tissue, which would indicate that some spurious effect might have been the cause of Cazzamalli's results.

The above review raises the following arguments in the author's mind.

A. The "equivalent" average power density, say P, of the brain can be calculated from experimental values for the electric field (E) obtained from EEG recordings by means of standard EM theory. Assuming there is no impedance mismatch at the scalp/air boundary, and that the field is "viewed" at long distances from the source (i.e. brain), one obtains values in the 10^{-15} to 10^{-11} watt/cm^2 range for E's from 10^{-4} to 10^{-2} V/m, respectively. Values for E vary markedly and depend on location, individual and frequency. Strictly speaking, the values for P represent the power arising from E within the frequency bandwidth of the amplifiers used in the EEG recordings. The power radiated by the body at 9 GHz in a 100 MHz frequency band is approximately 10^{-13} watt/cm^2. This power density can be easily detected by radiometers; this radiation does convey a wealth of information about the state of the body over limited distances. This latter comment also applies to EEG frequencies. The topic of telepathy in particular and biocommunication in general, with reference to the radiofrequency (RF) and MW bands, has been discussed by Bigu[14] elsewhere.

B. The inverse-square law need not necessarily apply to the case of telepathy.[14] Of equal or greater importance, the inverse-square law is only applicable at distances from the source which are much larger than the wavelength of the emitted radiation, i.e. the far zone of the radiating element (brain).

C. The theories postulated to account for radiation of much higher frequency that that corresponding to EEG, EMG, and ECG frequencies, and hence corresponding to Cazzamalli's frequency, are totally unnecessary.

D. The brain plays a central and unique role in these EM theories of telepathy. In the author's opinion, the "state," in its most general sense, of a biological system must be described not only by the "activity" of the brain but by the EM activity of the entire body. This total state could be represented by an EM state function ψ. The EM fields produced by the muscle and the heart, as well as those very slowly varying and DC fields measured on the skin, are also related to the mental, psychological, emotional and health states of the individual. Hence, the argument raised in item D seems quite appropriate.

II. The Neutrino Theory

Hammond[15] proposed a theory of telepathy based on the rather unique properties of the neutrino, e.g. travel at the speed of light, no measurable mass and great penetration of matter. Tyson[16] pointed out that the body was a source of neutrinos (due to the decay of K^{40}, a naturally occurring radioisotope, present in tissue) and hence a neutrino theory of telepathy was feasible. A simple calculation based on the amount of K^{40} in the body (~0.031 mg) shows that the neutrino emission is only about 8×10^3 neutrinos/sec (i.e. ~0.4 neutrino/cm^2). Since the interaction cross-section of the neutrino with matter is extremely small (~10^{-44} cm^2) it seems unlikely that the combination of such a small interaction cross-section and limited neutrino flux can account for telepathic communication.

Ruderfer[17] has attempted to reformulate the neutrino hypothesis by postulating a hard scattering interaction of the brain with the *neutrino sea*, i.e. neutrinos of solar and interstellar origin. No formal attempt has been made by any of the above authors to deal with the neutrino theory from the informational standpoint. No discussion or suggestions have been made of how the neutrino would interact with living matter, and therefore how encoding (by the sender) and decoding (by the receiver) of information would be achieved.

III. Other Theories of Telepathy

The models examined above, all have a common feature: the carrier of telepathic information is a physically observable quantity. Other theories, which argue to be physicalistic in nature, postulate "physical" agents with properties currently not observed experimentally. The following are examples of this:

Wassermann,[18] based on quantum mechanical considerations, has postulated a "psi-field" which would enable one to have parapsychological experiences. The "psi-field" has "very narrowly-spaced energy levels" and occupies "wide regions of space." These fields receive and emit "extremely small quantities of energy," smaller than the quanta observed by matter fields. Wasserman concludes that his model allows radiation of "energy" over long distances without it becoming absorbed by matter fields. Roll[19] also proposes "psi-fields" (analogous to EM and gravitational fields), although in his case these fields interact with known physical fields and with each other. Mindons, psychons and psitrons[20] have also been postulated. Psitrons will be discussed below under theories of precognition.

Other theories have also been advanced, such as Marshall's theory of resonance[21] and the "collective unconscious" theory of Price.[22] An interesting idea, the Paranormal Matrix, has been put forward by Murphy. The discussion on theories of telepathy will end here. The interested reader should consult Rao[10] for more information about the subject.

B. Theories of Precognition

1. Advanced Potential Theory

Targ[23] has presented an hypothesis, based on advanced potential theory, in which significant events create a perturbation in the space-time continuum in which they occur, and this disturbance propagates forward and, to a small degree, backward in time. Since precognitive phenomena are rare, this disturbance, Targ argues, must die out quite rapidly in the negative time direction (i.e. advanced solution). The wave traveling in the positive time direction (i.e. retarded solution) is associated with causality as usually experienced. According to Targ's model, events closer in time (along the negative time direction) to their actual occurrence should be more easily "precognized" than further back events in this time direction. Eventually, events far back in the negative time direction could not be precognized. Although a commendable feature of this model is that it can be falsified, it raises several serious questions some of which are indicated below.

Targ does not elaborate on the specific shape of his hypothesized space-time decay function; rather it appears it should be acquired through experiment. The time cut-off of this function is also left unspecified. An analysis of scattered data available seems to argue, in fact, against Targ's precognition-time dependence.

It is well known in electrodynamics, acoustics and other branches of physics that the second-order differential equation

$$\nabla^2 \phi - (1/c^2) \frac{\partial^2 \phi}{\partial t^2} = \rho(x,t)$$

has two solutions described as the retarded and the advanced solutions, respectively. In the above Eq. ϕ is the amplitude of some space-time dependent wave phenomenon (e.g. electric field strength, spatial particle displacement accompanying a pressure wave). ν is the velocity of the perturbation in the medium (e.g. $\nu \simeq 340$ m/sec for sound waves in air at NTP). ρ represents the source of perturbation, electromagnetic, acoustic. It is not difficult to see that the advanced solution will give values for ϕ at advanced times t given by $t = L/\nu$ where L is the distance between the source and the observer. Taking $L = 2 \times 10^4$ Km (i.e. the semiperimeter of the Earth) and assuming that ϕ propagates along the earth's surface, with no energy loss, one arrives at $t = 6.7 \times 10^{-2}$ sec, for EM waves, and $t \simeq 16$ h, for acoustic waves. Thus, the advanced solution for EM wave is not likely to play an important role in precognition unless the wave encounters an "anomalous" region of space with properties which introduce a substantial time delay. The advanced solution for acoustic radiation is more relevant in the context of precognition, as will be indicated in a future section. Unfortunately, except for infrasonic frequencies, higher "sound" frequency is rapidly attenuated in most media, especially air.

Feinberg[24] suggested a theory, similar to that of Targ's, in which he combined advanced potential theory and short term memory. As the starting point, Feinberg assumes that when some sensory input reaches the brain, an oscillatory variation of certain patterns internal to the brain occurs which is specific to the input. This oscillatory pattern, he theorizes, has not only a retarded part which propagates forward in time (i.e. memory), but also an advanced part propagating along the negative direction of time (i.e. precognition). The relative amounts of the retarded and advanced solutions are not defined, but the latter would presumably be much smaller than the former. Both Feinberg and Targ impose this condition based on experience which indicates that precognition is a rare phenomenon and an ineffective faculty. Feinberg suggests that precognition would be the symmetrical counterpart of memory. Because of the rapid decay of the advanced part, precognition is the counterpart of *short term memory* and shows the same characteristic K-decay curve as the latter. Feinberg goes even further to speculate that individuals with good memory may be better precognition subjects.

The criticism given above for Targ's theory is also applicable to Feinberg's model. In addition, any attempt to link memory, a not so well understood topic itself, to precognition is speculative at this moment. The reader will also notice that, according to Feinberg's theory, precognition is not applicable to events beyond short time memory (i.e. in the seconds to hours range). Hence "prediction" in the order of months or years is not possible. This contradicts reasonably well documented evidence in some special cases. Another difficulty arises in connection with flashbacks and hypnotic hyperamnesia: How would precognition be related to memory in these instances?

II. Tachyons

Tachyons, particles that can only move faster-than-light, were postulated by Feinberg[25] when investigating the solutions of relativity for particles with $m^2 < 0$ (where m indicates mass). Contrary to common belief these hypothetical particles do not imply any contradiction of relativity. It has been argued that tachyons, in traveling faster than light, would violate the laws of causality, providing man with the possibility of signaling to his own past. Based on this, the suggestion has been made that the tachyon might be a good candidate for a model of precognition. Apart from the argument that a variety of (apparently) causal and time paradoxes might arise in a world where faster-than-light particles exist, there are other serious objections associated with a tachyon theory of precognition; some of these objections will be discussed below. (The literature on paradoxes associated with time reversals and faster than light particles is far too extensive to be reviewed here. The interested reader should consult ref. 26 and references therein.

It is open to question whether or not tachyons could convey useful information to us, in the usual sense that we understand it.

No mechanism for tachyon production is known. The existence of these particles is debatable. There has only been a *possible* confirmation on the existence of tachyons.[27] Even if they did exist, only the neutral tachyon would be of interest here because of its long lifetime. Neutral tachyons would have a very low interaction crosssection to interact with matter, although details on their interaction have not yet been worked out. Since some form of interaction of living matter (brain, body, etc.) with tachyons is necessary to convey information from the source of the subject, it is difficult to foresee, in view of the above discussion, how a neutral tachyon would play a role in precognition.

Other communication difficulties of negative mass (in the mathematical sense) particles will be discussed below when dealing with psitrons.

III. Psitrons

Dobbs[28] put forward a 2-D time theory of precognition. One time dimension is hypothesized to move deterministically, in the usual way to which we are accustomed, but the second time dimension moves in a probabilistic way. In Dobbs' theory, the second time dimension contains the objective probabilities of future outcomes, which incline or predispose the future to occur in certain specific ways. Hypothetical messengers called "psitrons" (operating in this time dimension) are radiated by the system transmitting information not only about the *actual* state of the system but also "pre-casts" of its inherently probably future state. The psitron, as the tachyon, has negative mass (in the mathematical sense) and thus, according to Relativity, can travel faster than light. Dobbs postulates that the psitron operates on the brain (neuron), but no specific interactions are suggested.

A drawback of this theory, and of most of the psi theories so far advanced, is that although "explaining" psi it does not explain common sensory perception. A consequence of a theory involving particles of imaginary mass (i.e. psitron and tachyon) is that it would rule out the possibility of harnessing psi as a new means of systematic communication. Of greater importance is the principle that no entropy change would occur in either the radiator or the receiver (due to absorption and emission); such transitions without entropy changes *cannot* carry information according to the accepted principles of physical communication theory.

With few exceptions most of the physicalistic theories outlined above either postulate physical agents or space-time structures with properties so far not experimentally observed or they do not take into consideration the most essential feature of psi, i.e. its intrinsic biological nature. It is the author's contention that psi phenomena cannot be dissociated from their biological essence. It is therefore suggested that a more promising avenue would entail the exploration of conventional physical agents-e.g. environmental stimuli—and their interaction with living organisms, particularly man.

The complexity of our environment is considerable. A systematic study of the wide variety of stimuli found in our environment is beyond the scope of this paper. Hence, a choice has been made to deal briefly only with those stimuli for which direct experimental evidence of their effects on biological systems is available. Several potentially interesting stimuli—in the context of this paper—have been intentionally omitted for reasons of space. The environmental stimuli discussed in this paper include part of the electromagnetic (EM) spectrum, acoustic radiation, noise and mechanical vibration, small ions, and particle radiation.

The Natural Environment

I. Electromagnetic Fields of Terrestrial Origin

There are a variety of sources of EM radiation which can be broadly classified as terrestrial (naturally occurring and manmade) or extraterrestrial (naturally occurring). Not all the radiation of terrestrial (extraterrestrial) origin escapes (reaches) the earth's surface; some of this radiation is absorbed in the atmosphere or reflected in the ionosphere.

EM fields of terrestrial origin can be subdivided into the following: 1) fields originating on the earth's surface, arising mainly from blackbody (BB) emissions of both inanimate and living matter; 2) "atmospheric" fields (i.e. spherics) due to metereological conditions, e.g. lightning, thunderstorms and tornadoes; 3) fields originating from stresses in the earth's crust, e.g. earthquakes; 4) fields in the atmosphere mainly due to gases such as O_2, O_3 and H_2O in excited states; 5) fields arising from high energy charged particles of extraterrestrial, mainly solar origin, trapped in the geomagnetic field, e.g. synchrotron radiation; and 6) fields caused by disturbances in the geomagnetosphere attributed to solar influences.

The lowest-frequency fields of natural origin measured on the earth's surface are associated with geomagnetic disturbances which give rise to magnetic fields in the frequency range from approximately 10^{-4} Hz to a few Hz. These fields are called micropulsations and have periods of between approximately 600 sec and 0.2 sec. The "high" frequency region, i.e. Hz range, seems to originate from solar plasma-induced disturbances in the outer magnetosphere. Maximum magnetic flux densities of about several hundred gamma (γ) at 10^{-4} Hz are found. The magnetic power density decreases during maximum sunspot activity.

It has been argued that during earthquakes, seismoelectric effects could result in EM fields in the range from 1 Hz to 10 Hz with a maximum spectral component of a frequency of about 1.5 Hz,[29] with power much less than one watt. Higher frequency transients with much higher power could be produced. The seismoelectric effect referred to above has been postulated to arise from stresses in piezoelectric components of the earth's crust, particularly quartz.

"Atmospherics" are EM fields generated by atmospheric activity, particularly lightning. The frequency range of atmospherics is large, from a few Hz to several GHz, with a maximum near 10 kHz. The amplitude of atmospherics decreases with increasing frequency and distance from the "source." Electric field strengths of up to a few thousand V/m at about 10 kHz can be attained in regions close to the location of lightning discharges.

The tropical regions are major centres of atmospherics, the intensity of which varies with latitude, decreasing towards high latitudes. There is also a diurnal periodicity. In general, thunderstorm activity is at a minimum in the morning hours and maximum at night. Thunderstorm activity also shows a seasonal periodicity. In addition, atmospherics have been correlated with solar activity. Thus, atmospherics peak with solar flares.

Although the magnetosphere and the Van Allen radiation belts are relatively strong non-thermal sources of EM fields, a substantial proportion of this radiation is reflected by the ionosphere back into space. In addition to the electromagnetic fields discussed above, steady (DC) electric and magnetic fields are also found in the earth. On the average, the surface charge of the earth is negative while the upper atmosphere (electrosphere) carries a positive charge. At ground level the average electric field E_e is about 130 V/m. E_e depends on geographical location, time of day or night, height above the ground and meteorological conditions. E_e is found to be greatest in central latitudes decreasing towards the poles and the equator. It is also found that E_e undergoes annual and diurnal variations ranging from approximately 70 to 250 V/m.

Thunderclouds cause a reversal of E_e at ground level: when thunderclouds approach, large variations in E_e occur which may first induce an increase in the field followed by a reversal of the field. This reversal can occur quite rapidly ($\simeq$ 1 minute), often lasting for the duration of the storm. Reverse values of E_e from 100 to 3000 V/m, and much higher, have been observed even in the absence of lightning.

Intense electric fields can also be induced in piezoelectric materials under stress during earthquakes. It has been argued[29] that in rock with high quartz content, and with typical seismic stress changes of 30-300 bars, electric fields of $5 \times 10^4 - 5 \times 10^5$ V/m could be induced by earthquakes. For distances of the order of one half seismic wavelength, the generated voltage is $5 \times 10^7 - 5 \times 10^8$ V.

The DC geomagnetic field is characterized by vertical B_n and a horizontal B_h component. The value of B_h is a maximum (0.3 − 0.4 G) at the magnetic equator and decreases to hundredths of a gauss at the poles. B_n is almost zero at the equator increasing to 0.6–0.7 G at the poles. Regions of magnetic anomalies, including negative anomalies, are not uncommon.

The DC geomagnetic field has been observed to undergo periodic fluctuation with a period ranging from seconds, i.e. micropulsations described above, to several years, i.e. 11-year cycle. The DC geomagnetic field also exhibits diurnal variations. All of these kinds of magnetic activity are associated with solar activity; sunspots and solar flares.

II. Naturally Occurring EM Radiation of Extraterrestrial Origin

Extraterrestrial radiation may be galactic or extragalactic. Major contributions arise from: 1) the 3°K cosmic background; 2) the sun and some planets in our solar system; 3) interstellar gases such as H, and free radicals such as OH; 4) synchrotron radiation in interstellar space; 5) stars, radio-galaxies, supernova remnants, and quasars. Although all of the above items are relevant only item (2) will be considered here. Only radiation from outer space in the RF and MW regions is relevant to this discussion.

Due to its proximity to the earth, the sun constitutes the most powerful RF and MW radiation emitter known. RF and MW radiation from the sun is caused by sunspots and solar flares. Emission from the disturbed sun can be split into a slowly varying component, which peaks in the 3–60 cm wavelength range, and a rapidly varying component, peaking at several meters wavelength, entailing bursts of radiation lasting a few seconds to several hours. The slowly varying components have two oscillatory parts, one which fluctuates with the eleven-year sunspot cycle, and one that varies over weeks (i.e. 27 day solar radiation cycle), connected with sunspots. Emission from the quiet sun occurs at times of little or no sunspot activity, and it is characterized by a steady base level of radiation in which power decreases with increasing wavelength.

Apart from the sun, only the planets Jupiter and Saturn are of interest here. These two planets are characterized by strong non-thermal radiation components in the MHz region. Peak intensities are at about 1 MHz for Saturn and around 10 MHz for Jupiter.[30] Thus only a portion of Jupiter's emission reaches the earth; the remainder is reflected in the ionosphere.

III. Natural Sources of Sound and Vibration

Sound of different frequencies (i.e. infrasound (IS), audiosound (AS) and ultrasound (US)) and vibrations are produced by several geophysical phenomena and also by the interaction of these phenomena with objects on the earth's surface such as trees, mountains and buildings.

The low frequency portion of the acoustic and vibration spectrum (i.e. IS) is particularly important because this radiation can travel over great distances through the lower atmosphere experiencing very little attenuation. The spectrum of atmospheric IS between 0.001 to 1Hz includes a great diversity of signal sources and types. IS intensity (pressure) is usually below 5 newton/m². Among natural IS species, microbaron (~0.2 Hz) are the most continuous background signals. Less continuous IS sources include sound radiated from 1) severe cyclonic storms and tornadoes; 2) high winds and regions of turbulent interaction between the jet stream (air flowing at a great height at about

4500 Km/h) and mountain ranges; 3) both the epicentral region and local Rayleigh wave ground motion from strong earthquakes; 4) volcanic activity; and 5) auroral shock fronts.

Generally speaking, high levels of infrasound and low-frequency noise are found to occur in any situation where there is a large mass of air flowing at high speeds.

IV. The Natural Ion Environment

Ions are produced in the atmosphere by 1) cosmic radiation, 2) the earth's natural radioactivity (i.e. radon and thoron leaving the earth's surface through diffusion), 3) shearing of water droplets such as occurs in waterfalls, 4) the rapid flow of great volumes of air over a land mass (e.g. the sharav, Santa Ana, foehn, chinook, or zonda), or 5) as a by-product of several geophysical phenomena such as thunderstorms and earthquakes. Only small ions, i.e. $\sim 10^{-8}$ cm radius, will be discussed because they have been shown to be biologically active. The number of air ions in mountain air or clean country air rarely exceeds 10^4 per c.c. and under ideal conditions these ions may have a life span of a few minutes.

The positive and negative ion densities (i.e. n(p) and n(n), respectively) and their ratio are dependent upon the type of weather. During snowfall n(p) is greater than n(n), as in fair weather, but during rainfall n(p) is smaller than n(n). During heavy showers and thunderstorms, the ion density is highest because of an additional production of small ions by push ionization in the high electric field which occurs temporarily during precipitation. At low altitudes, the stronger the speed of the horizontal wind (e.g. sharav and foehn), the larger the surplus of n(p).

V. Natural Radioactivity

Natural radioactivity is mainly due to the components of the three radioactive families of Th-232, U-235 and U-238. Ra-226, Rn-222 and radon daughters are among the most representative radioisotopes of natural origin uniformly distributed on the earth's crust and soil-air surface. Other radioisotopes of natural origin such as K-40, C-14 and H-3 are also found.

The Man-Made Environment

Dramatic changes in our environment have occurred since the advent of advanced technology. The contribution of a given country to the man-made environment largely depends on its state of industrialization, geographical position, orography and a number of other factors. Highly industrialized nations contribute more to the man-made environment than poorly industrialized ones.

The strength of man-made stimuli varies considerably from below to well above—several orders of magnitude in some cases—the values measured for the same stimuli of natural origin.

Electrical transmission lines of up to 765 kV (AC, 60 Hz) and up to 800 kV (DC) are in operation in the USA since the late 1960's. The maximum electric field at ground level under an operating 765 kV transmission line is about 10.000 V/m; the maximum magnetic field is about 0.5 G.

AM radio stations transmit powers up to 50 kW, inducing electric fields of about 0.6V/m at distances of 1.6 Km from the transmitting antenna. FM radio stations transmit powers up to 100 kW producing fields of about 1V/m at the same distance. VHF-TV stations and UHF-TV stations transmit powers of the order of 0.3 MW and 5 MW, respectively. At a distance of 1.6 Km from the antennae, the measured electric field is 0.2–0.8 V/m. Higher electric fields are found at closer distances.

Microwave sources (e.g. radar installations for military, communications and tracking, among other uses) have power capabilities that can attain values of the order of hundreds of MW, and beyond. The power densities near the transmitting antennae of these installations can reach values of several hundred mW/cm^2, and more.

Sound pressure levels of man-made origin can range from below the threshold of hearing to well above (e.g. up to 180 dB, and more) the threshold of pain (120 dB). Major contributors to man-made environmental noise and vibration are transportation systems, street traffic and industrial noise.

Man-made radioactivity can reach values many orders of magnitude larger than the natural background. The ion concentration in clear country or mountain air rarely exceeds 1×10^4 ions/cm^3. Ion concentrations of 5×10^6/cm^3, and higher, are commonly used to investigate the biological effects of these ions, or are produced as by-products in corona discharge and other mechanisms.

Effects of Electromagnetic Fields

The effects of EM fields on living organisms have been found to be strongly dependent on 1) the state of the organism (i.e., physiological, psychological and biological states); 2) physical parameters pertaining to the specimen, such as size and shape; 3) EM field parameters such as field strength, frequency, duration of exposure, mode of irradiation (i.e. CW, pulsed, pulse width, etc.); 4) structure of the illuminating fields; and 5) specimen-field geometry, i.e. orientation of the specimen relative to the field.

The effects of EM fields and other environmental stimuli on biological systems vary considerably from gross morphological changes induced at high intensity levels to the more subtle physiological and behavioral effects, observed at low intensity levels, reported in the literature. The effects induced at very low field intensity levels are particularly relevant in the context of this paper for two reasons. Firstly, the field intensity levels at which some of these effects have been observed are of the same order of magnitude, or lower, than some naturally occurring fields induced by certain natural phenomena. Secondly, this information provides indirect evidence on the possible role of these fields in paranormal experiences.

I. Effects of DC Electric and Magnetic Fields

The effects of DC fields are not easy to determine. The difficulty arises in connection with temporal and spatial field inhomogeneities caused by misalignment and vibration of the electrodes (coils) that produce the electric (magnetic) field. This is compounded with the unavoidable motion of the specimen in the field, e.g. walking, flying, changes in body posture, gestures or even breathing and involuntary muscle contractions. Thus electromotive forces (currents) are induced in specimens moving in an inhomogeneous magnetic (electric) field, according to Maxwell Eqs. It is known that the surface of man's body, as well as that of other homeothermic organisms, vibrates mechanically in the $4-12$ Hz frequency range with an approximate amplitude of $10\ \mu$; values of up to $50\ \mu$ have been observed under muscle tension.[32] Breathing and the heart beat produce vibrations of larger amplitude and lower frequency. Thus, living organisms in inhomogeneous DC fields are actually exposed to AC fields of frequency equal to that of the vibration of the body. The effects of ELF fields of frequency equal to the body vibrations have been well documented.[31] The same considerations apply to motionless organisms in time dependent fields, including the sudden switching on and off of the field, which is known to induce visual sensations known as the phosphene effect.

It is frequently argued that the effects induced by inhomogeneous fields are more important than those due to truly homogeneous DC fields. The effects of homogeneous DC fields have not been thoroughly investigated; it is at present a subject of controversy except at high field intensities for the case of electric fields. Altmann[33] presented evidence on the effects of DC fields on insects, fish, frogs, birds and mammals. He reported an increase in the metabolic rate (30% increase in O_2 consumption and an increase value in free amino acid concentration in muscle and liver in mice and guinea pigs) when specimens were subjected to a DC electric field (420 V/m), relative to shielded (Faraday cage) specimens. A variety of behavioral, and other effects, have also been ascribed to low-intensity DC electric fields (i.e. of the same order of magnitude as those of natural origin); the experimental evidence provided in these cases has not been conclusive. It is interesting to note that the estimated minimum DC electric field necessary to elicit a reaction in a biosystem has been calculated as 10^6 V/m. In contrast, the minimum experimentally determined field is in the order of 10^{-5} V/m for the case of fish with electric organs.

II. Effects of ULF, ELF and VLF Electric and Magnetic Fields

A variety of effects on biological systems induced by ULF, ELF, and VLF electric and magnetic fields have been reported in the literature. Reiter[34] has found correlations between natural fields in the 4–50 kHz frequency range, and reaction time, traffic accidents and industrial accidents. Hamer[35] has investigated the effect of 2–12 Hz (4 V/m) electric fields on the reaction time of humans. He has reported a relative increase in reaction time using the lower frequency range (~2 Hz). Experiments by Hauf and Wiesinger[36] have shown an increase in reaction time on human subjects exposed to artificial 50 Hz electric fields of 1–15 kV/m. Gavalas et al.,[37] have found that a 7 Hz electric field of 10 V/m produced significantly shorter inter-response time in non-human primates.

Persinger et al.[38] have discussed the variability in reaction time of human subjects due to low intensity 3 and 10 Hz electric fields (0.3 to 3 V/m) as a function of stimulus pattern sex and field intensity. Konig[39] has observed headaches, fatigue and tiredness in human subjects within a few seconds of being exposed to a 3 Hz (~5 V/m) electric field. A decrement in skin resistance was also noted. Wever[40] has shown that a gradual desynchronization and lengthening of the circadian rhythms can be induced in human subjects placed in underground bunkers. Resynchronization could be attained using an artificial 10 Hz (2.5 V/m) electric field.

Experiments by Persinger et al.,[41] by Ludwig and Mecke,[42] and by Altmann[33] demonstrated substantial changes in the ambulatory behavior of rodents.

The effect of weather and atmospheric conditions on the respiratory rate (O_2 uptake) of several biological species has been reported by several authors. In general a decrease in O_2 uptake has been observed, or correlated, with 1) labile weather conditions[43] 2) low pressure frontal movements with maxima in the 3–50 kHz frequency range[44], 3) increased geomagnetic activity probably associated with sub-ELF geomagnetic pulsations[45] and 4) artificial bad weather impulses characterized by 30–100 Hz pulses with 10–100 kHz carriers of amplitudes greater than 0.1 V/m. The ELF-EM component of weather fronts has also been implicated in human cardiovascular disorders such as "driving" and "clotting."

Popa[46] noted that guinea-pigs exposed to 50–100 Hz fields showed an activation of the adrenal cortex. Persinger et al.,[47] reported increased aggressive behavior and a variety of other behavioral and physiological changes, in rats exposed to a 0.5 Hz rotating magnetic field. These changes were most probably due to increased thyroid activity. Pre- and neonatal exposure effects of ELF fields in rats and ducks have also been investigated by the above authors. Smith and Justesen[48] have reported an increase in activity and an alteration of the circadian period of mice exposed for 120 sec to a 60 Hz EM field.

Recent interest has been focused on the effects of DC and 50–60 Hz fields due to the ever increasing demand for electrical power in industrialized countries. Marino and Becker[49] have found that rats exposed to 60 Hz electric fields (of strength comparable to that produced at ground level by a typical 765 kV line) exhibited hormonal and biochemical changes similar to those caused by stress. When continuously exposed for three generations, the rats showed increased infant mortality and severely stunted growth. From these results the authors concluded that the electric field primarily affected the CNS and activated the stress-response mechanism. Gann[50] has tested the effect in dogs of a 60 Hz (15 kV/m) electric field on some of the involuntary responses that are controlled by the CNS—e.g. pulse rate, temperature and arterial pressure. He observed a decrease in arterial pressure and pulse rate in the exposed animals.

III. Effects of RF and MW Fields

The irradiation effects of RF and MW fields on biological systems vary considerably from gross morphological changes induced at "high" intensity levels, which result in burns or cataracts, for example, to the more subtle physiological and behavioral changes, observed at low intensity levels, reported in the literature.

A variety of effects on persons working in RF fields have been reported in the eastern literature. These include, for example, the following: headache, eyestrain, muscle pain, fatigue, dizziness, disturbed sleep at night, sleepiness in daytime, general weakness, disturbance of equilibrium, moodiness, irritability, hypochondriac reactions, feeling of fear, anxiety, nervous tension, mental depression, memory impairment, loss of hair, breathing difficulties, increased perspiration of extremities, difficulties in sex life, drop in body weight and changes in ECG due to interference with the cardiac rhythm.

At MW frequencies, the following effects of weak MW fields on humans have been reported: periodic or constant headaches, irritability, increased fatigability, sleepiness during work, decrease in smell sensitivity, exhausting influences on the central nervous system (CNS), hypotension, bradycardia, disruption on endocrine-humoral and neuroendocrine processes (e.g. intensification of thyroid gland activity; change in secretions of the pituitary gland, the adrenal cortex, the gonads, etc.) and an increase in the histamine content of the blood.

Substantial research conducted on animals by the Russian and other eastern European workers has been summarized by several authors. Petrov has discussed the various effects of weak RF and MW fields on the blood system, digestive organs, cardiovascular system, and CNS of several animals. Changes were observed in the blood system of rabbits; excretory system, derived from studies on kidney function, of mice, dogs and rats; and digestive organs of dogs and guinea-pigs. The following effects were observed in the cardiovascular system: 1) bradycardia, sinus arrhythmia, retardation of auricular and ventricular conduction, changes in the P- and T-deflections, and broadening of the QRS complex, in dogs; 2) changes in heart rate and hemodynamic shifts in rabbits; 3) hypotensive effects in rats. The most significant results are, however, those related with the CNS. The most distinctive changes were observed in the conditioned-reflex activity in dogs and rats. Petrov has suggested that a change in the normal activity on the CNS is the primary link in the various functional disturbances, and that the endocrine-gland activity changes are secondary. Derangement of cardiovascular, gastric, and other functions, however, is a consequence of disturbed neuro-endocrine regulation. Tolgskaya and Gordon have discussed in some detail the physiological and morphological changes induced in animals after prolonged and repeated exposures to low-intensity RF and MW radiation.

A number of relevant experiments have been performed by western researchers, partly aimed at verifying Russian contentions pertaining to low-intensity field effects on humans and other living organisms. Among the most relevant findings so far reported are the several behavioral effects observed in cats, rats, rhesus monkeys and birds obtained with pulsed RF and MW fields; and the auditory effects elicited in humans, dogs, cats, guinea-pigs and chinchilla by pulsed MW radiation.

In 1961 Frey, using pulsed RF and MW fields of extremely low average power density, induced the perception of sound in normal and deaf humans. This effect was elicited with carrier frequencies of 425 MHz and 1.31 GHz with average power densities of the order of 400 μW/cm^2. The subjects illuminated by the pulsed field reported a hearing sensation described as being a buzz, clicking, hiss, or knocking depending upon the pulse width and repetition rate. This hearing phenomenon has been extensively studied by Frey and other researchers under a variety of EM field conditions.

The MW hearing effect is a relevant phenomenon from the communications, and hence psi phenomena, standpoint since it is possible to generate, in addition to clicks, the perception of tones in humans.

Certain behavioral effects induced on animals exposed to CW and pulsed MW fields have been reported by several workers. Bawin et al. demonstrated that EM fields at a frequency of 147 MHz (1 mW/cm^2) amplitude modulated at brain wave frequencies, influenced conditioned and spontaneous EEG patterns in cats. Tanner first observed behavioral effects of MW radiation on birds. The above experiments were conducted with power densities from a few μW/cm^2 to about 1 mW/cm^2. In view of the observed effects on birds, Bigu et al. conducted a study on the properties of bird feathers as dielectric receptors (aerials) of MW radiation of 10 GHz and 16 GHz. Recently Ondráček et al. have reported the importance of antennae for the orientation of insects in a non-uniform MW field. Avoidance effects to MW radiation of 2.375 GHz, at power densities of 6.6 mW/cm^2, were observed for several species of insects. A number of interesting effects on primates were observed by Baldwin et al. with CW radiation of 388 MHz. These effects consisted of agitation, drowsiness, akinesia, and eye signs, as well as autonomic, motor, and sensory abnormalities. EEG recordings showed that cerebral activity was markedly influenced during the irradiation period, and immediately after cessation of the stimulating EM field. No accurate power density measurements were made, although the authors report trivial temperature changes caused by radiation exposure.

Young et al.[51] exposed (whole body) rhesus monkeys to 2.45 GHz radiation pulsed at 10 Hz. The animals could "detect" average powers as low as 2 mW/cm^2. D'Andrea et al. studied the effect of 360 MHz, 480 MHz and 500 MHz EM(CW) fields on certain behavior in rats as a function of animal orientation relative to the imposed field. Greatest disruption of behavior performance—e.g. random interval schedule of food reinforcement—occurred when exposures were made with the animal aligned parallel to the electric field at 500 MHz. The dose rate absorbed per incident power density was in the range 0.026–0.59 mW gm^{-1}/mW cm^{-2}. Monahan and Ho observed avoidance behavior of mice to 2.45 GHz CW radiation by orienting themselves relative to the field so as to minimize power absorption.

IV. Effects Induced by Solar Disturbances

There are a variety of behavioral, physiological, biological and pathological effects that have been ascribed to solar disturbances. There are abundant references in the literature[52,53] in which correlations have been made between solar activity (e.g. sunspot activity and flares) and a number of 1) human behaviors such as marriage, crime, immigration, rhythms of production, cycles of prices, patterns of war, etc.; 2) physiological, biological and pathological effects such as death rate (e.g. from heart disease), oncological diseases, detection of new flu viruses and periodicity of particularly bad crops; and 3) changes in the intensity and occurrence of several geo-physical phenomena such as earthquakes and spherics, which are known to cause bioeffects.

Specifically, correlations have been made by Friedman et al. between psychiatric ward behavior and some component of cosmic radiation[54], and between psychiatric hospital admission and geomagnetic parameters.[55] However, since most of the cosmic components reaching the earth's surface—which are responsible, among other things, for the disturbances of the geomagnetic field—are of solar origin, and since the sun activity is characterized by the emission of a host of physical variables (e.g. charged and neutral particles, and EM fields of frequencies ranging from less than 1 Hz to 10^{16} Hz), the above correlations with a particular variable should be, at best, considered as tentative until more data becomes available.

Specific correlations of RF and MW radiation, of solar origin, with effects on living organisms are scant. Yagodinskiy[53] reports a remarkable correlation between the number of myocardial infarcts and the sun's radiation in the 100–200 MHz region. It was found that the EM flux reaching the earth increased by a factor of about 20 to 100 MHz and by a factor of approximately 100 at 200 MHz. These increases were due to a massive motion of sunspots toward the centre of the sun. Since solar activity is accompanied by strong fluctuations (by several orders of magnitude) in the RF and MW components reaching the earth's surface it is possible that some of the effects attributed to the activity of the sun might have been caused, or at least influenced, by RF and/or MW fields of solar origin.

Noise and Vibration—Their Effects on Biological Systems

Experiments have shown that noise and vibration of moderate and high power levels (>70 dB) produce a variety of effects on exposed individuals and test animals.[56] Effects on humans have been reported on the auditory response (AS and US), the startle response (IS and AS) and on sleep (IS and AS). Other effects include fatigue (IS and AS), and complaint and annoyance (IS, AS and US). Headaches, nausea, tinnitus, etc. have also been reported at US frequencies. Reactions to vibrations include: 1) reflex disorders (1 to >100 Hz); 2) effect on respiratory response (1 to ~100 Hz); 3) vibro-tactile sensations (~ 1 to 1000 Hz); 4) fatigue (< 1 to >100 Hz); and 5) complaint (<1Hz to ~1 kHz). An "uneasy" and "uncomfortable" feeling is often reported by human subjects exposed to noise and vibration. A brief review of the effects of noise on neurosensory and endocrine-biochemical processes, on the cardiovascular system and of other non-aural effects has been given by Anticaglia and Cohen.[57] It is interesting to notice that the major whole body resonances are in the infrasonic band of 1 to 10 Hz, especially at 4 to 5 Hz. Specifically, whole body natural frequencies are: 5 to 12 Hz (standing), 3 to 4 Hz (prone) and 4 to 6 Hz (seated).

Bryan and Tempest[58] have argued that in an ordinary car traveling at speed the IS noise is more than enough to mimic the effect of drunkeness in the driver: "With the sense of euphoria that IS also induces, it may therefore be responsible for many inexplicable motorway crashes." Feeling of sickness in people in buildings under certain weather conditions, has been observed. It was found that the building produced IS which reached 110 dB at 1 Hz in stormy weather, and over 100 dB at 4 Hz during a hailstorm.[59] Complaints of annoying vibrations in modern, long-span floors have been reported by several investigators. These effects have been associated with vibrations induced in floor by walking or street traffic. The natural frequencies of floors of long spans—typically 20 m—are usually 5 to 8 Hz. Besides floor vibration, tall buildings also have vibration natural frequencies between 0.5 to 1.0 Hz due to their height.

Some people have experienced a low throbbing background when the weather is cool and there is a light breeze, particularly in the morning. When measurements were carried out, a noise signal in the

30 to 40 Hz range was detected. From these data the suggestion has been made that this source of sound might be the jet stream.[60] There has also been some speculation that IS might account for some people getting bad-tempered during stormy weather. It has been noted that offices in certain locations experience a very high turnover in staff and in others morale is known to be consistently low for no apparent reason. Green and Dunn[61] have obtained high correlations between days of infrasonic disturbances (during severe weather conditions) and 1) car accidents, and 2) rate of absenteeism among school children.

Air Ions – Their Influence on Living Organisms

Hundreds of papers dealing with the influence of air ions on living organisms, including man, have appeared over the last decades. The discussion here is limited to a few examples of such influence recently reported in the literature. The interested reader who wishes to pursue this topic further should consult,[62,63] and the references therein.

Krueger and Smith[64] collected data which indicated that negative ions lowered tissue levels of 5-HT (i.e. serotonin). Serotonin is a very powerful neurohormone. It is capable of inducing profound endocrinal, metabolic and neuromuscular effects through the body. This chemical compound (which is concerned with the transmission of nerve impulses) is found in relatively large quantities in the lower midbrain, where it significantly affects sleep patterns and mood. Gilbert conducted studies of the effect of negative ions on the emotional behavior and brain serotonin content in rats. He found a significant reduction in emotionality and serotonin levels. Olivereau carried out experiments on the endocrine system and nervous mechanisms of rats treated with air ions. From his observations he concluded that air ion-induced alterations in blood levels of 5-HT account for very significant physiological changes in the CNS and in the endocrine glands. These alterations, in turn, substantially alter basic physiological processes. Olivereau also observed that negative ions exerted an anxiety-reducing effect on mice and rats exposed to stressful situations. The results of the authors referred to above are particularly important because they bridge the gap between laboratory observation and a possible role of ions in the natural environment.[62] It is therefore possible that several of the observed behavioral responses and subjective complaints by humans under certain weather conditions are accounted for by the above observations.

Several effects on humans, due to air ionization, have been reported in the literature.[63] These include systemic (i.e. whole organism) effects as well as specific effects on the nervous, circulatory and respiratory systems. In general, negative ions were associated with decreased blood pressure, drowsiness and a feeling of release (i.e. relaxation). Positive ions were found to induce headaches, perspiration, increased blood pressure, nasal obstructions, hoarseness, sore throat and dizziness. Effects on the blood, the skin (i.e. feeling of warmth—positive ions—, or cold—negative ions), the healing of wounds, and on body chemistry have also been reported in the literature. The action of air ionization on microorganisms and on mouse influenza has also been investigated.[62] Krueger and Reed[62] have suggested that an indirect effect of environmental pollution on man is possible due to ion-depletion of the atmosphere caused by air pollutants.

An interesting study on the effects of certain type of weather conditions known as the Sharav (hot dry heat) and Bora (cold and rainy) on the functioning of the autonomic system has been conducted by Sulman et al.[65] They have found that changes from normal weather to the Sharav or Bora evoked specific reactions of neurohormone secretion in weather-sensitive patients. Changes have been observed in the stress hormones adrenaline, noradrenaline, 17-KS and 17-OH, and in the "irritation" hormones 5-HT, 5 HIAA, histamine and thyroxine. Serotonin increased during the weather front inducing the serotonin irritation syndrome (migraine, etc.). Patients suffering from occult hyperthyroidism reacted with an increase of urinary thyroxine and histamine as soon as a weather front arrived, with clinical signs of slight hyperthyroidism, especially tachycardia. It has been suggested that the above weather effects are somewhat related to the state of ionization associated with the weather front.

Effects of Ionizing Radiation

Individuals are continually exposed to natural radiation that comes both from sources external to the body and from naturally occurring radionuclides deposited within the body. The external sources are primarily cosmic radiation (electrons and muons are the major components of the cosmic background at sea level; fast protons and neutrons are also found, but in far lower numbers) and gamma radiation from materials naturally present in the ground and in building materials. From drinking water, foods and in the air, several radionuclides are deposited in the body including uranium and its decay products, and thorium and its decay products, K-40 and C-14. Natural radiation results in an estimated average annual dose equivalent to individuals of approximately 125 mrem,[66] 100 mrem external and 25 mrem internal. This figure is substantially larger for individuals living at high altitudes or in unusually large radioactive soil backgrounds such as those found in Kerala State in India and Minas Gerais in Brazil.

Environmental contamination by artificially produced radionuclides also finds its way to humans through the food chains and other ways. Its contribution can be quite large.

Aside from the visual sensations elicited by some components of cosmic radiation and of some reported correlations between solar activity and human behavior, there is little information on the effects of natural radiation on humans.

A considerable amount of information is now available on the bioeffects (somatic and genetic) of artificially produced radionuclides. However, to the knowledge of the author no behavioral effects, as those found with non-ionizing radiation, have been, to date, reported in the literature. The implication is that either such effects have, so far, not been investigated or that no effects at all have yet been found.

A Biophysical Theory for PSI Phenomena

The material presented in the previous sections has clearly shown that a variety of effects result from the interaction of certain environmental factors and living organisms. Psi phenomena on the other hand are, as far as we know, biological phenomena, i.e. they manifest themselves in man and perhaps in other living organisms as well. It is the contention of this paper that the complex environment in its interaction with man might be partly responsible for eliciting certain paranormal experiences. This contention is not based on direct experimental evidence, since little or no experimentation has so far been conducted to verify it. Rather, this theory is based on the extrapolation to psi experience of certain reasonably well documented results, given above, obtained in several fields of research such as the biophysical sciences. The discussion given below is an attempt to formulate a theory of psi based on biophysical arguments. It is not aimed at explaining all the manifestations of psi phenomena, but merely to indicate that certain alleged cases of telepathy and precognition (the two phenomena investigated here) could be in principle explained by conventional science without the need for invoking non-physical entities as the carriers of psi information. Undoubtedly, our understanding of psi phenomena will improve as our knowledge of the influence of the complex environment on man becomes more complete. Relevant to this discussion is a theory of psi

phenomena based on geophysical arguments (ELF-EM fields) formulated by Persinger,[67] and the theoretical and experimental studies on
biocommunication at RF and MW frequencies conducted by Bigu,[13,16]
and a discussion on unusual animal senses given in Appendix A.

I. A Biophysical Theory of Telepathy

Simply stated the theory presented here suggests that the complex
environment could be *modulated by the state of the human subject* by some
specific, although as yet undefined, kinds of biophysical interactions.
These interactions would result in the encoding of messages whose
informational content could then be carried to other geographical
locations where other subjects could conveniently decode them. Thus,
in this theory the environmental factors and their biointeractions are
presumed to be the carriers of information, and the encoding
(modulation) and decoding (demodulation) mechanisms, respectively.
An alternative theory, where no actual transmission of messages is
necessary, will also be discussed.

Encoding, transmission, and decoding of messages, three crucial
mechanisms in telepathic communication, have been discussed by the
author elsewhere.[14] Although the discussion dealt preferentially with
physical carriers (EM radiation at RF and MW frequencies) of
biological origin, the same arguments can be applied to physical
carriers of environmental—naturally occurring or man-made—
origin.

Reference to the *state* of a subject is understood to include
biophysical, physiological and psychological components. However,
the state itself is far too complex to be analyzed directly. An assumption
made in this paper is that certain measurable biophysical variables are
correlated with this state and therefore can be used to provide
pertinent information about the latter. In addition, it is suggested that
these variables might also be modulation factors involved in encoding
and decoding of messages. (The variables would include DC electric
and magnetic fields, EM fields from ULF to UV frequencies, and
acoustical and chemical "envelopes" around the body, to name but a
few examples.) The different physical and chemical variables
associated with the body have been discussed in some detail by Bigu
elsewhere.

Furthermore, rather than singling out a particular environmental
stimulus as a psi carrier, the theory proposed here suggests that a
complex set of stimuli, acting simultaneously, might provide the
explanation for the rarity and apparent unpredictability of certain psi

experiences. This contention is made in view of the material presented in several sections above in which the bioeffects of several stimuli were discussed. This material reveals that different stimuli acting independently on a given organism induce similar or identical effects. Hence, a theory based on single stimulus-single response relationships would contradict experience. It should also be noted that a great deal of effort has been made to investigate the effects of certain stimuli on several organisms, keeping other environmental factors constant. While this method is quite appropriate, the results obtained from these experiments do not entirely reflect those which would be obtained in a real situation where both the state of the organism and the complex environmental background are continuously changing. Hence, any conclusions drawn from such experiments should be viewed in their proper perspective, especially when they are to be applied to such subtle situations as psi phenomena. It is also important to note that stimulus-response relationships vary with the state of the organism, the environment, and their complex interrelationships. Thus a given stimulus may elicit different responses under different circumstances. The strength of the stimulus will also partly determine whether "perception" of stimuli occurs at a conscious or subliminal level (an area where lack of knowledge becomes more evident). This is an indication of the non-linear processing that occurs in the stimulus-response relationships. In contrast to the case of a single stimulus, the situation consisting of several environmental stimuli simultaneously acting on a subject would, of course, be considerably more complex: an example of the breakdown of the principle of linear superposition. It is, however, this very complexity with its "redundancy" of biointeractions, and the information derived from them, which could make the realization and selectivity of certain kinds of psi phenomena possible.

Perhaps the most far reaching consequences of the theory proposed above is that transmission of messages (thoughts, emotions, feelings, mental imagery, etc.) from the "sender" (S) to the "receiver" (R) is no longer necessary to account for certain forms of telepathy. It is only sufficient that the result of the interaction between the function Ψ, describing the state of the individual, and the function Φ, describing the environment, for both S and R be equal. In symbolic form this can be expressed as

$$\Psi(S)[X]\Phi(r,t) = \Psi(R)[X]\Phi(r',t') \tag{1}$$

where the symbol [X] indicates interaction between the lhs and rhs of the symbol, r and r', and t and t' indicate space coordinates (i.e.

geographical location) and time, respectively. For telepathy $r \neq r'$ but $t = t'$ where t and t' refer not to local time but to Universal Time. The function Φ entails both natural and man-made environments. Strictly speaking, the function Ψ should include such attributes as character, personality, patterns of behavior, and biophysical components, microscopic and macroscopic, of the subjects, among other variables of S and R.

Eq. (1) allows for four possibilities according to whether the functions Ψ and Φ are equal, or unequal, for the S-R pair and different spatial coordinates, respectively. The most general case is that for which $\Psi(S) \neq \Psi(R)$ and $\Phi(r,t) \neq \Phi(r',t)$. The degree of "dissimilarity" between the Ψs and the Φs, and the strength of [X] will determine the alleged selectivity between S and R for telepathic communication. If this were not so we would be continuously bombarded by telepathic messages from individuals totally indifferent and unrelated to us. Other consequences of Eq. (1) will not be discussed here.

For the case where Φ (the psi carriers) is modulated by the function Ψ, i.e. *for actual transmission of messages between S and R*, the following should be noted. A set of stimuli impinging on a subject will result in the modulation of Φ. The various components of the modulated signal will travel from S to R with different velocities, undergoing different interactions, according to the nature of both the stimuli and the intervening medium. A detailed discussion of this topic is beyond the scope of this paper, but does not present insurmountable difficulties. One advantage associated with a theory of multiple stimuli is that the stimuli would provide for an adequate combination of penetrability and bandwidth to account for some form of biocommunication.

It has been argued that penetrability is a necessary condition that a physical carrier of psi information must attain. Based on this argument Persinger[67] has made the suggestion that EM fields of ELF might provide the hypothetical carrier. It might be added that penetrability, although an important property, is not a sufficient one because high penetrability also indicates little interaction with matter. Thus, although ELF-EM fields can travel over long distances, and through heavy shielding, with little attenuation by virtue of their low interaction cross-section with matter, this very fact also indicates that little information would be extracted and/or conveyed as a result of biophysical interactions. The same argument also applies to other theories such as the neutrino hypothesis.[68] High penetrability through heavy shielding (an accepted pre-requisite derived from experiments carried out in telepathy), contrary to what might be expected, is not limited to EM fields of ELF. Barometric pressure, air-ions and other stimuli, such as vibrations of the earth's crust induced by several mechanisms, can make their effect felt under conditions of heavy shielding provided by ordinarily designed Faraday structures, for example.

Another difficulty arising in connection with ELF-EM fields is their extremely narrow bandwidth, which would make the transfer of reasonable amounts of information virtually impossible, unless transmission continues for prohibitively long periods of time. Thus, it is difficult to see how the informational content of a complex message, such as a telepathic message, could be transmitted under narrow bandwidth conditions. It should be noted, however, that conventional information theory is of limited value in the context of psi phenomena.

II. A Biophysical Theory of Precognition

Much of the material covered in the preceding section on telepathy also applies to the case of precognition. An understanding of the way certain precognitive knowledge is acquired is particularly less complex, in the context of our model, for the case entailing natural phenomena than for the case of a human sender. The study of several geophysical phenomena such as earthquakes, tornadoes, volcanic activity, thunderstorms, tidal waves, etc. show that these phenomena are accompanied by various physical variables that readily propagate through, and/or above, the earth's surface. In addition, the above phenomena also induce changes in the physical characteristics of the earth's crust and the atmosphere. Of particular importance for the case of precognition is the fact that the above physical variables often precede the actual occurrence of the phenomena. Persinger[67] has suggested that ELF-EM fields, generated by piezoelectric stress of the earth's crust, that precede an earthquake could act as the "warning signal" from which a precognitive knowledge of this future event could be extracted. Again our model based on multiple stimuli-multiple response relationships provides further insight into this problem. Although the main emphasis, below, is placed on earthquake phenomena, similar arguments also apply to other phenomena.

A variety of effects premonitory to earthquakes such as crustal movements, and anomalous changes in such phenomena as electrical and magnetic fields, radon emission, electrical resistivity and natural electric currents, tilt, fluid pressure, seismic velocities and the frequency of occurrence of small tidal earthquakes have been observed before various earthquakes. Scholz et al.[69] have shown that the precursory effects referred to above, previously regarded as seemingly

unrelated premonitory phenomena, have a common physical basis.
Their data, partly taken from Russian and Japanese studies, show that
the premonitory effects occur at a characteristic time before
earthquakes that increases with the earthquake's magnitude and that
appears to be related to the time needed for the formation of cracks
and for the diffusion of fluids through the volume of rock in the
earthquake region. The above data appears to lead to earthquake
prediction which is deterministic rather than probabilistic. The
interested reader is referred to[69,70] for a comprehensive discussion on
earthquake prediction. Some of the above premonitory effects are
discussed below. They are the following:

1. The ratio of seismic velocities v(P)/v(S) decreases to anomalously
low values (10–20% of their original value) before an earthquake. The
decrease in this ratio is mainly attributed to a decrease in v(P), the
compressional wave velocity. Typical values for the seismic velocity
ratio are ~1.75 (normal value) and ~1.5, the minimum value attained
before the earthquake. Typical values for v(S) and v(P) are ~3 Km/sec
and 4 6 Km/sec, respectively. The P- and S-waves can travel thousands
of Km from the epicentre. The precursor time for the above ratio is up
to several years. Changes in seismic velocities are important because
the seismic power, to which some individuals might be sensitive,
propagating away from the epicenter, depends on these velocities.

2. In general it has been found that earthquakes are preceded by a
decrease (~15%) in crustal electrical resistivity. The precursor time in
this case is in the order of several months.

3. Rapid increases in the radon (a radioactive gas with 3.8 days
half-life) content in water wells has been measured several years prior
to an earthquake.[69,70] For the case cited in these references the amount
of radon more than doubled its initial value; from about 6×10^{-10} to
approximately 1.5×10^{-9} Curies/liter. Radon release is important
because it increases the ionization of air to which living organisms are
responsive.

4. Anomalous rates of change of the magnetic field have also been
observed for a period of several years prior to an earthquake.[69] This
phenomenon seems to be related to piezomagnetic effects produced by
an increase in effective rock stress. It is also believed that the change in
the magnetic field could be caused by the changes in the electrical
resistivity of the crust referred to above.

5. A reduction in the natural electric currents inside the earth has
been also measured a few days prior to the earthquake.[70] Changes of
about 50 mV/Km between points several Km apart have been
measured. This phenomenon is affected by the earth's resistivity
discussed above.

6. In addition to items 1 to 5, other phenomena have been observed.

These include crustal movements such as uplifting and tilting. These phenomena appear a few hours to several years before the occurrence of the earthquake.

Scholz et al.[69] have plotted graphs connecting the duration (T) of the precursory anomaly with the 1) magnitude (M) of the earthquake and 2) length of the aftershock zone. These graphs show that log T is linearly related (with positive slope) to M. As an example one obtains T ~14 years for M = 7 and T ~3 months for M = 5.

There is considerable experimental evidence which suggests that some animals (e.g. horses, dogs, birds, and other higher vertebrates) are able to "sense" major natural phenomena. Thus erratic behavior, stress and other effects have been observed to precede several natural phenomena such as earthquakes, thunderstorms, tornadoes and solar activity. Weather "sensitive" people are not uncommon. It is therefore possible that some sensitive people, also, may possess similar faculties for detecting these precursors of geophysical phenomena. It should be noted that some individuals in addition to merely predicting a natural phenomenon also report having strong mental imagery (e.g. during dreams) associated with it. A satisfactory explanation cannot be offered for this other than noting that single, and "simple," stimuli may elicit complex responses. Thus, a tremor or sequence of the crust's vibrations may induce the feeling in the subject that a major natural phenomenon is approaching. The subject may then add (entirely on his own and at an unconscious level) a number of occurrences that are known to him to be usually associated with this phenomenon. For instance, the "feeling" of an earthquake can be easily associated (based on learning, experience, and inference) with such occurrences as fires, accidents, loss of human life, visions of wounded persons, buildings collapsing, yelling, etc. Similar arguments to those given in this section would also apply to other geophysical phenomena, such as tornadoes and the like. These phenomena are preceded by changes in the barometric pressure, air temperature, EM activity, air ionization, atmospheric vibrations and other effects.

Final Remarks

Although there is unquestionable evidence that shows that the environment affects the behavior of living organisms in a number of ways, extrapolation of these findings to psi phenomena does not necessarily follow. There are several areas of research, crucially important in the context of this paper, where lack of information is most evident. Some of these areas are indicated below.

A. Environmental effects on man. It has been shown above that at any given time and geographical location living organisms are subjected to an extremely complex spectrum of environmental stimuli, both naturally occurring and man-made, in a continuous state of change. Laboratory controlled experiments, however, are preferentially aimed at determining the bioeffects of one kind of stimulus, two stimuli at most, on a rather restricted variety of biological species. The restriction imposed on both the number of stimuli used and the biological species examined depends on such factors as practicality, simplicity and availability of equipment and specimens. It would therefore be a gross error to extrapolate the results obtained under the above experimental conditions to man in his complex environment. (Notice that, owing to moral and ethical principles, no direct experimentation on human subjects is usually conducted.)

B. *The role of the state of the individual.* There is considerable uncertainty as well as lack of information with regard to the effects which might be induced by environmental stimuli in higher living organisms under a variety of psychological and physiological states.

Data on the effects of external stimuli on man under the following states is, at best, scant: 1) altered states of consciousness, e.g., sleep, daydreaming, trance, hypnosis, meditation and mystic rapture; 2) drug-induced states, e.g. general anaesthesis, hallucinations, delirium; 3) mental disorders, e.g. schizophrenia, epilepsy, neurosis, psychosis; and 4) extreme states of stress and anxiety.

There is some indirect experimental evidence which indicates that while some of the above states act effectively as stimuli inhibitors, making man quite insensitive to their effect, other states can make him extremely sensitive, and therefore susceptible, to the same stimuli— e.g. these stimuli might elicit "strange" phenomena such as auditory and visual sensations. This is a subject of extreme difficulty which cannot be dealt with here for reasons of space. It will be sufficient to add that certain states of consciousness have been reported to enhance psi ability.

C. *Studies on Behavior.* The application of the material presented in some former sections of this paper to the problem of paranormal experiences is somewhat limited at present because of the following. Firstly, the studies on the influence of environmental stimuli on behavior and behavior patterns (which are the most relevant effects in the context of our theory) have been restricted to a few psychological tests and behavioral responses which include interresponse and reaction time; aversion, feeding, sleeping, mating, social, ambulatory, operant-conditioned and orientation behaviors; learning, vigilance and locomotor activity; and some measurments of EEG, ECG and VER changes, among other observations. Secondly, and most important, the above studies have been conducted on animals. Hence, the relevant information such as mental imagery, feeling, emotions, thoughts, mental processes and so forth in man cannot possibly be extracted from studies carried out on rats, mice, monkeys and the like.

D. *Frequency and energy "windows"–resonance effects.* There is some experimental evidence on resonance or enhanced effects induced at particular frequencies and energies.[71] This subject has been little investigated and deserves considerably more attention, as it is theoretically possible for some phenomena to take place only within a narrow frequency band and/or energy range.

Conclusions

A theory of psi phenomena based on the interaction of environmental stimuli and man has been outlined. Although far from refined, this theory can account in principle, for certain supposed telepathy and precognition phenomena. In addition, the above theory could also be extended to other paranormal experiences. For example, the "phosphene" effect (e.g. caused by EM fields, and transient electric and magnetic fields), the auditory sensations induced by electrical currents and fields, and the visual sensations elicited by charged particles and heavy ions could explain some kinds of hallucinations and alleged materializations.

One advantage of the theory proposed here is that it can be experimentally tested by investigating, for example, possible correlations between psi occurrences and environmental variables. Hence, *the theory is falsifiable.* For instance, it would be interesting to compare the occurrence of spontaneous psi experiences in the tropical regions (centers of major atmospheric activity) and the polar regions (centers of high auroral displays) with data from other, "quieter," geographical locations. A similar study could also be conducted during periods of quiet and strong solar activity.

A consequence of our biophysical theory of psi phenomena is that changes in environmental man-made pollution should be expected to affect the occurrence of psi phenomena. It is, however, not possible at present to predict whether the considerable increase in the environmental background brought about by our technological age would enhance or interfere with psi ability or psi occurrence. Finally, the dynamic nature of both the environmental background and man could account for the unpredictability of paranormal events.

The author does not wish to convey the false impression that the theory presented here, or an extension of it, can satisfactorily explain seemingly genuine psi phenomena. Rather, the purpose is only to point out the general usefulness of such a biophysical approach to ostensible paranormal experience.

BIBLIOGRAPHY

1. Bigu, J., "A Biophysical Theory for Psi Phenomena", *J. Research in Psi Phenomena*, vol. 2, no. 1, pp. 22–53, 1977.
2. Ullman, M., Krippner, S. and Feldstein, S., "Experimentally-Induced Telepathic Dreams: Two Studies Using EEG-REM Monitoring Technique", *Int. J. Neuropsychiatry*, vol. 2, pp. 420–437, 1966.
3. Vasiliev, L. L., *Experiments in Mental Suggestion*. Galley Hills, Hampshire, UK, 1963.
4. Targ, R. and Puthoff, H., "Information Transmission Under Conditions of Sensory Shielding", *Nature*, vol. 251, pp. 602–607, 1974.
5. Schmidt, H., "Precognition of a Quantum Process", *J. of Parapsychology*, vol. 33, no. 2, pp. 99–108, 1969.
6. Walker, E. H., "Consciousness and Quantum Theory", *In Psychic Exploration* (J. White, Ed.), G. P. Putnam's Sons, New York, 1974, 544–568.
7. Ehrenwald, J., "A Neurophysiological Model of Psi Phenomena", *J. Nervous and Mental Disease*, vol. 154, no. 6, pp. 406–418, 1972.
8. Schmidt, H., "Toward a Mathematical Theory of Psi", *J. Am. Soc. Psychical Research*, vol. 69, no. 4, pp. 301–340, 1975.
9. Chari, C. T. K., "The Challenge of Psi: New Horizons of Scientific Research", *J. of Parapsychology*, vol. 38, no. 1, pp. 1–15, 1974.
10. Rao, K. R., *Experimental Parapsychology: A Review and Interpretation*, Charles C Thomas, Springfield (Ill.), 1966.
11. Berger, H., "Ueber das Elektroenkephalogram des Menschen", *J. Psychol. Neurol.* (Leipzig), vol. 40, pp. 160–179, 1930.
12. Cazzamalli, F., *Neurologica*, vol. 6, p. 193, 1925; *Arch. Neurology*, Series 27, no. 3, p. 113, 1935; *Quaderni di psichiatria*, vol. 16, no. 5–6, p. 81, 1929; *Neuropsychiatrica*, p. 47, 1934. See also T. Jaski, *Electronics*, p. 43, Sept. 1960.
13. Bigu, J., "Thermal and Non-Thermal Electromagnetic Fields of Biological Origin-Their Role in Biocommunication . . .", Proc. 1976 Parascience Conf., London, UK, 1976.
14. *Ibid.*, "Radiofrequency and Microwave Radiation of Biological Origin-Their Possible Role in Biocommunication", Psychoenergetic Systems, 1977.
15. Hammond, A. L., "A Note on Telepathic Communication", Proc. I.R.E., vol. 40, p. 605, 1952.
16. Tyson, G. N., "On the Possibility of a Neutrino Communication System", Proc. I.R.E., vol. 41, p. 294, 1953.
17. Ruderfer, M., Private Communication, 1977.
18. Wassermann, G. D., *In* Ciba Foundation Symposium on Extrasensory Perception. Boston, Little Brown, 1956.
19. Roll, W. G., "The Psi Field", Presidential Address, 7th Annual Conv. of Parapsychological Association, Oxford University, England, 1964.
20. Smythies, J. R. (Ed.), *Science and ESP*. Routledge and Kegan Paul, 1971. See also. A. Koestler, *The Roots of Coincidence*. Pan Books Ltd. (London), 1974.
21. Marshall, N., "ESP and Memory:A Physical Theory", *Brit. J. Phil. Sci.*, vol. 10, pp. 265–286, 1960.
22. Price, H. H., "Some Philosophical Questions About Telepathy and Clairvoyance", *Philosophy*, vol. 15, pp. 363–374, 1940.
23. Targ, R., "Precognition in Everyday Life—A Physical Model", *In Proc. Int. Conf. on Parapsychology and the Sciences*. Parapsychology Foundation, Inc., 1972, pp. 251–265.
24. Feinberg, G., "Precognition—A Memory of Things to Come", *In Quantum Physics*

     and *Parapsychology*, L. Oteri (Ed.). Parapsychology Foundation, Inc., New York, 1975, pp. 54–73.

25. *Ibid.*, "Particles that Go Faster than Light", *Sc. Amer.*, vol. 222, no. 2, pp. 69–77, 1970.
26. Gardner, M., "Can Time Go Backward?", *Sc. Amer.*, vol. 216, no. 1, pp. 98–108, 1967.
27. Clay, R. W. and Crouch, P. C., "Possible Observation of Tachyons Associated with Extensive Air Showers", *Nature*, vol. 248, pp. 28–30, 1974.
28. Dobbs, A., "Two-dimensional Time and Probability Patterns", *Proc. S.P.R.*, vol. 54, p. 196, 1965. See also pp. 225–254 of ref. 23.
29. Finkelstein, D. and Powell, J., "Earthquake Lightning", *Nature*, vol. 228, pp. 759–760, 1970.
30. Desch, M. D. and Carr, T. D., "Dekametric and Hectometric Observations of Jupiter from the RAE-1 Satellite", *Astrophysical J. Lett. Ed.*, vol. 194, no. 1, pt. 2, pp. L57–59, 1974.
31. Sheppard, A. R. and Eisenbud, M. (Eds.), *Biological Effects of Electric and Magnetic Fields of Extremely Low Frequency*. New York University Press, 1977, pp. 3–3/3–4.
32. Rohracher, H., "Warmehaushalt und Koerpervibration", *Umschau*, vol. 22, p. 691, 1955.
33. Altmann, G., "Untersuchungen der Physiologischen Wirkung Elektrischer Felder auf Tiere", *Umschau*, p. 69, 1969. See also "Die Physiologische Wirkung Elektrischer Felder auf Organsimen", *Arch. Met. Geoph. Biokl.*, Ser. B, vol. 17, pp. 269–290, 1969.
34. Reiter, R., "Atmospheric Electricity and Natural Radioactivity", in *Medical Climatology*, S. Light (Ed.). Waverly Press, Inc., Baltimore (MA), 1964, pp. 280–316.
35. Hamer, J. R., "Effects of Low Level, Low Frequency Electric Fields on Human Reaction Time", *Commun. in Behav. Biol.*, vol. 2, pp. 217–222, 1968. See also "Biological Entrainment of the Human Brain by Low Frequency Radiation", Northrop Space Laboratories (Hawthorne) Rept. NSL65-199, 1965.
36. Hauf, R. and Wiesinger, J., "Biological Effects of Technical Electric and Electromagnetic VLF Fields", *Int. J. Biometeor.*, vol. 17, no. 3, pp. 213–215, 1973.
37. Gavalas, R. J., Walter, D. O., Hamer, J. and Adfy, W. R., "Effects of Low Level, Low-Frequency Electric Fields on EEG and Behavior in Macaca nemestrina, *Brain Res.*, vol. 19, pp. 491–501, 1970.
38. Persinger, M. A., Lafreniere, G. F. and Mainprize, D. N., "Human Reaction Time Variability Changes from Low Intensity 3 Hz and 10 Hz Electric Fields: Interactions with Stimulus Pattern, Sex and Field Intensity", *Int. J. Biometeor.*, vol. 19, no. 1, pp. 56–64, 1975.
29. König, H. L., "Ueber den Einfluss Besonders Niederfrequenter Elektrischer Vorgaenge in der Atmosphare auf die Umwelt", *Z. Angew, Bader. -u. Klimaheilk.*, vol. 9, pp. 481–501, 1962.
40. Wever, R., "Ueber die Beeinflussung der Circadianen Periodik des Menschen durch Schwache Elektromagnetische Felder", *Z. Vergl. Physiol.*, vol. 56, pp. 111–128, 1967. See also "Gestezmaessigkeiten der Circadianen Periodik des Menschen, Geprueft an der Wirkung eines Schwachen Elektrischen Wechselfeldes", *Pfluegers Arch.*, vol. 302, pp. 97–122, 1968.
41. Persinger, M. A., Ossenkopp, K. P. and Glavin, G. B., "Behavioural Changes in Adult Rats Exposed to ELF Magnetic Fields", *Int. J. Biometeor.*, vol. 16, pp. 155–162, 1972.
42. Ludwig, W. and Mecke, R., "Wirkung, Kuenstlicher Atmospheric auf Sauger", *Arch. Met. Geoph. Biokl.*, Ser. B. vol. 16, pp. 251–261, 1968.
43. Lotmar, R. and Ranscht-Froemsdorff, W. R., "Intensitaet der Gewebeatmung und Wetterfaktoren", *Z. Angew. Badar. u. Klimaheilk.*, vol. 15, pp. 1–10, 1968.
44. Damaschke, V. K. and Becker, G., "Korrelation der Atmungsintensitaet von Termiten zu Aenderungen der Impulsfolgefrequenz der Atmosperics", *Z. Naturforschg.*, vol. 19, pp. 157–160, 1964.

45. Barnwell, F. H., "A day-to-day Relationship Between Oxidative Metabolism and World-Wide Geomagnetic Activity", *Biol. Bull.*, vol. 119, p. 303, 1960.
46. Popa, M. M., "Response of Guinea-Pig Adrenals to Continuous and Arrhythmically Interrupted Low Electromagnetic Fields", in Proc. 5th Biometeor. Congr. S. W. Tromp and W. H. Weihe (Eds.). Springer-Verlag, Amsterdam, 1969, vol. 4. p. 129.
47. Persinger, M. A., Glavin, G. B. and Ossenkopp, K. P., "Physiological Changes in Adult Rats Exposed to an ELF Rotating Magnetic Field", *Int. J. Biometeor.*, vol. 16, pp. 163–172, 1972.
48. Smith, R. F. and Justesen, D. R., "Effects of a 60-Hz Electromagnetic Field on Locomotive and Aggressive Behaviors of Mice", 1976 URSI Meeting (Oct. 11–15, Amherst, Massachusetts), Symp. Proc., p. 146, 1976.
49. Becker, R. O. and Marino, O., "Electromagnetic Pollution", *The Sciences*, vol. 18, p. 15, January 1978.
50. Gann, D. S., Final Report, Electric Power Research Institute Project, RP 98-02, 1977.
51. Young, R. W., Middleton, G. R. and Currant, C. R., "The Detection of Pulsed Microwaves by the Monkey (Macaea mulatta)", *In Proc. Biol. Effects of Electromagnetic Waves*, Boulder (Co), Vol. I, Oct. 1975, pp. 158–159.
52. Dewey, E. R. with Mandino, O., *Cycles*, Manor Books Inc., New York, 1973.
53. Yagodinskiy, V. N., *Cosmic Pulse of the Biosphere.* Znaniye, Moscow, 1975 (in Russian).
54. Friedman, H., Becker, R. O. and Bachman, C., "Psychiatric Ward Behavior and Geophysical Parameters", *Nature*, vol. 205, pp. 1050–1052. 1965.
55. Ibid., "Geomagnetic Parameters and Psychiatric Hospital Admissions", *Nature*, vol. 200, pp. 626–268, 1963.
56. von Gierke, H. F. and Wright-Patterson, "On Noise and Vibration Exposure Criteria", *Arch. Environm. Health*, vol. 11, pp. 327–339, 1965.
57. Anticaglia, J. R. and Cohen, A., "Extra Auditory Effects of Noise as a Health Hazard", *AIHAJ*, vol. 31, no. 3, pp. 277–281, 1970.
58. Bryan, M. and Tempest, W., "Does Infrasound Make Drivers Drunk?", *New Scientist*, vols. 52/53, pp. 584–586, 1971/1972.
59. *New Scientist*, p. 414, Nov. 8, 1973 (cited by R. Brown).
60. Ibid., p. 415 (cited by J. Hanlon).
61. Green, J. E. and Dunn, F., "Correlation of Naturally Occurring Infrasonics and Selected Human Behaviour", *J. Acous. Soc. Am.*, vol. 44, no. 5, pp. 1456–1457, 1968.
62. Krueger, A. P. and Reed, E. J., "Biological Impact of Small Air Ions", *Science*, vol. 193, pp. 1209–1213, 1976.
63. Pavlik, I., "Significance of Air Ionization", in *Medical Climatology*, S. Light (Ed.). Waverley Press Inc., Baltimore (MA), 1964, pp. 317–342.
64. Krueger, A. P. and Smith, R. F., *J. Gen. Physiology*, vol. 44, p. 169, 1960.
65. Sulman, F. G. et al., "Effects of the Sharav and Bora on Urinary Hormone Excretion in 500 Weather-Sensitive Females", *Int. J. Biomet.*, vol. 19, no. 3, pp. 202–209, 1975.
66. Barnes, E. C., "Ionizing Radiation", The Industrial Environment—Its Evaluation and Control USDHEW, chapter 29, pp. 377–397, 1973. Better estimates are given in Rept. UN Scientific Committee on Effects of Atomic Radiation, Supp. No. 40A/32/40, NY 1977.
67. Persinger, M. A., *The Paranormal:* Parts I and II. MSS Information Corporation, New York, 1974. See also "Geophysical Models for Parapsychological Experiences", Psychoenergetic Systems, vol. 1, pp. 63–74, 1975.
68. Ruderfer, M., *J. Am. Soc. Psychical Res.*, vol. 62, pp. 84–86, 1968 (Letter to the Editor).
69. Scholz, C. H., Sykes, L. R. and Aggarwal, Y. P., "Earthquake Prediction: A Physical Basis", *Science*, vol. 181, pp. 803–809, 1973.
70. Press, F., "Earthquake Prediction", *Sci. Am.*, vol. 232, no. 5, pp. 14–23, 1975.
71. *Soviet Physics (USPEKHI)*, vol. 16, pp. 568–579, 1976. See also "The Electric Sense of Sharks and Rays", *J. Exp. Biol.*, vol. 55, pp. 371–381, 1971.

APPENDIX

Unusual Animal Senses

This Appendix reviews some well documented sensory modalities observed in several biological species. This discussion, although relevant to psi phenomena, has not been included in the main body of this paper for simplicity.

Sensory perception is considerably more complex than it may seem at first glance. For example, it is known that a given sense organ can respond to more than one kind of stimulus. Quite often these stimuli are of a widely different nature. Such examples abound in the animal kingdom, as the following cases indicate. The human eye, which is extremely sensitive to light of wavelength between 400 and 780 nm, is also known to respond to other stimuli such as UV and X-ray radiation. It is believed that the eye can detect these stimuli through a fluorescence mechanism.[1] In the intact (human) eye, the cornea absorbs most energy at wavelengths shorter than 300 nm. The crystalline lens, however, has a very sharp cut-off at about 380 nm. Hence persons that have their crystalline lens removed during cataract operation can see objects using UV radiation only. They have a sensation of violet when viewing UV. Some degree of UV vision in subjects with their crystalline lens intact does not seem infrequent. A variety of visual sensations have been elicited in humans by the passage of relativistic charged particles (e.g. μ-mesons) through the vitreous humor.[2,3] This phenomenon seems to be caused by Cerenkov radiation generated in the eye by the passage of these particles. Other mechanisms which have been postulated are scintillation in the crystalline lens or vitreous humor and direct excitation of the retina. Furthermore, non-relativistic high energy helium, nitrogen, oxygen and neon ions, as well as secondaries from fast neutrons, produce light sensations of stars and streaks in the dark-adapted human eye when their energy loss is more than about 10 keV/μm^{-1}. The above visual sensations have been frequently reported by astronauts and individuals working in accelerator sites.[4,5] Visual sensations, although of a diffuse kind, have also been reported to be induced by X-rays down to a dose of 90 μRads.[4] In addition, extraretinal light perception by animals with no eyes has been shown to affect their circadian rhythms.[6] There is also experimental evidence[7] indicating that the olfactory system of the rat plays an important role in X-ray detection. There are other examples in the animal kingdom of multiple stimuli perception by a given sensory organ, but reasons of space preclude further discussion of this subject.

Relevant to a discussion of ESP and sensory perception is the fact that what we may classify as an extrasensory means of perception and/or communication may be a common modality necessary to the survival of some biological species in their particular environments.[8] The animal kingdom is laden with such examples, a few of which are discussed below.

Several species of snakes, fish and insects are known to have highly developed IR receptors. These sensors are chiefly used for locating prey and optimum environmental conditions. Experimental work[9] has shown that boa constrictors, and probably other species as well, are maximally sensitive to IR radiation at a wavelength of about 10 μ. This is the wavelength at which living organisms most strongly emit radiation. Calculation shows[9] that the boa constrictor can respond to IR radiation levels as low as about 84 μW/cm^2, with a response time of about 35 msec. Several snake species can detect environmental temperature changes of a few tenths of a degree Centigrade. Fish are also quite sensitive to IR radiation. They can sense water temperature differences of about 3×10^{-2}°C. Mosquitoes are credited with detecting temperature difference of approximately 2×10^{-2}°C at about 1 cm from an IR source, such as warm-blooded animals.

In at least three unrelated fish families, the *Mormyridae*, *Gymnotidae*, and *Gymnarchidae*, a weak electric field is generated for environmental scanning and communication. These fields are produced as pulses of variable duration and frequency. Some fish generate low-frequency bursts, while others emit continuously. The frequency may range from 55 Hz to 1300 Hz. Communication in certain fish is incredibly complex. The *Sternarchus* (a *Gymnotidae*) produces electric fields at two well separated frequencies of approximately 800 Hz and 1300 Hz, respectively. When another fish of the same species approaches, it shifts its frequency slightly to avoid jamming. The fish using weak electric fields (*Gymnotidae* and *Mormyridae*) can detect electric fields of strength as low as 0.03 μV/cm, sharks (*Scyliorhinus canicula*) and skates (*Raja clavata*), as low as 0.01 μV/cm, and bullheads (*Ictalurus nebulosus*), as low as 30 μV/cm [1c].

Unlike the "well established" electrical sense, the question of whether or not a magnetic sense exists at all is controversial. Experimental research conducted in the last one or two decades, seems to confirm that such a magnetic sense operates in some complex animals. Snails respond to weak DC magnetic fields as low as 40 mG by shifting 2–15° from their main path.[11] A variety of other weak-field effects have also been observed.[12] Recently, migrating birds have been observed to turn or change their altitude more frequently when approaching a low frequency A-C signal produced by a large antenna.[13] This signal had a frequency in the 72 to 80 Hz range. The above animal behavior was observed when the birds were at a distance from the antenna for which the calculated electric and magnetic field strengths were 70 mV/m and from 1 to 5 mG, respectively. It has been shown[14,15] that the orientation of homing birds is affected by naturally occurring disturbances in the geomagnetic field within the range of 10^{-5} to 10^{-2} Hz. The strength of the disturbance is much smaller than the undisturbed geomagnetic field. A magnetic biosensor based on the Josephson effect (assuming that superconductive biological junctions exist) has been suggested by Beischer[16] to account for the alleged high sensitivity of certain biological species, e.g. birds, to magnetic fields. A well "designed" biosensor might attain a sensitivity of about 10^{-10}G! More recently, Leask[17] has proposed an alternative mechanism to account for the orientation behavior of migratory birds and homing pigeons. He suggests an optical/RF double resonance process involving the lowest excited molecular triplet state of, say, the rhodopsin molecule.

Bats use ultrasound to locate prey and for orientation purposes. This is done by using highly developed echolocation techniques.[18,19] The majority of the orientation sounds are emitted at frequencies from 10 to 150 kHz. (Human hearing in adults is confined to the 20 Hz to 10 kHz region. The threshold for hearing is about 10^{-16} w/cm^2). Some species of bats (e.g. horseshoe bats) use sounds that are nearly monochromatic and which may range from 60 to 120 kHz, depending on the species. The individual sounds last usually from 50 to 100 msec. Other species of bats (e.g. "FM bats") use sounds beginning at a very high frequency, e.g. 90 kHz, dropping rapidly to about 45 kHz in only a few msec. Another group of bats emit sounds of complex frequency ranging from 10 to 150 kHz, lasting from less than 1 msec up to 3 msec. Other bats (e.g. *Eptesicus*) have a peak power output of about 10 μW and can detect targets of approximately 1 cm in diameter at about 2 meters distance! Some bats can detect wires as small as, or smaller than, 0.12 mm.[18,20] Ultrasound echolocation and communication is not limited to bats alone. Moths have ears that can hear the ultrasounds emitted by bats at distances up to 33 meters. Moths use their ultrasound sense in various ingenious ways to avoid being preyed upon by bats.[21] Porpoises, dolphins and small whales, to mention only a few of the sea-living mammals, pip to locate obstacles. Each sound pulse contains frequencies up to 200 kHz—possibly even 300 kHz.[19] Porpoises can echolocate fish 15 cm in size by means of ultrasound.[18]

Certain baleen whales use very low frequency (VLF) sound at about 20 Hz, with 3–4 Hz bandwidth, for long range acoustic signalling.[22] It is calculated that these signals can propagate up to several hundred Km. The human ear is virtually deaf at these VLF's. At 20 Hz, the threshold for human hearing, the sensitivity of the adult ear is about 100 dB below the maximum sensitivity for human hearing at about 3 kHz.

Bees, some moths and the horseshoe crab "see" in the UV region of the electromagnetic (EM) spectrum. Patterns of color contrasts in flowers due to differential adsorption and reflection of UV light in the 300–400 nm range (invisible to the human eye), can be perceived by honeybees and some other insects and are important cues to foraging honeybees.[23] Patterns of polarized light are also used by some insects, including bees, for orientation.[24]

Certain biological species exchange complex messages by means of chemical communication. By a wide margin, the most effective chemical communication system employed by animals is the use of pheromones: chemical substances, secreted externally by special glands under endocrine control.[25] Some female butterflies release certain "sex" pheromones (e.g. bombykol and gyplure) which can be detected by males at distances of up to 11 Km. It has been calculated that only a few hundred molecules per cc are sufficient to stimulate the males. This means that only a few of these molecules from time to time need to hit the antennae of the male butterfly. Pheromones are also used, among other chemicals, as food attractants, shock and warning substances, messengers and territorial-marking substances. Many other insects and other animals make use of pheromones. Chemical communication in man is a controversial issue.

In addition to the "unusual senses" discussed above, certain environmental stimuli can also elicit auditory and visual phenomena —among other phenomena—without the direct intervention of the ear and the eye. Recently, Adrian[26] has reported that auditory (electrophonic) and visual (phosphene) sensations can be generated in human subjects through direct transcranial stimulation by low-frequency currents. The minimum threshold of current for the phosphene effect was about 0.5×10^{-2} mA(rms) at 18 to 22 Hz. The threshold for the auditory effect was approximately 0.45 mA(rms) at 60 to 90 Hz. Sensations of color can also be induced over a narrow range of frequencies centered at about 30 Hz. The threshold current to elicit a color response is about 0.2 mA(rms).[26]

Hearing sensations elicited by AC electric fields in the audiofrequency region, similar to those previously reported by Frey in the RF and MW regions, have also been reported by Sommer and von Gierke.[27] The threshold for the hearing effects decreases if a DC bias field is superimposed to the AC field. A human sensation in humans is elicited by an electrode situated 1.25 cm from the head carrying a voltage of about 3.5 V at 700 Hz in the presence of a DC voltage of 7.5 kV. This threshold increases to approximately 300 V at 350 Hz in the absence of a DC bias field.

REFERENCES

1. Bornschein, H., Pape, R., and Zakovsky, J., *Naturwiss.*, vol. 40, p. 251, 1953.
2. D'Arcy, F. J. and Porter, N. A., "Detection of Cosmic Ray μ-Mesons by the Human Eye", *Nature*, vol. 196, pp. 1013–1014, 1962.
3. McNulty, P. J., Pease, V. P. and Bond, V. P., "Visual Sensations Induced by Cerenkov Radiation", *Science*, vol. 189, pp. 453–454, 1975.
4. McNulty, P. J. et al., "Particle Induced Visual Phenomena in Space", *Radiation Effects*, vol. 34, pp. 153–156, 1977.
5. Tobias, C. A. et al., "Some Studies on Visual Perception and Pathologic Effects of Accelerated Heavy Ions", in *Radiation Research* (Nygaard, Adler and Sinclair, Eds), Academic Press, New York, 1975.
6. Underwood, H. and Menaker, M., "Extraretinal Light Perception: Entrainment of the Biological Clock Controlling Lizard Locomotor Activity", *Science*, vol. 170, pp. 190–193, 1970.
7. Hull, C. D. et al., "Role of the Olfactory System in Arousal to X-Rays", *Nature*, vol. 205, pp. 627–628, 1965.
8. Bigu, J., Editorial, *J. Research in Psi Phenomena*, vol. 1, no. 1, pp. 1–4, 1976.
9. Gamow, R. I. and Harris, J. F., "The Infrared Receptors of Snakes," *Scientific American*, May 1973.
10. Cited by McCleave et al., "Weak Electric and Magnetic Fields in Fish Orientation," in *Annals of NY Acad. Sci.*, vol. 188, p. 270, 1971.
11. Brown, F. A. et al., *Bio. Bull.*, vol. 127, pp. 221–231, 1964 and *Biol. Bull.*, vol. 118, pp. 367–381, 1960.
12. Cited by Conley, C. C., "Effects of Near-Zero Magnetic Fields Upon Biological Systems," in *Biological Effects of Magnetic Fields*, vol. 2 (M. F. Barnothy, Ed.), Plenum Press, New York, 1969, pp. 29–51.
13. Larkin, R. P. and Sutherland, P. J., "Migrating Birds Respond to Project Seafarer's Electromagnetic Field," *Science*, pp. 777–779, 1977.
14. Keeton, W. T., Larkin, T. S. and Windsor, D. M., *J. Comp. Physiology*, vol. 95, p. 95, 1974.
15. Southern, W. E., *Condor*, vol. 74, p. 102, 1972.
16. Beischer, D. E., "The Null Magnetic Field as Reference for the Study of Geomagnetic Directional Effects in Animals and Man," *Ann. N.Y. Acad. Sci.*, vol. 188, pp. 324–329, 1971.
17. Leask, M. J. M., "A Physicochemical Mechanism for Magnetic Field Detection by Migratory Birds and Homing Pigeons," *Nature*, vol. 267, pp. 144–145, 1977.
18. Griffin, D. R., *Echoes of Bats and Men*. Anchor Books, New York, 1959.
19. Sales, G. and Pye, D., *Ultrasonic Communication by Animals*. Chapman and Hall, London, 1974.
20. Griffin, D. R., "More About Bat 'Radar'," *Scientific American*, July, 1958.
21. Roeder, K. D., "Moths and Ultrasound," *Scientific American*, April, 1965.
22. Payne, R. and Webb, D., "Orientation by Means of Long Range Acoustic Signalling in Baleen Whales," *Ann. N.Y. Acad. Sci.*, vol. 188, pp. 110–141, 1971.
23. Thorp, R. W. et al., "Nectar Fluorescence under Ultraviolet Irradiation," *Science*, vol. 189, pp. 476–478, 1975.
24. Wehner, R., "Polarized-Light Navigation by Insects," *Scientific American*, vol. 235, pp. 106–116, 1976.
25. Wilson, E. O., "Pheromones," *Scientific American*, May 1963.

26. Adrian, D. J., "Auditory and Visual Perceptions Stimulated by Low-Frequency Electric Currents," *Radio Science*, vol. 12, no. 6(S), pp. 243–250, 1977.
27. Sommer, H. C. and von Gierke, H. E., "Hearing Sensations in Electric Fields," *Aerospace Medicine*, pp. 834–839, Sept. 1964.

DISCUSSION

HONORTON: I'm having a great deal of difficulty, which maybe you can help me with, in relating your theory to the empirical data in the field; in particular the idea that there could be biophysical carriers of psi. I certainly can see that in many of the spontaneous cases and in many situations dealing with macroscopic effects. But, for example, what do you do in the case of a card-matching experiment, where the subject is matching words in a language he doesn't know against key cards in the language that he is familiar with, where what seems to be going on is a meaning rather than a transmission of discrete stimuli?

BIGU: The theory, of course, is merely applicable to spontaneous psi occurrences. You are referring to some control experiments, which of course, is a different thing. But even in the case of a control experiment, you have environmental stimuli, because I think that's what it is although it may sound like strange terminology. It is bound to affect and is known to affect the performance of the individual. So I haven't incorporated these in the case of a control experiment; these are rather for the case of spontaneous psi experiences.

HONORTON: Does your theory relate to the process by which the information gets from point A to point B, or are you primarily concerned with how the information is mediated once it's available to the organism? If the latter, then I can see it. I don't see how it could possibly account for more than a very small percentage of the experimental work to date.

BIGU: Experimental data is practically absent. When you come to review papers to find the effects of very low levels of any stimuli on humans, there are very few and for testing animals there is very little. So you don't know exactly what level of any given environmental stimuli affects what animals.

HONORTON: But what kind of stimuli could you conceive of that would enable a North Carolina high school student to translate the Telegu word for "fish" into its English equivalent? That's the kind of problem I'm referring to.

BIGU: Well, of course, you would then have to resort to the complexity of the central nervous system. I haven't mentioned these things in my discussion, although some of them are in my paper. I'm trying to extrapolate a little from the behavioral effects, the physiological effects to psi phenomena which may not be fundamentally different.

TART: The examples you present of certain spontaneous events which, in a sense, are mislabeled "paranormal," are interesting. Extension of our current physical explanatory systems along some of the lines you suggested will probably turn out to be sufficient to explain them. However, the bulk of parapsychological experimentation, I think, is in a quite different category. We have telepathy experiments where the sender and receiver are separated by hundreds or thousands of miles, and the target to be sent is a random set of numbers. There are no very obvious physiological correlates of thinking of numbers.

In engineering terms, there are two simultaneous problems to be faced in trying to extend current physical explanations. One is the signal-to-noise ratio problem of any known kind of energetic carrier. All the ones I can think of, that I've seen mentioned, have dropped many levels of magnitude down below the natural noise level by the time you talk about that sheer distance. The second related factor is the question of selectivity. If you have a card-guessing experiment between Europe and California, for example, there are millions and millions of people thinking of numbers all over the planet. I don't know of any mechanism whereby you can tune into one and not the other.

Now, the problem is even worse when you get into pure clairvoyance experiments, where the information only exists as, say a pattern of ink on some pieces of cardboard in a sealed box. It's difficult to visualize a modulation mechanism there for environmental energies. And in the case of precognition experiments, the problem gets even worse, because the kind of precognition dealt with in parapsychological experiments involves, by definition, a randomizing operation before the selection of the stimuli, so that it can't be inferable on the basis of any currently existing cues. Can you make some comments on the extension of your approach to this kind of experimental data?

BIGU: Yes. Say, for instance, in one of the cases, you actually don't need any transmission. You do away with the noise or losses in transmission because you need only an interaction of the immediate environment with the state of the system.

TART: Is this the precognition example you gave earlier?

BIGU: Yes, that would be equally applicable to both precognition and telepathy.

TART: The example you gave struck me as an example of mislabeling. There was a common environmental stimulus.

BIGU: Which example are you referring to now?

TART: In any precognition experiment you have to rule out the possibility of access to all sorts of current information, a knowledge of which might allow you to infer the later state of the system. So you introduce a randomizing operation, usually a thorough shuffling of the cards, the introduction of an electronic random number generator, or something like that to destroy any such inferential ability. So you have the problem that future data is being commented upon to a statistically significant degree when by definition, it's *not* inferable from any knowledge of current information, even a knowledge much more extensive than you think a person would ordinarily have.

BIGU: From the informational standpoint, I would have serious doubts about some of the published papers in which different drawings are compared and similarities are stated as being significant at a certain level. To me it is still a mystery that when some of the drawings are compared, people can see any degree of similarity. Now, I have never seen thus far any serious attempt to apply conventional information theory to this kind of thing. I cannot see how a comparison like this can induce people to say that this is clear case of clairvoyance or precognition or telepathy or whatever you want to call it, because, in specific examples of drawings I cannot see at what point there is a similarity between the message sent and the drawings received.

BELOFF: If an earthquake produces so many physical precursors such as you describe, how is it that seismology isn't further advanced? I mean, for example, last week's earthquake in Santa Barbara, which we read about in the papers, how far in advance were they able to produce a warning about this? My very slight knowledge of seismology leads me to suppose that the predictive devices aren't very good. But why aren't they better, if there are all these effects that a machine could pick up?

BIGU: That's a very good point. There is an article that appeared in *Science*, that said they were very optimistic in the beginning about being able to predict earthquakes, but it turned out to be a bit more difficult than they thought. But you are right. However, we are talking about two different things. What these people are trying to do is to predict earthquakes with some kind of apparatus, some kind of instrumentation. But we're talking about humans now. A mouse doesn't have any apparatus to measure anything. Horses and other animals have been observed to become very disturbed whenever a major meteorological or other natural phenomenon occurs. That is one of the ways by which some people used to recognize when something was going to happen. So this is purely anecdotal, if you want to put it that way, and you probably have read this many times. There is a difference between technological means of predicting an earthquake and a living organism being able to sense when something may happen. You see, these are two fundamentally different issues here, and the fact that someone says that our techniques are incapable of predicting an earthquake, would not invalidate the theory, I think.

EHRENWALD: A psychiatric friend of mine used to say, "A theory should be like a bathing suit: elegant, brief, and cover the whole territory." We have heard here another distinguished contribution to physical theory, but it is a theory which selects only the data which it can supposedly explain, and when we come to data which it cannot explain, then Dr. Bigu told us "it is a complete mystery to me." Information theory falls short of answering the question of how, for instance, symbolic interpretations or symbolic messages get across and are understood. An example of this is one that Chuck Honorton gave us before. When it comes to catastrophic, physical events, then, as Dr. Beloff pointed out, such big events cast their shadows ahead of time in terms of information theory, in terms of transmission of well-known physical forces, environmental or otherwise. But precognitive dreams are another matter. Dreams are admittedly physical events involving the brain. But how can you, with the help of information theory, account for the fact that a patient of mine dreams ahead of time an event like my moving into a new apartment and drawing a picture of the apartment, which she has never seen nor known about, which contained certain systematic distortions, while giving the essential core of the information intact? It is true that the reproduction of the target material is often incomplete. But it is the very incompleteness of the telepathic response which is significant and incompatible with physical theories.

BIGU: I think I emphasized that the theory is not supposed to explain everything. Moreover as I applied these facts to spontaneous psi occurrences, I didn't put any emphasis at all on control conditions and therefore we have to accept this limitation. I am only trying to point out the advantage of applying a biophysical theory, because, as far as I know, people overlook the obvious every time. For example, there are some phenomena such as the visual sensations elicited by low levels of UV radiation, X-rays and highly energetic charged particles, which could, in principle, explain some kinds of alleged hallucinations and "materializations." You also have sensations of color and auditory effects evoked by the transcranial flow of low-frequency microcurrents produced by externally applied voltages. Another example is provided by the experiments on "primary perception" in plants. In some of these experiments brine shrimps were used to prove this perception (the details of this experiment can be found in the literature as it was well publicized). However, it is possible that the alleged response of the plant, as recorded by the apparatus used, might have been due to EM signals generated by the electrical motors or other electric and electronic gadgets used, and picked up by the recording apparatus.

EHRENWALD: I object to a theory which selects the data that it's supposed to explain and has, by necessity, excluded data which cannot be explained by the preconceived theory from which it started. A theory which focuses on physical events and environmental factors is fine, but when it says that it is a mystery why telepathic drawings are distorted, then it is clear that the theory has fallen short of what it is supposed to do. By the same token, I object to Jung's theory of synchronicity because it cannot account for the ESP type of card experiments. Nor do I see any merit in Spencer Brown's theory of mathematical resonance in ESP experiments, because it does not account for so-called "need-determined" incidents of the type we see in the psychoanalytic situation or in many spontaneous phenomena. A theory, unless it explains everything, falls short of its purpose.

BIGU: First of all, let me settle one point. There is no theory in the world in any field of science that can account for all the phenomena, so any and every theory falls short most of the time; it explains one thing and doesn't explain the other. Another thing is that I didn't selectively gather any experimental material because I didn't give any description of the biophysical interaction, inasmuch as I said I was going to skip it for the sake of time. But perhaps I didn't make myself clear in my response to Dr. Tart. What I said was that in the comparison of drawings in telepathy it is difficult for me to understand how some conclusions can be drawn from a purely informational standpoint. Some people have tried to do some studies, and the only thing they have managed to do is to write a commonly used equation in communication theory—nothing else. In discussing my theory, I pointed out that it would apply in principle to spontaneous psi occurrences. There are many limitations to the theory because of lack of data, so I'm not saying that it is right. I am just saying that the theory may help to explain some kinds of telepathy or precognition.

DIXON: I think your theory is logically and psychologically viable. It seems to be based on Hegel's Axiom of Internal Relations—the idea being that if, for example you move your clock on your mantle in Montreal it could presumably affect say, a tiger in the Burmese jungle, the grand idea being that everything is in a sense related to everything else. The second point is a psychological one. And that is that human organisms are extremely good at monitoring much more than they think that they are monitoring in their normal transactions with the environment. Though the mechanisms of attention tend to restrict entry into consciousness, it's been shown that in communication we may acquire a lot of unconscious incidental learning about the relationships between what we're receiving and what we're transmitting. The third point seems to me very valid—that we are adept at making use of available information from the physical environment when we need to, even though we don't appear to be responding to it at other times. If, then, you put these points together (while accepting the fact that paranormal phenomena are statistically very rare) it seems to me not entirely surprising that every now and then you might come across people who monitor the total environment (and the correlates of their communications) so well that they will from time to time produce these astonishing results. But the only thing against that is that, as far as I'm aware, people who were in outer space and tried to send messages did apparently succeed, and this seems to me something which cannot be explained in terms of biophysical, terrestrial data.

BIGU: Then one could always extrapolate and say we're not dealing with the earth environment now, we're talking about the extraterrestrial environment. I'm stretching the thing a little bit but surely you have in space as many environmental factors as you have here on earth. You have there plasmas, electromagnetic radiation of various frequencies (e.g. RF, MW, IR, visible, UV, X-rays and gamma radiation), highly energetic charged particles of various kinds, simple and complex molecules, dust, etc. Some of the above environmental factors are "stronger" above ground than on ground. You may also have things up there that you don't have down there.

GOEGEBEUR: I studied wild life in British Columbia and found one particular wasp that has the habit of making its nest a few inches above the snow line over the winter. I wonder how the wasp would be able to do that. I studied this particular wasp for three consecutive years and each time it made its nest a few inches above the snow line over the whole winter.

PRIBRAM: The future snow line?

GOEGEBEUR: Yes. I wonder how the wasp could do that. In other words, it seemed to know where the snow would fall.

BIGU: I don't know about that particular thing, but animals are known to do tremendously difficult things.

RUDOLPH: Information theory does not presuppose a signal transmission model. Shannon had a signal transmission model in mind when he created the theory, but his theory does not require that and is perfectly compatible with things like precognition.

BIGU: The only comment that I made is that this formula had been applied in principle to psi phenomena but there have been no further elaborations on the results.

SERVADIO: Just a word of praise for Dr. Bigu's paper, which has taken up a line that was practically abandoned for many years since the time when Dr. Tromp in Holland and in Italy Dr. Mackenzie and Dr. Cipriani did something along these lines. I've been helped by Dr. Bigu's paper to get a few more ideas about the famous "sender/receiver" concept which has always puzzled me very much, and to which I have never found a satisfactory alternative in ideas like the collective unconscious, the mind-at-large, or things like that. Ideas such as collective unconscious or synchronicity, have never really taken environmental and natural stimuli into account. The idea of a planetary psi component linking biophysiological and biopsychological dimensions to the natural environmental dimension, could perhaps correspond with what some ancient philosophers meant by the concept of an *anima mundi*, where you find components of psi and environment linked together.

VOLUNTARY MOVEMENT, BIOFEEDBACK CONTROL AND PK

JOHN BELOFF

The question I want to raise in this paper is the following: Is the power which enables us to influence the target system in a PK experiment the same power, basically, as that which we deploy every time we voluntarily move our limbs (using the word "power" in its most general and noncommittal sense)? Or, in other words, can PK be regarded as the extrasomatic (and hence paranormal) extension of what, in ordinary volitional activity, is endosomatic (and hence normal)? The question was first explicitly raised, I believe, by Thouless and Wiesner in their classic paper of 1947, where they also put forward the idea that ESP is the extrasomatic extension of what occurs in normal perception and cognition where the mind extracts information from the brain to create a meaningful conscious percept or thought. Here, however, we shall be concerned exclusively with the problem of PK. If the answer to this question is no, if the Thouless-Wiesner thesis is mistaken, then, presumably, PK represents some special power or faculty that is *sui generis* and radically different from anything else that forms part of our ordinary mental life. The question is, I consider, worth raising again both because of the light it may throw on the nature of PK and because of its implications for the mind-body problem.

At first it may seem that there is little to commend the analogy. In the first place, whereas voluntary movement is a universal fact of life, PK is an exceedingly rare and dubious phenomenon, at any rate insofar as it can be demonstrated experimentally. Secondly, the amount of conscious control that can be exerted in the case of PK is almost nil. This is so even in those exceptional cases of directly observable or macro-PK effects, where objects move or metals bend. Indeed, it may be doubted whether we can rightly speak of "willing" in connection with PK. At most the subject can wish for a certain result to come about, but there is not much he can then specifically do to make it come about. In the case of RSPK phenomena even the conscious wish may be absent, so that it is only by a process of elimination and inference that we identify a particular individual as the subject or "poltergeist focus." In view of these obvious differences between voluntary movement and PK many would wish to argue that there was nothing to be gained by pressing the analogy and subsuming both under the same rubric.

Nevertheless, in spite of such asymmetries, there are important respects in which the two processes resemble one another. In the first place, they are both goal-oriented or teleological-type processes, in the sense that a given state of affairs is achieved without there being any awareness on anyone's part as to the precise means necessary for such an achievement to be possible. Thus, when I stretch out my hand to pick up an object off the table, I know nothing at all about the sequence of physiological events starting in the motor cortex of my brain and leading up to the contraction of muscle groups in my arm and fingers that must precede any action on my part. But, even with regard to the overt movements which I then proceed to execute, I am largely dependent on a stock of tacit knowledge which never enters my focal awareness. In much the same way, the successful PK subject becomes aware of the results which he produces while remaining totally ignorant of the micro-processes, mechanical or electronic, which must take place in the target-system for such results to be possible. In the second place, voluntary movement and PK are intimately bound up with the provision of feedback. Our muscles are not just effectors but also receptors, so that with every contraction of the muscles there is some proprioceptive feedback and, at least in the case of the manipulatory skills we perform with our fingers, there is usually some visual feedback as well, although touch-typing would be an exception. To what extent PK is dependent on the visual or auditory feedback that is usually provided by the experimental set-up is still a matter for speculation, but, for one school of thought, at any rate, that represented by the influential "observational theories" of PK associated with such theorists as Helmut Schmidt and Evans Walker, it is critical. According to these theories, it is not until feedback is received that the train of events leading up to the observed outcome is determined. This implies, paradoxically, a causal loop in time between aiming at a given result and observing its realization. Whether a similar "observational theory" of voluntary movement is conceivable is not a question I shall pursue here, as it would take me too far afield. In the present context I want only to stress that feedback enters into both voluntary movement and PK in this integral way in virtually every instance that we can cite.

I am going to suggest that we may be able to arrive at a better understanding of the connection between voluntary movement and

PK if we look at an intermediate class of phenomena which partakes of some of the characteristics of each. It is here I wish to introduce the topic of biofeedback control. We can now demonstrate that people can acquire control over certain physiological functions which, in the ordinary way, are beyond conscious control by adopting certain special techniques. The functions in question are mainly those associated with the autonomic nervous system, heart-rate, vasodilation, glandular secretion etc. but may include functions of the central nervous system such as brain rhythms and measures of arousal. There is one function, rate of breathing, which ordinarily operates automatically, but which can be consciously controlled without using any special technique, but here I shall be concerned only with those where a special training is required. There are a variety of such special techniques, the oldest of which are the systems of yoga, but the one with which I shall be concerned is that known as biofeedback, which is based on allowing the subject to monitor his own physiological output through appropriate visual or auditory displays.

Biofeedback is a normal phenomenon, in the sense that it does not, as far as is known, transcend any limits of what is considered within the natural capacity of the nervous system. Moreover, anyone can acquire a moderate degree of proficiency in biofeedback control; no special ability is presupposed. At the same time, from the psychological point of view, there are important respects in which the phenomenon resembles PK. I am thinking especially of its dependence on what Elmer Green (1976) has called "passive volition." One cannot produce a biofeedback effect, as one might the raising of one's arm, by a simple fiat of the will. Rather, one has to want the effect to come about and wait hopefully, in a half expectant yet relaxed frame of mind, for it to appear spontaneously. This is notoriously the case with the control of alpha rhythm, for it is one of the paradoxes of the biofeedback technique that alpha rhythm will vanish if the subject makes a conscious effort to produce it! There is a parallel here with the finding that the best scores in a PK test are often obtained when the subject is least trying to produce them. Rex Stanford coined the expression "release of effort" to cover cases in which significant scores are obtained by the subject after the termination of the official run when, unknown to the subject, the target generator is kept going, but others too, have noted that a state of relaxation is conducive to success. Thouless and Wiesner suggested that this might be due to the fact that active volition would have the effect of channeling the influence directed onto the target system back into the subject's own motor system.

Certainly, at a purely formal level, there is a striking similarity between the typical biofeedback set-up and the PK set-up as this has been developed especially by Helmut Schmidt and has since become standard laboratory practice. Of course, objectively, there is a world of difference, depending on whether the feedback display is coupled with the subject's own body, as with biofeedback, or with an electronic random event generator, as with PK, but this does not preclude the possibility that the same basic phenomenon underlies both. And this possibility begins to loom larger when we venture beyond biofeedback studies of the routine kind to consider certain virtuoso performances by those who, in one way or another, have learnt to control their own organism. Take, for example, such performers as Swami Rama or Jack Schwarz, to name but two who have both been tested in some depth at the Menninger Institute. Swami Rama has demonstrated differential control over the arteries of his right hand to the extent of producing changes of temperature in opposite directions on two spots of his right palm only a few inches apart amounting to a differential of about 10°F. He has also demonstrated control of his heart beat to the extent of completely arresting the circulation of his blood for as much as 17 seconds, having been dissuaded from prolonging the effect (Green et al., 1976). Jack Schwarz, a Dutch-American who belongs by rights to the Indian fakir tradition, has, for his part, demonstrated feats of self-wounding which not only fail to elicit any pain reaction or even any bleeding but, more surprisingly still, the wound never becomes infected no matter how severe or how soiled the implement used (Rorvik 1976). It is, further, of interest to learn that both Swami Rama and Jack Schwarz are credited with special powers of self-healing of a kind that psychic healers are supposed to be able to exert on an alien body.

But, to return to biofeedback proper, I want next to discuss one particular study which is linked with the problem of voluntary movement and to which Honorton drew our attention in his presidential address to the Parapsychological Association in 1975. I refer to the electromyographic experiments of John Basmajian as reported in *Science*, 1972. His experiments consisted of training his subjects to activate specific motor units within certain selected skeletal muscles; he used mainly the forearm, shoulder and neck muscles. His subjects were given both visual and auditory feedback of the varying myoelectric potential in the specific motor unit in question as recorded by means of microelectrodes planted in the muscle fiber. It transpired that any normal volunteer subject could, within a few minutes, learn to control the appropriate unit. From then on he could be taught increasingly difficult discriminations, for example activating one given unit rather than another neighboring unit, varying at will the rate at which it was firing and, finally, being able to control it even in the absence of any exteroceptive feedback. To quote the author: "Some persons can be trained to gain control of isolated motor units to such a degree that, with both visual and aural cues shut off, they can recall any one of three favorite units on command and in any sequence. They can keep such units firing without any conscious awareness other than the assurance (after the fact) that they have succeeded. In spite of considerable introspection they cannot explain their success except to state they thought about a motor unit as though they had seen and heard it personally."

This is an unusual application of the biofeedback technique, inasmuch as the effect involved is not some involuntary autonomic function, but rather a highly specific component of our ordinary voluntary motor activity. Ordinarily, all that we are able to do, voluntarily, is to control the gross movements of our limbs, but, after a Basmajian type training, we can, it seems, turn on or off at will the firing of a single motor unit. We have no idea how we do this any more than we know how we succeed in wagging a given finger. All we know, in both instances, is that, by taking thought we can bring about the desired effect. The relevance of the Basmajian work for our present purposes is that it shows how, at the microscopic level of analysis, voluntary movement and biofeedback control converge.

I want next to discuss a very different experiment which attempts, rather, to bring together biofeedback control and PK. This is an experiment of William Braud's which he reported at the 1977 P.A. Convention where he introduced his intriguing concept of "allobio-feedback." It is evident that any biofeedback set-up could be converted into a PK set-up by the simple expedient of coupling the feedback display to another person's body in place of the subject's own body. In Braud's experiment he himself acted as subject and his task was alternatively to increase or decrease, according to a random schedule of instructions, the GSR amplitude of a target-person whose GSR tracing he was meanwhile monitoring. The design of the experiment was a very complicated one, inasmuch as the target-persons were themselves acting as subjects with respect to a test involving clairvoyance and relaxation, but these complications need not detain us here. Suffice it to say that the allobiofeedback test was successful in that, out of the ten target-persons involved in the confirmation experiment, eight produced higher GSR amplitudes during those runs in which Braud was aiming to increase them and that a t-test of the difference between the two conditions was significant at the 1 percent level of confidence. Discussing his findings, Braud claims that the concept of allobiofeedback is the simplest way of conceptualizing the situation; in other words that what we have here is a feedback loop that is closed by a PK influence directed onto a live target-system. As is always the case, however, in a parapsychological experiment, there is enough ambiguity in the situation to permit other interpretations. As he points out, the results could have been due to a telepathic influence that he might have been exerting on the target-person's mind rather than on his body and even more devious interpretations are possible that we need not pursue here.

At all events, before the concept of allobiofeedback becomes established, several pertinent factors call for clarification. First, how critical was the provision of feedback in this instance? Could the subject have influenced the activity of the target-persons had he *not* been monitoring their output? It is noteworthy that, in another experiment by Braud and Braud reported at the same Convention, PK effects on a random event generator were obtained in the absence of feedback. Secondly, is a live target-system such as this a more sensitive detector of PK than an inanimate random event generator? On the Thouless-Wiesner hypothesis that PK is essentially the power we normally use to control our own brain, we should expect this to be the case, since one brain is more like another than it is like an electronic machine. However, since the great majority of PK experiments have been done with artificial target-systems we have little basis for comparison. There may even be a flaw in the argument which would lead us to expect better results from a live target-system since, if we adopt an observational theory of psi, it would make no difference in the last resort what processes were involved in the production of a given PK effect; all that counts is the final awareness of the effect that has been produced. Whatever the outcome may be, we must hope that many more allobiofeedback experiments will be forthcoming in the years ahead. It would be of particular interest to take a subject who had first mastered autobiofeedback control and switch him without warning to the allobiofeedback condition. Would there be a carry-over from the normal to the paranormal condition? Would he proceed to control both his own and the target-person's output in unison? Or would conflicting exteroceptive and interoceptive feedback make such a deception impossible, so that the experiment would founder with the subject in a state of total confusion?

Leaving such questions unanswered, let us revert to the familiar case of normal volitional activity. We must start by recognizing that, according to the orthodox view that still prevails alike in science and philosophy, there is, strictly speaking, no such thing as a volition. The distinction between voluntary behavior on the one hand and involuntary, automatic or reflex behavior on the other, depends on the kind of brain processing that goes on, not on whether such behavior is, or is not, preceded by, or accompanied by, an "act of will," whatever we are to understand by that phrase. For, ultimately, in the orthodox view, it is the brain alone which governs the activity of the limbs. The organism as a whole may be conceived of as a self-regulating cybernetic machine and the interaction of the organism and its environment constitutes a closed physical loop which admits of no extraneous influences and interventions of a nonphysical kind. As for the familiar experience of free-will on which we humans set such store, the experience of acting freely according to conscious decisions for which we as persons or selves take sole responsibility, that is no more than a subjective or epiphenomenal reflection of whatever physical brain states are the real causes of our behavior.

One notable brain physiologist of recent times who has never accepted this orthodox view of voluntary movement is Sir John Eccles, who gave the invited address to the P.A. Convention in Utrecht in 1976. Already in his Waynflete lectures in Oxford in 1952, that were later published as *The Neurophysiological Basis of Mind*, he shocked the scientific and philosophical establishment, which were particularly well entrenched at Oxford, by putting forward what he has called his "neurophysiological hypothesis of will." This is based on the observation that the situation at the synapse through which the neural impulse must pass is so delicately poised that factors at the level of quantum uncertainty may decide whether the impulse is discharged or not. In such a situation, a psychic influence might tilt the balance one way or the other since, whether or not there is a ghost in the machine, the brain appears to be just the kind of machine that a ghost might be expected to operate! Furthermore, given the prodigious inter-connectedness of our brain cells, even one such intervention might produce an appreciable effect on the overall output of the brain or, as he puts it (1970): "within 20 milliseconds the pattern of discharge of even hundreds of thousands of neurones would be modified as the result of an 'influence' that initially caused the discharge of merely one neurone." But there is no need to stop there. The same mind-influence could conceivably operate holistically by exerting spatio-temporal "fields of influence" on the cortex, which would be uniquely fitted to respond. It is of some interest to note, in passing, that more than a century before the great physiologist, Johannes Müller, had proposed a very similar conception of the will when he declared that: "the fibers of all the motor, cerebral and spinal nerves may be imagined spread out in the medulla oblongata and exposed to the influence of the will like the keys of the pianoforte."

Recently Eccles joined forces with the philosopher Karl Popper and last year the two of them published a large volume entitled *The Self and Its Brain* which bore the subtitle *An Argument for Interactionism*. In his section of this book, Eccles further elaborates, with plentiful anatomical detail, his ideas about the interaction between what it pleases him to call "the self-conscious mind" and the "liaison brain." The latter, he speculates, consists of complex modules of neurones in columnar formation, each module comprising some 10,000 neurons including many hundreds of pyramidal cells. In his chapter on "Voluntary Movement," Eccles draws attention to the work of H. H. Kornhuber, a German neurophysiologist, which, he claims, illustrates in its purest form the action of mind on brain. Essentially, what Kornhuber did was to get his subject, who had first been carefully trained to maintain a relaxed posture, to wag his right index finger at irregular intervals entirely of his own volition when care had been taken to exclude any possible triggering stimulus from the environment. While he was doing this, certain electrical potentials were recorded from various sites on the subject's scalp and these were then averaged over some 250 recordings. The resultant curve revealed a concentration of neuronal activity in the pyramidal cells of the motor cortex occurring at about 1/20th sec. before the muscular response, an interval which, as Eccles points out, is just about adequate for transmission of the impulse from the pyramidal cells down to the muscle fibers in the finger. This, then, provides at least a partial answer to the question of what goes on in the brain when a willed action is in process of being carried out. The more searching question is whether it provides evidence of the action of mind on brain.

Eccles repeatedly insists that it does, although he realizes that the upholders of the orthodox view will be reluctant to admit it. They will argue that, when the subject receives his instructions, the brain, like a computer, stores the information and duly programs the subject to emit the required response at irregular intervals. But Eccles will have none of this. "The stringent conditions of the Kornhuber experiment," he insists, "preclude or negate such explanatory claims. The trained subjects literally do make the movements in the absence of any determining influences from the environment and any random potentials generated by the relaxed brain would be virtually eliminated by the averaging of 250 traces." He concludes, therefore, that: "we can regard these experiments as providing a convincing demonstration that voluntary movements can be freely initiated independently of any determining influences that are entirely within the neuronal machinery of the brain." (1977, p. 294)

I think I need hardly say that not even the authority of an Eccles, nor yet the argumentative skill of a Popper, is likely to make much impact on the committed materialist. It is significant, however, that neither Eccles nor Popper is prepared to avail himself of the parapsychological evidence and bring it to bear on the issue, indeed neither is yet willing to acknowledge the existence of PK. Eccles, at one point, expresses some surprise that the activity of the "self-conscious mind" should be limited to a single individual brain, but he never pauses to consider whether this is indeed always and necessarily the case. Thus, much as I admire these two great men for doing battle on behalf of the autonomy of mind, I consider that their case is weaker than it might be for lack of this crucial prop and that, if, for our part, we can place the evidence for PK on a footing where it can no longer be ignored by official science, we shall succeed in clinching the argument in favour of treating voluntary movement as an expression of free will.

I have tried, in this paper, to show that the assumption that PK is a form of volitional activity directed onto the outside world has implications for the philosophy of mind and, conversely, the dualistic view of the mind-body relationship has implications for the study of PK. However, as I am always being reminded by my more experimentally minded associates, a theory is no use unless its implications are testable and so, in what remains of my time, I want to say a few words about the sort of lines along which such tests might hopefully be conducted, even if I cannot as yet be very explicit. If I am correct in thinking that in PK we use the same basic means to influence the target-system as normally we use to control the brain, then two possibilities suggest themselves. Either we might try preventing the subject from exercising normal voluntary movement hoping that, in desperation, he will be driven to exteriorize his powers in the form of PK or, alternatively, we could arouse the subject's normal volitional activities in such a way that the powers involved will spill over onto the target system. As it happens, support can be found in favor of each of these possibilties in the existing literature. With respect to PK of the microscopic or statistical kind, I have already mentioned the importance of adopting an attitude of passive volition suggesting, perhaps, that PK might here function as a substitute for normal voluntary effort. In that case, it may be worth testing those who either happen to be paralyzed or could be experimentally made so and would thus be physically debarred from control of their limbs, but it might also be worth seeing what happens to a random event generator during the REM stage of sleep when we are all of us paralyzed. However, with respect to PK of the macroscopic or directly observable kind, the evidence suggests that the successful subjects are usually in a state of high arousal. This was specially the case with Nina Kulagina, but even with a physical medium like Rudi Schneider, who was in a complete trance when he produced his phenomena, it was observed that both his breathing and heart rate underwent an astonishing acceleration. If this "spill-over" model of PK should prove more appropriate in certain circumstances we would have to find ways of arousing the subject.

While I was still engaged in speculating on these possibilities for research, I was happy to learn that Charles Honorton had been thinking along rather similar lines and had, indeed, already carried out some pioneering work in this connection which had yielded positive results. His particular strategy (as described in a paper he is presenting at this conference) was to use biofeedback in order to train his subjects to control their alpha rhythm. A random event generator is then brought into play and the experimenter finds out whether its output is significantly biased from the random baseline during the critical phases when control of the alpha rhythm is achieved. Honorton's experiments, which have already provided some promising data, are based on a rationale that is somewhat different from either the substitution model or the spill-over model that I discussed earlier. Presumably, like me, Honorton was impressed with the similarities he had observed as between the biofeedback situation and the PK situation and took this as his point of departure. But, be that as it may, he has added a further impetus towards searching for a common thread uniting the phenomena of voluntary movement, biofeedback control and PK.

BIBLIOGRAPHY

Barber, T. X., (Ed.,) *Advances in Altered States of Consciousness and Human Potentialities, Vol. 1.* New York, Psychological Dimensions Inc., 1976.

Basmajian, J. "Electromyography comes of age," *Science, 176,* 1972, 603–609.

Braud, Lendell and Braud, W., "PK effects upon a random number generator under conditions of limited feedback to volunteers and experimenter," *Research in Parapsychology 1977,* Metuchen, N.J., Scarecrow Press, 1978.

Braud, W., "Allobiofeedback: Immediate feedback for a PK influence upon another person's physiology," *Research in Parapsychology 1977,* Metuchen, N.J., Scarecrow Press, 1978.

Eccles, J. C., *The Neurophysiological Basis of Mind.* Oxford, Clarendon Press, 1953.

Eccles, J. C., *Facing Reality,* New York/Heidelberg/Berlin, Springer-Verlag, 1970.

Eccles, J. C. "The human person in its two-way relationship to the brain," *Research in Parapsychology 1976.* Metuchen, N.J., Scarecrow Press, 1977, 251–262.

Green, E. E., Green, A. M. and Walters, E. D., "Biofeedback for mind-body self regulation: Healing and creativity," reprinted in T. X. Barber (Ed.,) op. cit., 1976.

Popper, K. R. and Eccles, J. C., *The Self and Its Brain.* Berlin/Heidelberg/London/New York, Springer International, 1977.
Rorvik, M., "Jack Schwarz feels no pain," reprinted in T. X. Barber (Ed.,) *op. cit.*, 1976.
Thouless, R. H. and Wiesner, B. P., "The psi process in normal and 'paranormal' psychology," *Proc. S.P.R. 48*, 1947, 177–197.

DISCUSSION

EHRENWALD: Dr. Beloff's presentation is most appealing to me and has a high heuristic value. It is wholly in the footsteps of the Thouless-Wiesner theory and it is very close to my own thinking. As a matter of fact, my extension theory which I proposed some seven or eight years ago, is in complete agreement with the scheme developed by Dr. Beloff. I stated that the closer a stimulus is to the ego, the greater is the probability that it will be consciously and accurately perceived. The further it is removed from the ego, the less likely it is to be perceived correctly and accurately. Yet the impressions plotted on such an imaginary curve are subject to probabilistic and not the traditional causal laws. Of course, this is a purely descriptive statement, but it is in good keeping with the actual behavior of PK and ESP as well. In the extreme case—for instance, when I try to lift a paralyzed limb—the probability of succeeding goes down to zero. Still, it does so not in an arbitrary, unpredictable way. The same is true for PK, with the qualification that given powerful motivation, it is at least statistically likely to occur. The imaginary break or turning point in the curve postulated by the extension hypothesis can be described as the existential shift. It involves a shift from the standard, if you like Newtonian or Euclidean, frame of reference, to a new, non-Euclidean frame of reference which is capable of accommodating psi and which takes us to a paranormal level of experience.

HONORTON: First, in terms of the analogy between PK and biofeedback, the impression I get reading about feedback is that, particularly in studies involving thermal feedback, there very often is a tendency for the subject to go in the wrong direction initially. On an anecdotal level, the first time I tried to increase my hand temperature, it dropped 15 degrees in thirty minutes, so there may be another parallel here between psi-missing and biofeedback. In relation to Braud's allobiofeedback studies, this is something that I'd be interested in getting Tom to comment on. I wonder if some of the difference between biofeedback experimenters who show significant alpha control and those who don't, might not have something to do with this. I remember, at the organizational meeting of the Biofeedback Society in Santa Monica many years ago, listening to Joe Kamiya describe his initial experiments, how he would go in and interact with the subjects and break it up into short periods and also listen to the feedback. Is that a variable? Does anyone know to what extent experimenters doing biofeedback studies are monitoring the feedback that the subjects are getting and may in some sense be helping them along? Finally, John, you mentioned that unlike PK, anyone can learn biofeedback. I wonder if that's really true. Certainly, there are differences and there seem to be some people who are biofeedback stars and others who have very great difficulty in doing it. I wonder, at this stage in the development of biofeedback research, would there be some information in terms of individual differences predicting the likelihood of successful training or not?

BUDZYNSKI: There are some indications in the biofeedback literature as to which subjects seem to do better with biofeedback training. Unfortunately, these characteristics do not always hold when you go from normals to people with psychosomatic disorders. For example, people who are so-called internalizers as opposed to externalizers do better with biofeedback when they're from normal populations, but when you get into the psychosomatic disorders, then that dimension does not seem to predict how they're going to do, so it's a complex interaction. With regard to whether everybody can do biofeedback, the answer is probably "yes," if you give them enough training. Some people learn it very, very quickly and they're what Peter Lang calls "autonomic athletes." Others are "autonomic duffers," his words again, and they take a long time to train to control certain of these variables.

BELOFF: So you're saying that you never had a subject who couldn't eventually master the biofeedback.

BUDZYNSKI: Well, I don't know, because a lot of the people, of course, stop the training before they reach the level of mastery.

BELOFF: Well, I only wish this were true of PK. I think it would transform parapsychology if we could really teach PK by any technique and for any length of time, but I don't see that happening yet.

TART: I liked your paper very much, John, especially the idea of PK during the REM state. A particular thing I wanted to comment on is the argument that ordinary volition and PK may not be the same, because we can obviously do so much with ordinary volition. I don't think that's a valid comparison at all. When we compare ordinary volition, we're comparing the result of feedback training over hundreds of thousands of trials, spread over years, with a skill in which no learning time has been spent *at all* in most cases. I doubt if any PK subject is run for more than a few thousand trials, and the conditions under which conventional motor skills are learned are totally different. Let's assume that when you're born, you're biased toward ordinary motor ability. It's obviously survival adaptive. You're also in a cultural situation where the motivation to learn that kind of motor skill is enormous; your very survival depends on it. You're surrounded by people or examples of people who have ordinary motor skill, so there's not only social *permission* to learn to move your limbs that way, there's enormous social *pressure* for it. With PK, on the other hand, you don't have that kind of practice because the people around you don't show PK ability and, if anything, there is positive social discouragement against anything like that. So I don't think we can talk about an ordinary sort of comparison there until we start raising some people, perhaps, in cultures where PK is considered all right—where they think they see instances of it, or at least where they have had extremely long feedback training trying to do it.

BELOFF: Yes, I think that's a very valuable point you made. Our motor skills are some of the most highly learned things we have.

TART: But we take them for granted.

BELOFF: Yes, we do take them for granted. I think this illustrates so clearly how ignorance of parapsychology and even related things like biofeedback has distorted a lot of current philosophical thinking. I just read Bernard Williams' book on Descartes. It's a very good study, but in the final chapter he tries to assess Descartes' interactionism. He dismisses it in a paragraph or two by saying, "Well, it's obvious nonsense to say that we can control our brains since the brains aren't the sort of things that can be an object of will." Therefore, this proved to him that there couldn't be anything in a mind/brain interactionist theory such as Descartes was proposing. But, you know, it seems to me even if you were aware of the sort of biofeedback techniques that Honorton was talking about this morning, with control of alpha rhythm, etc., these are things that you can learn to do and, therefore, can become in the full sense an object of will.

KELLY: First, I would rephrase Chuck's point in my own way, that it would be interesting to look and see whether people who are good at biofeedback tasks are also good at PK tasks. I would rephrase Charlie's point by saying that it would be interesting to look at certain kind of PK experiments that really went on for a substantial amount of time, much more than we have typically tried. Another possible and related implication concerns the possibility of working with human infants. I'd just like to mention an experiment that we started to do. Unfortunately we didn't get very far with it for logistic reasons. The idea was that we would work with a, say, six-month old child, who has lots of intentions, but not much control of his motor apparatus. He might still have the capacity to influence his environment in other ways. The particular setup we arranged was one in which the baby was linked to a random number generator, so he would be lying in his crib looking up at a screen and on each of a sequence of trials, he would either see or not see a picture exposed by a slide projector, depending on the decision of a random event generator. And the idea was that if the baby really wanted to see those pictures, maybe he would find a way to influence the generator. Now, as I said, unfortunately we didn't get very far with that, but the few sessions that we did do were very encouraging. We had a good overall score—something over 55 percent for a relatively small number of trials—and what was particularly encouraging was that the rate was substantially higher on those trials where the baby was actually looking at the target area, so we had some reason to suppose he might actually be particularly interested in what was happening at that moment.

One other thing I wanted to mention to add to your arsenal of facts was that Graham Watkins in the mouse-ether experiments had gotten some preliminary physiological observations consistent with your spilling-over idea. That is, people tended to be successful when they were highly aroused, heart rate was up, etc. But not *too* aroused.

Last, however, I must disagree with your statement in which you argue that if evidence for PK were absolutely convincing, we would have "clinched the argument in favor of treating voluntary movement as an expression of free will." I think that statement could readily be resisted by someone who wished to resist it.

BELOFF: Yes, that was putting it too strongly. Yes, I withdraw it.

BIGU: I wonder if Dr. Beloff would say a few words on how you would extend your theory on voluntary movements in a case where you have strong PK and where you have no direct physical contact between subject and target.

BELOFF: In a PK experiment you never have physical contact with the target, so what is the question?

BIGU: Well, you have effects which happen in your own body and you may call them PK effect and you may call them uncontrollable.

How may some biofeedback control affect some poltergeist phenomena? What is the link between subject and target?

BELOFF: I did not want to imply in my paper that feedback is always necessary, either for voluntary movement or for PK, but in an ordinary way it plays an important part. It comes to the fore in the case of the biofeedback control situation which is, I believe, a connecting link between these two situations, because in a biofeedback control, you have to learn a new task. It's something familiar to you. It's not something that you're born with or very rapidly acquire. But if PK occurs, it's conceivable to me that it can occur in the absence of feedback.

PRIBRAM: First, most voluntary movement takes place in relaxed consciousness. If one tries to type and watch one's individual fingers, one very quickly messes it up. If one tries to drive a car and watch what one is doing every moment, pretty soon one is driving poorly. So that condition doesn't differ in ordinary voluntary movement and in PK phenomena.

Second, biofeedback is adding a feedback to an already existing internal feedback loop. If one connects two feedback loops in parallel then one obtains what is called "feedforward," an open loop system, and that provides voluntary control. Your argument is a telling one.

A third point closely related to this is that the motor cortex encodes environmental events. It doesn't encode muscular contractions. The motor cortex encodes the relationship of the total motor system to environmental events—e.g. adding weights to a lever produces a proportional increase in the firing of a cortical cell—the shortening of a muscle does not. Thus the cortex encodes how much force is being exerted on the organism—not whether or how much the muscles are contracted or relaxed. So it isn't such a big leap to go from what the motor cortex might be doing with regard to a muscle system to PK because it's the environmental consequence of the operations of that muscle system that are encoded. So, again, I don't see, from my neurophysiological stance, that there's such a gap between what's going on normally and in PK.

BELOFF: So these parts are really reinforcing.

PRIBRAM: They're all reinforcing.

BELOFF: Minimizing the discrepancies that we are trying to account for.

PRIBRAM: These were the four points in support of what you were saying. Now a fifth point really isn't addressed to you, but to Popper and Eccles, regarding the mind/brain problem. I'm not arguing that some interactionist position should or should not be taken; I just think they did a poor job of it. There are two things that are being said by them, as I noted earlier. One is that mind is an emergent property and the other is that it acts on brain. Now, when mind acts on brain, when one takes that position, the way Eccles does, one is doing the same thing as saying that gravity acts on one's body. We say that the gravitational pull of the earth is what's pulling one's body down. Now, that's perfectly all right to say in a colloquial sense. But, basically, the concept of gravity was conceived as an interaction term in the first place, so the term *derives* from the interaction of two bodies, the earth and a small mass, which is one's body in this instance! Then we turn the statement around and say that gravity is *pulling* me down, that gravity is acting on one's body. In the same way, mind is derived from minding, the *interaction* of an organism with its environment, then the statement is turned around and "mind" now operates *on* the organism. That is not a very careful way to state the proposition.

BELOFF: Yes, I think one could say that gravity was regarded as an inherent property of matter, and I think that, by analogy, people like Eccles, and I would go along with this, would say that willing is a property of mind.

PRIBRAM: Earlier we noted that the dematerialization of matter leaves that argument rather bare. The materialist view thus becomes a rather naive one.

BELOFF: However dematerialized, matter still has certain acknowledged properties, powers in the old sense.

PRIBRAM: They're not all that different from mental properties.

BELOFF: Well, there I'm afraid I would have to disagree with you.

HONORTON: On this matter of passive volition, and relating to what Karl Pribram said about voluntary action generally being very relaxed—what we normally do in PK experiments at the very beginning, to give the subject the idea of what we want him to do, is to ask him to very carefully attend to the act of raising his hand to his forehead to see how that feels, and then to *try* very hard to raise his hand to his forehead, and to interact with the PK feedback in the way that you would raise your hand to your forehead if your forehead itches, i.e., passively, without thinking about it or trying. But there is one additional point here that I feel is important to make. Although the passive volition concept seems to work for us in our laboratory and in others reported also, I think you'll recall when Helmut Schmidt was speaking in St. Louis, he was talking about a very active type of "getting the subject to push the light in the right direction." I wonder to what extent these strategies may be analogous to Jan Ehrenwald's doctrinal compliance with dream symbolism. They may apply more to the expectations within the laboratory than they do to any intrinsic characteristic of the phenomena. I also wondered to what extent the same thing may occur in conventional biofeedback work where the type of strategy that works best may, in fact, vary from laboratory to laboratory on the basis of the predilections of the investigator.

BELOFF: I would like to remind you of the extreme difficulty that experimenters have had getting people to produce macro-PK effects by simply consciously wanting it to happen. You know, it nearly always happens in an unguarded moment, so that's the thing that leads one to say it has to be passive volition in the last resort.

BRAIN LATERALIZATION AND BIOFEEDBACK

Thomas H. Budzynski

Every 25 years or so the discovery of a new technique, procedure or model excites most, if not all, the researchers involved in that area of science. Often this initial excitement leads to somewhat exaggerated claims for the new factor. Eventually, a second wave of research leads to disclaimers based on negative or minimal results. It should be noted however, that second wave scientists get their academic accolades not for replications but rather for failures to replicate. Ultimately, a third wave of researchers comes closer to the truth. This wave is not so influenced by the positive and the negative biases of the first and second waves respectively.

The findings of those scientists initially involved in the area called brain lateralization caused such excitement that it quickly found its way out of this select circle of researchers and into the fertile imaginations of the lay public. For the most part, these findings were concerned with the specification of the functions of the left and right cerebral hemispheres of the human brain. And even though the brain research scientists are now riding the second wave of hypercriticality, the lay public insists on prolonging its romance with the phenomenon of brain lateralization.

Biofeedback, a new technique of approximately the same "age" as modern brain lateralization research, has already passed through the first two waves and has just begun to evolve more realistic expectations. We will see later how these two intriguing conceptualizations have begun to interact in such a fashion that the combination may prove to have great practical, as well as heuristic value.

The Functions of the Cerebral Hemispheres

Brain lateralization refers to the separate functions found in the two cerebral hemispheres. The more lateralized, the more distinct the functions. In general, men appear to be more lateralized than women, and the right-handed (dextrals) more so than the left-handed (sinistrals) (Levy, 1977).

The hemisphere which has most of the functions of speech, logic, critical judgment and sequential ordering is often called the dominant hemisphere. The other hemisphere, labeled the nondominant, appears to mediate intuitive, emotional, visuospatial relationships, pattern recognition, and parallel rather than sequential functions (Ornstein, 1972). In almost all dextrals and approximately 67% of sinistrals the left hemisphere is the dominant one. A lesser degree of lateralization implies that the same functions may be present in both hemispheres, although not necessarily to the same degree. Thus, the highly lateralized right-handed male may never recover speech after a left hemisphere stroke destroys the speech centers. In contrast, a left-handed female has a good chance of recovering speech after such a stroke since she will have speech centers in the uninjured right hemisphere as well.

Cortical Specificity and Eye Movements

Differences between the cortical hemispheres also have been demonstrated by means of observing the direction of lateral eye movements. These responses, labeled CLEMS (conjugate lateral eye movements), appear to be reflexive in nature. For example, a flick of the eyes toward the right indicates that the left hemisphere is activated. Conversely, if the eyes move quickly and momentarily to the left when a cognitive task is presented, it signals that the right hemisphere is activated.

A study by Schwartz, Davidson and Maer (1975) involved the presentation of 40 reflective questions. The dimensions encompassed by these questions included verbal versus spatial and emotional versus nonemotional. Thus subjects were asked verbal-nonemotional, verbal emotional, spatial-nonemotional, and spatial emotional questions. The results showed that verbal questions elicited more right-eye movements than spatial questions, while nonemotional questions were associated with both a greater number of right-eye and fewer number of left-eye movements compared with emotional questions. Additionally, spatial-emotional questions were associated with the greatest overall right-hemisphere activation (fewest number of right-eye and greatest number of left-eye movements), while verbal-nonemotional questions were associated with the greatest overall left-hemisphere activation (fewest number of left-eye and greatest number of right-eye movements).

Davidson, Schwartz and Weinberger (1977) later replicated this study, supplemented by an independent measure of affective arousal (skin resistance) to confirm that the emotional questions actually produced arousal. These affective questions were indeed associated with significantly greater response amplitude (less resistance) than the comparable nonemotional questions. No significant differences were found between the verbal and spatial questions.

It would appear from these CLEM studies that eye movements can correctly indicate which hemisphere is being used or activated in considering questions asked of the subject. This phenomenon is true if the experimenter does *not* face the subject but rather remains out-of-sight. If, however, the experimenter (questioner) sits *in front* of the subject there is a tendency for the subject to look consistently in the same direction no matter what the question (Gur, 1975). Several findings have emerged from the "in-front" questioning. For example, Gur and Gur (1974) have found evidence that left-looking (activated right hemisphere) is related to hypnotizability. Duke (1968) found less consistency of eye movements in females than males and Kinsbourne (1972) showed that left-handers have less consistency than right handers.

Do CLEMS reflect personality dimensions? Bakan (1971) found that left-lookers were more spontaneous and emotional, less verbal and logical than the right lookers. Furthermore, the left-lookers considered themselves to be more musical and more artistic, while right-lookers tend to be better in left-hemisphere skills, such as the SAT Mathematics Subtest, and tend to major in "hard" science areas (Bakan, 1969).

Differences in conjugate lateral eye movements seem to relate to differences in cognitive or conceptual style. Krashen (1975) has noted that right-lookers may be Cohen's "analytic" thinkers (Cohen, 1969) and left-lookers her "relational" thinkers. Krashen also goes on to suggest that different approaches to learning may be necessary for each kind, or alternatively, different strategies need to be made available within the same classroom.

Intonation Contour Processing

A less well-known function of the right or nondominant hemisphere is that it has an advantage over the left with regard to the processing of auditory intonation contours and emotional material (Heeschen and Jürgens, 1977; Blumstein and Cooper, 1974). Embedding short phrases and sentences in a simple *melodic* pattern results in significant improvement in the expressive ability of severely aphasic patients (Albert, Sparks and Helms, 1973; Keith and Aronson, 1975). In fact, it is not uncommon for aphasic patients to be able to sing a melody or hum a tune (Benton and Joynt, 1960). This statement however, has to be qualified somewhat. It is a fact that totally aphasic patients can recite *well-known* verses, sing simple, *familiar* songs and emit curse words. Levy (1974) has suggested the presence of whole auditory Gestalts in the right hemisphere. Usually these patients cannot recite verses or sing songs unless they start at the beginning.

Using the Wada procedure of injecting amobarbital sodium into the right carotid arteries of six subjects with definite right handedness, Bogen and Gordon (1971) found marked depression of ability to sing the melody of well-known songs. These results provided additional support for the hypothesis that certain musical abilities are controlled by the right hemisphere.

One final word on this subject—an interesting article appeared in *The Unesco Courier* in January, 1976 entitled "Our Split Brain." It was written by Vadim Lvovich Deglin, an eminent Soviet neurophysiologist. Beginning in 1967, the staff of the psychiatric clinic of the I.M. Sechenov Institute of Evolutionary Physiology and Biochemistry of the USSR Academy of Sciences has been administering *unilateral* EST (electric shock therapy). By shocking first on one side of the brain and then on the other side in the next treatment, the patient is less debilitated then if both hemispheres were shocked simultaneously. Dr. Deglin noted that after a unilateral shock the patient feels, behaves and thinks only with the unshocked hemisphere. An EEG (electroencephalogram) recorded after the shock reveals that one hemisphere is "asleep" whereas the other remains active and can be described as "awake."

Deglin then describes the average single hemisphere patient. If the right hemisphere was shocked for example (in a right-handed patient), the voice becomes monotonous, colorless and dull; the *intonation* is less expressive. This speech defect is known as dysprosody. In addition to the loss of affective coloring of his speech, this "left hemisphere" patient has difficulty understanding the intonation of words spoken to him. He is unable to identify the tone of the voice as angry or interrogative, etc., or to distinguish a male from a female voice. He also ceases to recognize well-known tunes or even to hum them if he hears the music. If asked to hum, he begins to hum wrong notes and ultimately prefers to tap out the rhythm without the melody.

The patient with only the left hemisphere active is *not* typically depressed. Instead of being preoccupied with his own symptoms, he becomes interested in topics unconnected with his illness. He takes an optimistic view of his own situation, believes he will be cured and regards the future as an encouraging prospect.

Deglin next discusses the same patient after his left hemisphere has been shocked. Now a "right hemisphere" person, he speaks poorly—in simple sentences and often with isolated words. He prefers to respond by mime or gestures. It is necessary to speak to him in *very short* or *simply constructed* sentences. However, his voice intonation is unchanged and he can hear and distinguish *better than before* the prosodic elements of speech. He is attentive to and can easily recognize non-verbal sounds. He recognizes melodies and feels an urge to hum along. Unfortunately, his mood tends to decline in a direction opposite to that when his left hemisphere was active. He becomes morose and pessimistic about his present situation and his future prospects and he complains of feeling unwell.

These composite descriptions of the typical patient with first a left hemisphere and then a right hemisphere directing him provide us with valuable insights into the functioning of the normal, intact human whose hemispheres interact continuously across the corpus callosum and other commissures. We can begin to see how conflict could arise between these "computers" which process the same data in different ways and which may arrive at totally different emotional tendencies.

Language and the Minor Hemisphere

Can the nondominant or minor hemisphere comprehend language? The answer is a qualified yes. Without referencing all of the many studies which have dealt with this question, we can list some of the characteristics of language comprehension by this hemisphere. As noted above one of these is voice intonation—the minor hemisphere understands better if the dynamics and emotionality of the voice communication are increased. A flat monotone voice therefore would not excite, arouse, or even be understood very well by this hemisphere, although such a presentation would be understood and perhaps preferred by a left-hemisphere oriented individual. Revival preachers, Baptist ministers, certain politicians, military leaders and good lecturers know that the secret of "moving" audiences is the dynamism of the speech and not so much the content.

Geschwind (1972) has observed that the comprehension of speech appears to be mediated by the region of the brain called Wernicke's area. It is possible that the intonation of the voice is subserved by the mirror area (Werwicke's) in the right hemisphere. The preliminary report of Albert, Sparks and Helm (1973) mentioned above was a description of a technique of improving language comprehension in certain kinds of aphasic patients. Later, this procedure was labelled Melodic Intonation Therapy (MIT). Basically, the procedure involves "singing" the message with the melody and rhythm of simple melodic patterns with a range of three to four whole notes. MIT has a slower and *more lyrical* tempo than speech, with a more precise *rhythm* and *more accentuated points of stress.*[1] (For a detailed description of this new speech therapy, see Sparks and Holland, 1976.)

Still other factors mediating minor hemisphere language absorption are: redundancy, concreteness, use of high probability or common words, direct, positive (rather than negative) statements (Schnell, Jenkins and Jimenez-Pabon, 1964). A sentence spoken at one-third the normal rate and punctuated with frequent pauses also improves comprehension. Active affirmative sentences (The man is kissing the girl) are absorbed better than passive negative (The girl is not kissed by the man) (Lasky, Weidner and Johnson, 1976).

What is the limit of vocabulary and syntactical ability in the minor hemisphere? Zaidel (1976) showed that the right hemisphere comprehends spoken language better than had been previously believed. This research indicates a minor hemisphere *vocabulary* roughly equivalent to that of a *14 year old* and the *syntactical ability* of a *four or five year old.* If Levy is right about language Gestalts residing in the right hemisphere, then we might surmise that the language of choice for the minor hemisphere would be that which was commonly used in the patient's *early environment.*

Arousal Level and Hemispheric Functioning

Leaving language comprehension for a moment, let us now move to an area not generally considered in discussion of hemispheric differences. Arousal level refers to the degree of activation of the various physiological systems of the body. A high arousal implies heightened muscle tension, increased heart rate and blood pressure, greater stress hormone output and so on. Changes also occur in the brain during high arousal. The EEG pattern assumes a beta configuration with low amplitude, high frequency rhythms. Although high arousal helps to prepare us for fight-or-flight emergencies, it can be overdone. A common example is the test-anxious student who is so "high" that she can't think during the exam. The common phrase "paralyzed with fear" suggests not only cortical dysfunction but skeletal motor as well. Crowd behavior—lynch mob mentality—is another example of how heightened arousal decreases certain mental abilities. In his book *Persuasion and Healing*, Jerome Frank (1973) notes that most religious healing procedures involve a systematic increase in arousal often to the point of exhaustion, ". . . leading to an altered state of consciousness that increases susceptibility to outside influences."

Frank also noted another interesting fact. He observed that the people who had been cured at Lourdes included the deserving and the sinful and believers and apparent sceptics, but they tended to have one common characteristic: they are " . . . almost invariably simple people—the poor and the humble; people who do not interpose a strong intellect between themselves and a higher power." He further noted that these people are not detached or *critical.* He found that persons who remained entirely unmoved by the ceremonies did not experience cures.

After studying many different religious and primitive healing ceremonies, Frank concluded that the apparent success of healing methods based on *various* ideologies and methods compels the conclusion that the healing power of faith resides in the patient's *state of mind*, not in the validity of its object.

Considering Frank's conclusions along with the well-known phenomenon of a regression to more primitive behavior patterns and a decrease of critical, judgmental, logical faculties under conditions of high arousal, we might permit ourselves a speculative leap—that such conditions appear to disturb, disrupt, or disengage the normal functions of the left, dominant hemisphere. But, what about the right, nondominant hemisphere when all this is going on? There really is not a lot of "hard" data, but a host of anecdotal accounts. A favorite example is the mother who accidentally backs her car over her young child and then in a moment of extreme panic actually lifts the bumper and the car off the child. It is not *logical* for this to happen and yet it did. Does the regression to childlike behavior (and at times childlike speech) under conditions of extreme stress sound like a minor hemisphere takeover of behavior? Is it not possible that our less conscious hemisphere, which does not arrive at conclusions through deductive reasoning, could serve as a backup computer in times of extreme stress?[2] Is it possible that primitive shamans, medicine men, charismatics and healing preachers induce a state of rhythmic high arousal so as to produce a functional suspension of dominant hemisphere critical faculties (Budzynski, 1977)?

Could it be that, having suspended the major hemisphere faculties in their patients, these healers can now communicate more optimally with the still-functioning minor hemisphere by a rhythmic, emotional, concrete, direct language? Since the minor hemisphere, as far as we know, does not employ deductive reasoning to test the credibility of the incoming message, it may accept, absorb, or act upon the directive as though it were true or possible.

If high arousal functionally disables the major hemisphere, does low arousal do the same? Quite obviously it does, as when we are sleeping. However, for this procedure to be effective the minor hemisphere must be able to absorb the directive at this low arousal level. In several publications (Budzynski, 1972, 1976, 1977) I have attempted to document that in the "twilight" zone between wakefulness and deep sleep such conditions pertain.

The Twilight State

This transition zone has been called a reverie state, fringe of consciousness, pre-conscious, offconscious, transliminal experience, and hypnagogic state by various researchers or writers.

Foulkes and Vogel (1965) speak of the drowsy period just preceding stage 1 sleep as characterized by a slowing of the alpha rhythm and slow, rolling eye movements. As the sleeper passes into stage 1 sleep, the slowed alpha rhythm begins to break up and is replaced by even slower smaller amplitude theta rhythms (4–7Hz). These two researchers also questioned subjects upon awakening them from these twilight states. Their replies to the questions about control over mentation and loss of contact with the external world indicated that loss of volitional control over mentation tended to occur first; then loss of awareness of surroundings; and, finally, loss of reality testing occurred. Later, Vogel, Foulkes and Trosman (1966) also scored subject reports for two ego functions: the degree of maintenance of nonregressive content and the maintenance of contact with the external world. Report content was rated as nonregressive if the mentation was plausible, coherent, realistic and undistorted. Examples of regressive content would be: single isolated images, a meaningless pattern, an incomplete scene or bits and pieces of a scene, bizarre images, dissociation of thoughts and images and magical thinking. The results showed that there was a statistically significant tendency for each EEG state (alpha, stage 1 and stage 2) to be associated with a different combination of ego functioning. In the first combination (ego state) usually found during an alpha pattern, the ego maintained *both* functions, or, at most, showed an impairment of only one function. A second ego state in which both functions were impaired was associated with descending stage 1. The third ego state usually occurred during stage 2 and was characterized by a return to less regressive content; however, contact with reality was completely lost.

Summarizing the findings of Vogel, Foulkes and Trosman we can see that:

1. As individuals become drowsy and pass into sleep, their brain rhythms change from predominantly alpha, to fragmented alpha, to low-amplitude theta.
2. Paralleled (though not perfectly) with these EEG patterns are three

ego states showing an increasing impairment of ego functioning (as defined above).

3. Individuals with rigid, repressive, dogmatic personality traits report *less* sleep fantasy material.

These characteristics could be descriptive of the gradual loss of at least major hemisphere functioning. The generation of vivid visual imagery and sometimes voice Gestalts is also characteristic of the hypnagogic or twilight state. This sounds like the minor hemisphere is still operative. There is, in fact, at least one study that bolsters this surmise. As reported by Dimond and Beaumont (1973), the left hemisphere showed a decline in performance on a vigilance task of 80 minutes duration. In contrast, the right hemisphere beginning with a less than 100 percent performance does *not* show a decline across the 80 minutes. These researchers concluded that the right hemisphere appears to provide a skeleton service in vigilance, a minimum service capable of maintaining performance after decrement occurs in the left hemisphere.

Can Language by Absorbed in the Twilight State?

Given that the low cortical arousal has functionally suspended the dominant hemisphere processing, can the nondominant hemisphere still absorb an auditory message? T. X. Barber's dissertation helped answer this question (1957). He found that subjects were just as suggestible when in a light sleep or in a drowsy condition as when hypnotized. One of his subjects said, "I was just sleepy enough to believe what you were saying is true. I couldn't oppose what you wanted with anything else." He stated that, at the therapeutic level, it is possible that suggestions could be presented to people while they sleep for purposes of helping overweight people reduce, getting heavy smokers to cut down and helping timid people gain confidence.

A Yale dissertation added more data. Felipe (1965) tested the effects of attitude-change information presented via tape recording to subjects during waking, drowsy and deep sleep conditions. A portion of the attitude presentation concerned interracial dating. Felipe used several pre-post attitude scales to measure change that may have occurred during the three conditions. In only one of the three arousal conditions did the attitude *change* reach significance—the *drowsy* condition. This finding is consistent with the premise that attitude change is potentiated in a drowsy or light-sleep state because of a decrease in critical screening. Felipe's research demonstrates the relatively uncritical acceptance of information even though the information may differ from the subject's present belief system.

Other examples of procedures which involve the generation of low arousal and subsequent re-programming include the use of sensory deprivation coupled with psychotherapy suggestions (Suedfeld, 1977; Gibby and Adams, 1961; Adams, 1965); Suggestopaedia (Ostrander and Schroeder, 1970) a Bulgarian tutorial method involving among other things deep relaxation, listening and focusing attention on classical music, and absorbing (though not attending to) the learning material which is presented by a teacher who adapts her voice *intonation* to the music; Russian sleep-learning (Rubin, 1968, 1970) and, of course, hypnosis.

Twilight State Biofeedback

Ordinarily, individuals pass through the hypnotic state in 5–10 minutes. If, indeed, this transition zone represents a segment of the arousal continuum which is characterized by hypersuggestibility and the possibility of dramatic change in attitudes, goals, and values, then it may be advantageous to prolong the state for this purpose. In 1971 we began to work with a biofeedback device which would sense the brain wave pattern and automatically turn on a tape recorder when theta waves occurred over the major hemisphere. The tape contained a specially prepared message for the minor hemisphere (Budzynski, 1972, 1976). This device, called the "Twilight Learner," would automatically increase the volume of the minor hemisphere message if the EEG began to show slower and/or larger theta or delta waves. This "sleep guard" causes the sleepy trainee to rouse momentarily into alpha or beta. Of course, the device turns off the tape recorder in less than one second when this arousal occurs. The arousal, or "bump" effect, acts to consolidate in long term storage the material presented to the drowsy brain (Koukkou and Lehman, 1968; Rubin, 1970).

Our clinical case study data over the years since 1971 indicate that material presented during twilight states may not be available to recall after the session. However, it seems evident to us that the material hopefully absorbed by the minor hemisphere only, "shows" itself in attitudinal or even behavioral change at some future time, perhaps delayed as long as several months. This delayed effect has been seen in dream research as well (Cohen, 1976), where incorporated dream material (a positive attitude change) resulted in a behavioral change some four weeks later, even though no such tendency was found right after the dream incorporation.

The duration of the period required for the appearance of attitudinal or behavioral change may be a function of the importance of the change. For example, a simple twilight learning suggestion such as "Your nose itches," while not consciously perceived, may result in an immediate behavioral response—a scratch. On the other hand, a message suggesting a positive change in self-image may take weeks to surface. Speculating freely, one could imagine that material affecting deeply held beliefs or values would require more "integration time" than would material involving a simple behavioral response.

Why Attempt to Reprogram the Minor Hemisphere?

In order to answer this question we must consider two factors: the inhibition of one hemisphere by the other and the concept of hemispheric conflict. First of all, consider the description of the brain given by Dimond and Beaumont (1974): "Each hemisphere is an information processing system which works its way through the information it receives. At this stage, no facility appears to exist for passing unanalyzed information across to the opposite hemisphere. Each, therefore, is seen to act independently of the other. The process of integrating the products of the work of each hemisphere presumably occurs at a later stage following the completion of visual analysis."

Moreover, Bogen and Bogen (1969) have stated that ". . . the possession of two independent problem-solving organs increases the prospects of a successful solution to a novel situation although it has the hazard of conflict in the event of different solutions."

Other brain researchers have warned of possible conflict. Levy, Trevarthen and Sperry (1972) noted that commissurotomy studies have revealed that the two disconnected hemispheres, working on the same task, may process the same sensory information in distinctly different ways, and that the two modes of mental operation, involving spatial synthesis for the right and temporal analysis for the left, show indications of *mutual antagonism*.

Galin (1974) noted the compelling similarity between hemispheric dissociations seen in the commissurotomy patients and the phenomenon of repression. In Freud's early "topographical" model of the mind, repressed mental contents functioned in a separate realm which was inaccessible to conscious recall or verbal interrogation, functioning according to its own rules, developing and pursuing its own goals, affecting the viscera and insinuating itself into the stream of ongoing consciously directed behavior. Galin further notes that many aspects of right hemisphere functioning are congruent with the mode of cognition psychoanalysts have called primary process. Freud originally called this the *unconscious*.

Continuing with his argument, Galin suggests that the isolated right hemisphere in the commissurotomy patient can sustain emotional responses and goals divergent from the left (e.g. assaulting with one hand and protecting with the other). Galin furthermore proposes the hypothesis that in normal, intact people, mental events in the right hemisphere can become disconnected functionally from the left hemisphere (by inhibition of neuronal transmission across the corpus callosum and other cerebral commissures) and can continue a life of its own. This hypothesis, according to Galin, suggests a neurophysiological mechanism for at least some instances of repression and an anatomical locus for the unconscious mental contents.

Can One Hemisphere Block the Other?

The phenomenon of inhibition of selected functions in one hemisphere by the opposing hemisphere is well known. Galin quotes Bogen and Bogen (1969): ". . . certain kinds of left hemisphere activity may directly suppress certain kinds of right hemisphere action. Or they may *prevent access* to the left hemisphere of the products of right hemisphere activity." This should of course be reciprocal—at certain times right hemisphere processes could interfere with or suppress certain left hemisphere activity.

We do not know all the reasons why one hemisphere selectively inhibits the other or under what conditions it does so. It may be that if a function in a particular hemisphere develops a history of positive reinforcement, then it will come to dominate in that situation. In our society we get lots of this reinforcement for using our left hemisphere and therefore it may come to dominate (even when it should not) over the right hemisphere most of the time.

Galin speculated about the way the left hemisphere could inhibit the right for the conscious memory of unpleasant events. He gives the hypothetical example of a mother hatefully spanking her child. The child's left hemisphere processes the words, "I'm only doing this because I love you," while the right hemisphere absorbs the non-verbal cues such as hate expression in the face and tone of voice, body posture, etc. The Gestalt of the right brain's memory is something like "I hate you and will destroy you." Galin offers the conjecture that, based on the conflicting conclusions and the high stakes involved, both hemispheres will attempt to implement a different course of action (to approach or to flee). The left hemisphere usually wins control of the output channels, but, if the left is not able to inhibit the right completely, it may settle for *disconnecting the transfer* of the conflicting material from the right side. The mental process in the minor hemisphere, even though cut off from major hemisphere consciousness, may nevertheless continue a life of its own. Quite probably its emotional reactions, expectations and action tendencies will make themselves felt when similar situations happen in the future. One can imagine many situations in which the two hemispheres develop conflicting action tendencies requiring the inhibition of one by the other. It is also easy to see why the left brain's plan is more often accepted in our culture. The question becomes—what can result from a storehouse of repressed, conflicting motor, emotional and attitudinal tendencies? Will the mute minor hemisphere eventually make its tendencies known? Perhaps it must do so non-verbally for the most part. Ferenczi (1926) claimed that most hysterical disorders appeared on the left side of the body—the side controlled by the right hemisphere. However, the right hemisphere has approximately 10 percent control over the right side of the body as well, so it may not be limited to the left side.

Minor Hemisphere Programs and Psychosomatic Disorders

If we go out on the limb far enough to say that hysterical symptoms are a resultant of a frustrated right hemisphere, dare we go a little out and say that most, if not all, psychosomatic disorders are the result of repressed tendencies? To be more specific, could it be that the minor hemisphere can express its frustration through our skeletal motor and autonomic systems and, perhaps, even through our immune system? Gross speculation to be sure, but a model which is receiving much attention these days.

A little more speculation now. If we "buy" the model outlined above, i.e., there are maladaptive programs in the minor hemisphere which cannot be accessed (easily) through the conscious major hemisphere —are there ways of sidestepping the major hemisphere in order to identify and then change (reprogram) these maladaptive tendencies?

The answer to this last question is a very qualified yes. When we are able to train clients with the twilight learning system to maintain themselves in primarily a theta state, the reprogramming seems to work quite well in changing self-images and lifting depressions. Some individuals do have difficulty in learning to maintain the theta state. These people are not good candidates for this type of therapy. Gradually we are learning to use the language style of the right hemisphere. Thus, the twilight learning tape messages are short, concrete, redundant, slowly spoken with frequent pauses, using high frequency words (common usage words) and spoken in a sing-song fashion. Positive reactions to the twilight learning may occur immediately or be delayed by several months.

Another possible way of accomplishing successful reprogramming is to *overload* the left hemisphere with a meaningless task such as repeating random numbers heard in the right ear at a fast rate while the change message is presented to the left ear. This dichotic listening task is based on the assumption that by overloading the dominant hemisphere it will be unable to prevent the nondominant hemisphere from absorbing the message. Of course, another possibility is that the left hemisphere may inhibit the right from absorbing any auditory material. Research with this technique is just beginning and we do not yet have a clear answer to the question of its efficacy.

Many of the new "body therapies" are essentially right brain change procedures. Taking advantage of all types of non-verbal responding, these therapies attempt to break through the left-brain defenses and allow the right-brain to respond. Gestalt therapy, Primal Scream, Re-Birthing, Z-therapy, Rolfing (Structural Integration) and even Transactional Analysis with its "parenting" procedure are examples of this general approach. Certainly Suedfeld's suggestions presented while clients undergo a 24-hour sensory restriction is another example of reprogramming while the left brain is temporarily unable to act upon the suggestions.

Although the high arousal end of the continuum is a more difficult state to generate and maintain under clinical conditions, it may be possible to implement reprogramming while doing rhythmical physical exercise. For example, it is not uncommon for joggers to chant a repetitive phrase in rhythm with their respiration and stride. Joggers who use such chants say that the phrases are very effective if used consistently. It is likely that the chanting is better absorbed as the runner approaches the point in the run (after thirty minutes) when thought processes become more flowing and less concentrated (Budzynski, 1978).

In concluding this section it is fair to say that the model presented (Budzynski, 1977), though quite provocative, is at the same time based on relatively "soft" evidence. "Harder" research may help answer these questions:

1. Are there segments of the cortical arousal continuum in which left hemisphere functioning is weakened or suspended, yet right hemisphere functions remain intact?

2. Given that (1) is true can the right hemisphere then absorb and implement suggestions which are aimed at psychological and physical change?

3. Are there ways of functionally suspending left hemisphere functioning without producing cortical arousal extremes?

4. Can changes produced by these procedures alleviate or cure certain psychosomatic disorders?

Cognitive Styles Across Three Occupational Groups

We can turn now to research employing a new measurement tool—the precise determination of alpha EEG amplitude over each hemisphere. Galin and Ornstein (1972) were among the first researchers to note that alpha amplitude decreases somewhat (approximately 10 percent) over the hemisphere in use for a particular task. Thus, a spatial task would result in a decrease of alpha amplitude over the right hemisphere while a verbal task decreases alpha over the left hemisphere. The decrease is at times relative to the amplitude of the other hemisphere, i.e., given a new situation involving a verbal task you may see a decrease in alpha over each side, but a greater decrease on the left side.

Our study compared three general occupational groups as they focussed their attention on six tasks. We measured alpha amplitude bilaterally with monopolar placements at C3 and C4 and mastoid references. The alpha rhythm (8–12 Hz) was filtered by two AT-1 alpha/theta biofeedback units which fed their outputs to two DQ-1 Digital Quantifiers which, in turn, provided a digital readout of 30-second samples of integrated alpha.[3] This instrument package thus involves only four small units, yet allows a precise quantification of bilateral alpha amplitude.

Right-handed subjects sat in a semidarkened room with their eyes closed. Alpha-alpha measurements were taken approximately every minute. A six minute stabilization period was followed by presentation of six cognitive tasks each taking about three minutes. Three of the tasks were left hemisphere oriented and the other three right hemisphere oriented. The three left hemisphere tasks were: counting backwards as fast as possible, presenting a rationale for or against some cause (psychic phenomena, sexism, etc.), and repeating aloud random numbers as fast as they were presented by the experimenter. The three right brain tasks were: visualizing a friend or relative whose face looked sad, visualizing yourself in a life-threatening situation and listening to music with no lyrics. Left and right hemisphere alpha scores were averaged separately for the three dominant hemisphere tasks and for the three non-dominant hemisphere tasks. An "S" score for each subject was then derived from the following equation:

$$S = (R \text{ ave.} - L \text{ ave.})\text{Dom} - (R \text{ ave.} - L \text{ ave.})\text{NDom}$$

For example, if subject Jones had a lower average alpha of 10 over his left side during the dominant tasks and a lower average alpha of 5 over his right side during the nondominant tasks, his S score would be +15. On the other hand, subject Smith produced a relatively lower average of 4 over her left side during the dominant tasks and a higher average of 7 counts over her right hemisphere during the nondominant tasks. Thus, her S score would be $(+4 - (+7) = -3$.

Our subjects fell into three groups which we labelled BLA (business, law, accounting), TMP (technical, medical, psychological), and C (creative). Subjects in the BLA group were business persons, lawyers, accountants, business secretaries, etc. Subjects in the TMP group (our most diverse group) included medical doctors, engineers, scientists, nurses, and psychologists. The C group included artists, dancers, writers and entertainers.

An analysis of variance of the S scores showed significant differences among the three groups and a test for linear trend proved significant as well. This latter test allowed us to see if the groups ranked C > TMP > BLA as the pilot data had led us to believe. The creative group came out with the highest S scores and the BLA group with the lowest. The range of scores was greatest in the TMP group. These results simply indicate that these three groups do tend to use their brains somewhat differently when processing the same task material. It is not possible to tell from this study whether your occupation trains you to think a certain way or whether you tended to think that way and therefore you chose that type of occupation.

There was also a significant difference in alpha amplitude between the BLA and the C groups, with the C group showing the greater amplitude of alpha. Overall, we can say that this experiment showed that people engaged in what are considered to be rather left-brained occupations produced smaller S scores and lower amplitude alpha EEG than did people in the creative or right-brained occupations. We are continuing to gather data on more subjects so as to be able to break down these general categories even further, e.g., teachers, nurses, applied physicists, lawyers, etc. Perhaps, with refinement of this type of procedure, we can evolve a good physiological predictor of job performance and/or satisfaction.

Biofeedback Produced Differential Control of Hemispheric Activation

Something in the brain appears to switch arousal levels in the hemispheres in order to activate or inactivate one or the other. If the task is verbal, the left hemisphere is activated and the alpha amplitude over the frontal, temporal or parietal area on the left side will decrease slightly in the fully alert subject. The reverse tends to happen if the task requires a right hemisphere process. Ordinarily, this switching of cortical activation happens automatically. Levy (1974) believes that a stimulus input to a hemisphere appears to alert and arouse that hemisphere, and when that hemisphere lacks the functions for adequately processing the stimulus, some signal must travel to the reticular formation which, in turn, must stop arousal input to one hemisphere and shunt it to the other. We have found differences among occupational groups with regard to the way they manipulate this switching of arousal for different cognitive tasks. Perhaps this indicates that there are optimal differential hemispheric arousal patterns for any given task. If this is so and these patterns can be identified, then one can wonder if biofeedback could be used to teach an individual who does not produce the appropriate pattern to do so.

Erik Peper (1972) was one of the first biofeedback researchers to attempt to shape differential alpha characteristics over the two hemispheres. Subjects received a high tone when alpha occurred in one hemisphere and a low tone when alpha occurred in the other hemisphere. In two sessions one of eight subjects was able to switch alpha (and therefore hemisphere activation) back and forth. Peper concluded more sessions were necessary for most individuals, but that it was possible to learn to consciously switch alpha. Ray, Frediana and Harman (1977) used a computer-generated visual feedback of hemispheric asymmetry. Subjects were more successful in this study and the investigators concluded that most individuals can selectively control the EEG output of one hemisphere in comparison to the other.

Are there sex differences in ability to control differential alpha? Suter, Krone and Matthews (1978) found that males regulated the left hemisphere alpha (20 percent change) better than females (11 percent change), while the females controlled the right hemisphere alpha (15 percent change) slightly better than the males (12 percent change).

Perhaps the most intriguing example of the potential application of differential hemispheric arousal level control is the work of Murphy and his co-workers at Oklahoma State University. Using alpha frequency biofeedback, these researchers asked subjects to increase or decrease alpha frequency over one or the other hemisphere. In general, decreasing alpha frequency (decreasing arousal) enhanced the plasticity of the functioning of that hemisphere, i.e., task performance either increased or decreased after the training. In contrast, increasing alpha frequency (increased arousal) seemed only to stabilize task performance at pre-training levels. One result which stood out was that arousal decrement training of the left hemisphere improved performance on a verbal multiplication task.

Taking their cue from this result, Murphy, Darwin and Murphy

(1977) trained 10 learning disabled adolescents to decrease or increase arousal over the left hemisphere. Using before-after math tests, Murphy *et al* showed that only the decreased arousal training improved the scores on the mathematics test. Increased arousal training produced no significant change. Post tests conducted at the end of the academic year showed a +0.33 change in GPA (grade point average) for the decrease group but a −0.33 change for the increase group.

One case study by these same researchers illustrates the flexibility of this approach. A 16-year-old male showed a 30 point discrepancy between his WAIS Verbal and Performance IQ, with Performance lower than Verbal. Resting EEG rhythms showed a dramatic asymmetry in alpha frequency with the left hemisphere producing a dominant 10Hz alpha and the right showing a 14Hz dominant alpha. The subject was involved in 35 weekly-biweekly sessions of EEG biofeedback over 11 months. He learned to both increase and decrease the alpha frequency. At the end of 10 sessions, his right hemisphere alpha frequency had decreased from 14 to 10Hz. A comparison of academic performance from sophomore to junior year showed a GPA improvement from 2.0 to 4.0. A six-month follow-up showed his GPA to be 3.8. His Performance IQ increased from 107 to 117.

This case study, plus the larger study with the learning disabled adolescents, hints at the possibilities inherent in the new application of biofeedback to differential hemispheric functioning. The biofeedback units can be used to identify certain brain dysfunctions and then employed to correct the dysfunction if it involves primarily a maladaptive arousal level.

Concluding Remarks

A brain model which hypothesizes separate functions for the left-right hemispheres and which further postulates that the dominant hemisphere has a more restricted effective arousal level continuum than does the nondominant hemisphere, offers at least a partial explanation of many of the phenomena which result in sudden or dramatic psychological or physical change. Research with aphasics and commissurotomized patients indicates that the speech characteristics which maximize comprehension by the right hemisphere are very similar to the voice qualities of many of the better known preachers or ministers who specialize in healing.

The model also suggests that the hemispheres can inhibit one another, but that the left side is more effective in this regard. Certain of the inhibited contents of the right hemisphere may be relatively inaccessible to consciousness, according to Galin. If these memories constitute attitudes or action tendencies which are opposed to these qualities in the conscious left hemisphere, then the resulting conflict may produce emotional or even psychosomatic disturbances.

Some of the newer therapy procedures which feature temporary suspension of left hemisphere functions and reprogramming of the right hemisphere may result in the alleviation or elimination of some of the more recalcitrant psychological and psychosomatic disorders.

If, as some people believe, the minor hemisphere also subserves *psi* phenomena, then these same procedures should allow the enhancement of paranormal abilities. Specifically, the suspension of the critical, logical faculties may release the more intuitive, creative minor hemisphere functions, one of which may be the ability to receive or transmit *psi* energy.

In a more pragmatic vein, some recent research using bilateral alpha measurements shows that people from business, law and accounting professions differ from individuals in creative professions in the way their hemispheres process cognitive tasks. Those in scientific, medical and psychological professions fall somewhere in between these two groups. This technique may result in a physiological test which might have predictive value in job performance and/or satisfaction.

Biofeedback procedures involving differential control of hemispheric arousal levels may prove to be extremely useful in the diagnosis and correction of certain brain dysfunctions related to maladaptive differential activation in one or both hemispheres.

FOOTNOTES

1. Compare these characteristics of a procedure for optimal comprehension of language by the right brain with the voice characteristics of a good revival meeting preacher.

2. *The Origin of Consciousness in the Breakdown of the Bicameral Mind*, 1976, p. 93. Julian Jaynes speculates that during the bicameral eras (earlier than 2000 B.C.) the threshold for stress which released the control of consciousness to the minor hemisphere was much lower than today.

3. Bio-Feedback Systems, Inc., 2736 47th St., Boulder Co. 80301.

BIBLIOGRAPHY

Adams, H. B., "A case utilizing sensory deprivation procedures," in L. P. Ullman and L. Krasner (Eds.), *Case Studies in Behavior Modification*, New York: Holt, Rinehart & Winston, 1965, Pp. 164–170.

Albert, M., Sparks, R. and Helm, N., "Melodic intonation therapy for aphasia," *Archives of Neurology*, 1973, *29*, 130–131.

Bakan, P., "Hypnotizability, laterality of eye movements, and functional brain asymmetry," *Perceptual and Motor Skills*, 1969, *28*, 927–932.

Bakan, P., "The eyes have it," *Psychology Today*, 1971, *4*, 64–69.

Barber T. X., "Experiments in hypnosis," *Scientific American*, 1957, *196*, 54–61.

Benton, A. L. and Joynt, R. J., "Early descriptions of aphasia," *Archives of Neurology*, 1960, *3*, 205–222.

Blumstein, S. and Cooper, W., "Hemispheric processing of intonation contours," *Cortex*, 1974, *10*, 146–158.

Bogen, J. E. and Bogen, G. M., "The other side of the brain III: The corpus callosum and creativity," *Bulletin of Los Angeles Neurology Society*, 1969, *34*, 191–220.

Bogen, J. and Gordon, H., "Musical tests for functional lateralization with introcarotid amobarbital," *Nature*, 1971, *230*, 524–525.

Budzynski, T. H., "Some applications of biofeedback-produced twilight states," *Fields within Fields within Fields*, 1972, *5*, 105–114. Republished in D. Shapiro, T. X. Barber, L. V. DiCara, J. Kamiya, N. Miller and J. Stoyva (Eds.), *Biofeedback and Self-Control*, 1972. Chicago: Aldine-Atherton, 1973.

Budzynski, T. H., "Biofeedback and the twilight states of consciousness," in G. E. Schwartz and D. Shapiro (Eds.), *Consciousness and Self-Regulation Vol. 1*. New York: Plenum, 1976, Pp. 361–385.

Budzynski, T. H., "Tuning in on the twilight zone," *Psychology Today*, August, 1977.

Budzynski, T. H., *"Running and Reprogramming,"* in preparation, 1978.

Cohen, R., "Conceptual styles, culture conflict, and nonverbal tests of intelligence," *American Anthropologist*, 1969, *71*, 828–856.

Cohen, D. B., "Dreaming: Experimental investigation of representational and adaptive properties," in G. E. Schwartz and D. Shapiro (Eds.), *Consciousness and Self-Regulation*, Vol. 1. New York: Plenum, 1976.

Davidson, R. J., Schwartz, G. E. and Weinberger, D., "Eye movement and electrodermal asymmetry during cognitive and affective tasks," Paper presented at the meeting of the American Psychological Association, San Francisco, August, 1977.

Deglin, V. L., "Our split brain," *The Unesco Courier*, Jan. 1976.

Dimond, S. J. and Beaumont, J. G., "Differences in the vigilance performance of the right and left hemispheres," *Cortex*, 1973, *9*, 259–265.

Dimond, S. J. and Beaumont, J. G., "Experimental studies of hemisphere function in the human brain," in S. J. Dimond and J. G. Beaumont (Eds.), *Hemisphere Function in the Human Brain*, London: Elek Science, 1974, Pp. 48–88.

Duke, J., "Lateral eye movement behavior," *Journal of General Psychology*, 1968, *78*, 189–195.

Felipe, A., "Attitude change during interrupted sleep," Unpublished doctoral dissertation, Yale University, 1965.

Ferenczi, S., "An attempted explanation of some hysterical stigmata," in *Further Contributions to the Theory and Technique of Psychoanalysis*, London, 1926.

Foulkes, D. and Vogel, G., "Mental activity at sleep-onset," *Journal of Abnormal Psychology*, 1965, *70*, 231–243.

Frank, J. D., *Persuasion and Healing: A Comparative Study of Psychotherapy*, Baltimore: Johns Hopkins University Press, 1973.

Galin, D., "Implications for psychiatry of left and right cerebral specialization. A neurophysiological context for unconscious processes," *Archives of General Psychiatry*, 1974, *31*, 572–583.

Galin, D. and Ornstein, R., "Lateral specialization of cognitive mode: An EEG study," *Psychophysiology*, 1972, *9*, 412–418.

Geschwind, N., "Language and the brain," *Scientific American*, 1972, *226*, 76–83.

Gibby, R. G. and Adams, H. B., "Receptiveness of psychiatric patients to verbal communication," *Archives of General Psychiatry*, 1961, *5*, 366–370.

Gur, R., "Validation and personality correlates of conjugate lateral eye-movements as an index of hemispheric activation," *Journal of Personality and Social Psychology*, 1975, *31*, 751–757.

Gur, R. C. and Gur, R. E., "Handedness, sex and eyedness as moderating variables in the relation between hypnotic susceptibility and functional brain asymmetry," *Journal of Abnormal Psychology*, 1974, *6*, 635–643.

Heeschen, C. and Jurgens, R., "Pragmatic-sermantic and syntactic factors influencing ear differences in dichotic listening," *Cortex*, 1977, *13*, 74–84.

Jaynes, J., *The Origin of Consciousness in the Breakdown of the Bicameral Mind*, Boston: Houghton Mifflin, 1976.

Keith, R. L. and Aronson, A. E., "Singing as therapy for apraxia of speech and aphasia: Report of a case," *Brain and Language*, 1975, *2*, 483–488.

Kinsbourne, M., "Eye and head turning indicates cerebral lateralization," *Science*, 1972, *176*, 539–541.

Koukkou, M. and Lehmann, D., "EEG and memory storage in sleep experiments with humans," *Electroencephalography and Clinical Neurophysiology*, 1968, *25*, 455–462.

Krashen, S. D., "The left hemisphere," *U.C.L.A. Educator*, 1975, *17*, 17–23.

Lasky, E. Z., Weidner, W. E. and Johnson, J. P., "Influence of linguistic complexity, rate of presentation, and interphrase pause time on auditory-verbal comprehension of adult aphasic patients," *Brain and Language*, 1976, *3*, 386–395.

Levy, J., "Psychobiological implications of bilateral asymmetry," in S. J. Dimond and J. G. Beaumont (Eds.), *Hemisphere Function in the Human Brain*, London: Elek Science, 1974. Pp. 121–183.

Levy, J., "Variations in the lateral organization of the brain," Master Lecture presented at the 85th Annual Convention of the American Psychological Association Meeting, San Francisco, California, August 26–30, 1977.

Levy, J., Trevarthen, C. and Sperry, R. W., "Perception of bilateral chimeric figures following hemispheric deconnexion," *Brain*, 1972, *95*, 61–78.

Murphy, P. J., Darwin, J. and Murphy, D. A., "EEG feedback training for cerebral dysfunction," unpublished, 1977.

Ornstein, R., *The Psychology of Consciousness*, San Francisco: Freeman, 1972.

Ostrander, S. and Schroeder, L., *Psychic Discoveries Behind the Iron Curtain*, Englewood, Cliffs, N.J.: Prentice Hall, 1970.

Peper, E., "Localized EEG alpha feedback training: A possible technique for mapping subjective, conscious and behavioral experiences," in D. Shapiro et al (Eds.), *Biofeedback and Self-Control: 1972*. Chicago: Aldine, 1973.

Ray, W. S., Frediani, A. W. and Harman, D., "Self-regulation of hemispheric asymmetry," *Biofeedback and Self-Regulation*, 1977, *2*, 195–199.

Rubin, F., *Current Research in Hypnopaedia*, London: MacDonald, 1968.

Rubin, F., "Learning and sleep," *Nature*, 1970, *226*, 447.

Schnell, H., Jenkins, J. J. and Jimenez-Pabon, E., *Aphasia in Adults: Diagnosis, Prognosis, and Treatment*, New York: Hoeber, 1964.

Schwartz, G. E., Davidson, R. J. and Maer, F., "Right hemisphere lateralization for emotion in the human brain: Interactions with cognition," *Science*, 1975, *190*, 286–288.

Sparks, R. W. and Holland, A. L., "Method: Melodic intonation therapy for aphasia," *Journal of Speech and Hearing Disorders*, 1976, *41*, 287–297.

Suedfeld, P., "Using environmental restriction to initiate long-term behavior change," in R. B. Stuart (Ed.), *Behavioral Self-Management: Strategies, Techniques and Outcomes*, New York: Brunner/Mazel, 1977.

Suter, S., Krone, A. and Matthews, S., "Hemispheric, cognitive, and sex differences in biofeedback regulation of occipital alpha," Presented at the Ninth Annual Meeting of the Biofeedback Society of America.

Vogel, G., Foulkes, D. and Trosman, H., "Ego functions and dreaming during sleep onset," *Archives of General Psychiatry*, 1966, *14*, 238–248.

Zaidel, E., "Auditory vocabulary of the right hemisphere following brain bisection or hemidecortication," *Cortex*, 1976, *12*, 191–211.

DISCUSSION

STORM: I have two questions for you. One is on the matter of people who appear to be strongly lateralized. Do you ever find any evidence that a sort of verbal argumentativeness, verbal aggressiveness tends to manifest itself? The second question is, are there any interesting personality characteristics about the people who are at the other end of the scale of lateralization, who are least lateralized?

BUDZYNSKI: The impression that one gets from talking to people who are working in this area is that the highly lateralized individual can be either more or less a left-brain dominated or a right-brain dominated individual; however, the extremes are found among left-handers, according to Jerry Levy. She says that because left-handers generally are less lateralized, they can have the same functions in both hemispheres. Thus, you may have what appear to be double left-hemisphere people; that is, extremely logical, extremely abstract and analytical in their thinking and at the other extreme the double right-hemisphere people who should be very good in sports, or perhaps do very well in the creative arts.

Dr. Levy in fact, found support for this theory in a study carried out at Cal. Tech. in the Engineering School. She reasoned like this: the entrance examinations required to get into Cal. Tech. and, in fact, the exams you would have to take to get even that far, were very left-brain oriented. So, if left handers got that far they were probably "double-lefts," i.e., very bright in a left-brained way, but perhaps less talented at right-brain processing. Using the WAIS I.Q. test she compared right-handed with left-handed engineering students. In the right-handed students the Verbal/Performance scores were balanced, something like 132/133, whereas among the left-handed students the average Verbal score was approximately 142 and the Performance score average was only about 116. Since the Verbal scores reflect more of the left hemisphere's abilities, Dr. Levy's hunch was supported.

McGUINNESS: I'm delighted that you bring up the question of male-female, because I think it's terribly important when you're working with paranormal phenomena, where the traditional stereotype is the intuitive clairvoyant female. This goes all the way back to Greek mythology. There are three points bearing on this, all making the same general point about the male-female brain. The first point you made about the control of heart rate, where you got results going in opposite directions, also raises another issue about EEG. When you filter alpha—you can get alpha diminishing as your slow wave activity goes up, but you can also get alpha diminishing because you have fast activity coming in, and unless you have some measure on the outside, the females might be shifting slow waves versus the males shifting fast waves or some difference in the relationship might be taking place. I think the variable of sex is terribly important if one is going to do EEG work with people in paranormal situations. Another point was your left-right lookers. The logical left-brain person and the intuitive right-brain person are opposite with respect to sex. The female is the verbal person *and* intuitive. Then the final point dealt with the singing results that you got. Again, there's the sex difference that I've come up with sometimes in my own work, and that other people have also found that females are singers as well as the speakers which, in a sense, bears out your comments about the bilateral female. Females are almost never monotones.

DEAN: Before Einstein's discovery of relativity in 1905, physicists worked on spatial problems and on time problems as if they were separate. Then Einstein showed that there was no such thing as separate space and time; that there was only space-time, and brought in all the equations to show it. Now, the question arises, was Einstein discovering something about the true reality out there as we picture physicists discovering the objective reality of space-time in 1905, or was he discovering something about his brain—that we now know seventy-three years later—that the left hemisphere deals with time and the right hemisphere deals with space, and that the hemispheres are joined by the corpus callosum?

BUDZINSKI: I have a few relevant impressions of Einstein. One came from Karsch, who photographed him. He mentioned that when he called upon Einstein in his office he heard a very musical voice ask him to enter. This sort of voice is said to be typical of right-hemisphere dominated people. He also had trouble with algebra when he was quite young. Algebra is very much a left-brain type of mathematics whereas geometry is best handled by the right brain. This would lead one to believe that Einstein had a little difficulty, perhaps, overriding his dominance of right hemisphere functioning at several phases in his life. Of course, a man of his genius no doubt possessed unusual ability in both hemispheres.

HONORTON: One of the studies that we're planning involves bilateral EEG training. Are there any studies that show that, if you differentially train activation on the right hemisphere and quieting of the left, you can demonstrate significant changes in relevant performance, and if so, how much of a differential is necessary in order to show a change in performance?

BUDZYNSKI: In what kind of performance?

HONORTON: Increase in visual pattern recognition ability, for example. Another similar kind of question has to do with mutual feedback. Do you know whether there have been any studies in which two people have simultaneously been given the same biofeedback conditions as a technique for facilitating empathy, so that they both must be meeting, say, alpha conditions in order for the feedback to occur?

BUDZYNSKI: Barbara Brown has been exploring that latter problem for a number of years. I'm not sure what kind of results she has obtained. She was trying to get two people to produce alpha at exactly the same time in an attempt to produce empathy. To answer your first question—you can train people with biofeedback to change cortical arousal level, but with regard to research on performance at that point, all we have so far is the work of Philip Murphy, which showed math scores going up as this particular group of learning-disordered adolescents *decreased* arousal over the left hemisphere. We have some further clues from work being done on meditation at the University of Washington at Bob Pagano's laboratory. He finds that after people meditated—and, of course, meditation is a way of quieting the left hemisphere, because you're simply reciting a mantra, which produces a numbing effect of the verbal hemisphere—they improved on right-hemisphere abilities. I think one of the tests was a pattern recognition task of some kind. I know that the Seashore Battery was one of the tests as well. The other thing that occurred that was intriguing was that the subjects decreased a bit on left-hemisphere performance as a result of meditation. So meditation is probably very good for those of us who spend too much time in our left hemispheres, and is possibly not advocated for those who are too right-hemisphere oriented, to begin with.

SERVADIO: We all know, at least in the West, that to say that music is not logical would be a great mistake. Certainly, the music of Bach and Beethoven is all very logical and even the avant-garde music is not just a succession of sounds. So there is a talking, a "saying something" in Western music. There is, I think, a great deal of difference between Western and Eastern music. When I arrived in India, I was very much surprised because I couldn't understand what they were aiming at with their music. Then I realized that they don't want to convey a particular message, but just to create a state of feeling. I would predict that a comparative study of Western composers and Eastern composers would show a much more important function of the right hemisphere in the East than in the West.

SMALL: There has been some speculation in relation to paranormal phenomena and I'm wondering how we can put ESP ability in proper perspective, as to whether it's a remnant of some kind or whether it's something we're in the process of developing. Regarding Julian Jaynes' book, about the origins of this lateralization historically, I'm wondering if you would comment on whether there was any evidence as to how this has been developed in terms of cross-cultural studies or animal studies. Can we speculate on some kind of evolutionary advantage there might be in this lateralization?

BUDZYNSKI: Jaynes' book is very interesting and in a course I teach in this area of lateralization I have everyone read it. His book presents a model, a very speculative one that has certainly not been very well accepted by his peers, but it's a very exciting concept. One of the things he states is that the people who lived in the bicameral era two to three thousand years B.C., were people who very easily shifted into right hemisphere consciousness in order to make decisions. He says that they did this when stress would increase somewhat. Today we tend to do this only if stress builds up to a very high level. We have to reach a high threshold before we'll trip off into right-brain dominated behavior. We're thinking logically as things begin to happen to us and then, all of a sudden, say in automobile accidents or near accidents, we very quickly trip off into non-dominant hemisphere automatic reactions and later say it seemed as though it happened in slow motion. Perhaps this is because the right brain does not perform sequential processing as does the left. However, Jaynes noted that in bicameral days we had a much lower threshold of stress which would allow us to trip into a right-hemisphere dominated consciousness, and that type of con-sciousness was very different from today's. It did not involve logical reasoning—at least hypothetical deductive reasoning—but, rather, it was very directive. In fact, the ancients called it the "god mind." If a man had to make a decision, the gods would speak to him and most often it was brought to the person's attention by hallucinatory voices. Perhaps, in some ways, this resulted in a much more tranquil existence, because when you don't spend a lot of time in your left hemisphere, you're living more in the present rather than in the past or the future. You don't feel anxious or guilty so much; you're enjoying yourself in the here and now. Sometimes I think it might be better to return to a kind of bicameral era, at least part of the time.

EHRENWALD: Let me point to a striking parallel between the predisposing factors that are favorable for a therapeutic response on the one hand and for psi phenomena on the other. In my *History of Psychotherapy* I came across a virtually omnipresent pattern that is conducive to a therapeutic response. It can be described as the "Therapeutic triad," consisting of 1) a healer with a powerful motivation to help and a conviction of being able to do so; 2) the patient, with a corresponding strong faith in his therapist, and 3) the tribe surrounding the two, participating in the act, and reinforcing results. This, in a nutshell, is the *modus operandi* of psychotherapy. Exactly the same configuration seems to be responsible for the emergence of need-determined psi pheomena: there is the experimenter's motivation to succeed; there is the subject—a Schmeidlerian "sheep" with his faith in the possibility of psi and the magic of the experimenter—and there are the surrounding people who are likewise "true believers" and thereby reinforce the psi conducive pattern.

DIXON: There have been a number of different theories of schizophrenia, at least two of which have had a very rough ride. One is that it's a left-hemisphere dysfunction. The other is that it's due to double-binding by a schizophrenogenic mother. However, it seems to me that what you've been talking about makes sense if you combine these theories. I wondered, therefore, if you have any information from studies of lateralization in schizophrenics?

BUDZYNSKI: There is some very recent research by Gur that indicates that schizophrenics have too high an arousal level in the left hemisphere. That's one of the factors. The other is that somehow that left hemisphere doesn't operate very adaptively at that high level. I've also heard that the corpus callosum has a larger cross-section in schizophrenics than it does in normal people, which is intriguing, you know. It's almost as though too much information gets transferred back and forth.

DIXON: So they would perhaps be subject to double-bind situations such as you were talking about, would they not?

BUDZYNSKI: Yes, where the memories that are stored in the right hemisphere are in conflict with the conscious memories.

KELLY: I have to confess I feel a certain amount of disappointment. I hoped that you would talk more about relationship of work in these areas to the specific things that we were to talk about here. Obviously, you can't go on to do that now, but I would like to ask one specific question, about your encounter with the "coin-bender." I'm wondering, do you have any further plans for work with him and, if so, what kind of things do you have in mind?

BUDZYNSKI: We hope to adapt him to the instrumentation to the point where he can actually bend a coin while we're measuring bilateral alpha. That's what our plans are for him. With regard to the other question, very briefly, there just is not that much data yet on biofeedback enhancing psi phenomena. The work of Charles Honorton is probably the only work I know of in that area. Perhaps Charlie Tart has done something in the realm of biofeedback, but those would be the only two people whose work I could mention.

TART: The split between right and left functions, especially as in the example you gave from David Galin's work, where a child might be getting a hostile message from the mother in a non-verbal way, may be a prototype of the reason we talk about psi apparently being relatively rare in ordinary life. Think of the early mother/child relationship, where the child is totally dependent on the mother. The mother usually *says* she's loving, she's taking care of the child's needs and all that, but being human, there are many times when the mother is in a rotten mood and would like to kill the little brat! That message may come through non-verbally and/or may come through by psi. In either case, the message is extremely difficult for the child to handle, so we may have right there a prototype of repression for psi phenomena starting to happen early in life and then continuing on through.

As for these changes in arousal level which may facilitate psi—it may be that a high arousal state or low arousal state per se is effective in aiding ESP, but also it should be remembered that high and low arousal conditions can destablize our ordinary state of consciousness and thus act as induction techniques from which some other state of consciousness develops, which is psi-favorable. We should measure the consequences of arousal, not just arousal per se.

A PROGRESS REPORT ON THE SCIENTIFIC UNDERSTANDING OF PARANORMAL PHENOMENA

Karl H. Pribram

Introduction

In 1968, I attended a conference on methodology in psi research organized by Roberto Cavanna. The participants contributing to the neurophysiological parts of the program included Monte Buchsbaum, Joe Kamiya, Don Lindsley, Alan Rechtscheffen, Julie Silverman and Grey Walter. We were seriously offering our services to the others in the gathering—the believers in paranormal phenomena. In our discussions among ourselves, we reassured each other of our scientific skepticism and integrity. Still, we had to face the fact that we had accepted the invitation to participate and that we were presenting our own work in good faith. At the time, I summed up our position—in an attempt to resolve the tension between skepticism and faith—as a scientist's willingness to suspend disbelief until the facts are in. My own current position remains essentially unchanged since the 1968 meetings. At the same time, however, I am much more comfortable with the putative phenomena concerning which my disbelief needs to be suspended. This increased comfort does not arise so much from any accretion in facts as it does from important new insights which have enhanced understanding. These insights, I believe, augur a paradigm shift in all of science—to use Kuhn's classic phrase—a shift which may make it feasible for scientific understanding to encompass paranormal experiences.

Note that I am addressing the problem of a scientific base for understanding. Such a base would allow the phenomena under consideration to be approached from a variety of directions with a variety of methods. Only in this way can experiences be truly shared. In saying this I do not mean to disparage sharing by experiencing *per se*, nor the attempts at proving (i.e. testing) reliability. Nonetheless, we must admit, that even one experience by one person, if it is believed, must be explained if scientific understanding is to be achieved. And belief will rest on prior understanding (shared values, etc.) and very little else.

The Hologram

In 1968, I ventured the suggestion that the holographic hypothesis of brain function held a hidden promise for understanding unmatched by other developments in the neurosciences. This suggestion was based on the fact that holography encodes waveforms and could therefore explain how organisms might tune-in on and "resonate-with" energy configurations other than those that give rise to our ordinary perceptions. The hidden promise is no longer hidden. Much has happened in support of the holographic hypothesis and a larger understanding of its import has been achieved.

Holograms were the mathematical invention of Dennis Gabor (1948) in the late 1940's. Gabor was attempting to improve the resolution of electron microscopy by recording, instead of images, the patterns of light diffracted by (filtered through or reflected from) the tissue to be examined. A decade or so later, Gabor's mathematics became realized in hardware when coherent light from lasers could be used to form optical holograms (Leith and Upatnicks, 1965). Also, the advent of inexpensive general purpose computers made it possible to simulate the holographic process in order to formulate a precise model of how it might be realized in neural tissue (Pribram, Nuwer and Baron, 1974). These hardware realizations made it obvious that object → wave storage → image construction is a linear process and that, according to Gabor's equations, the identical mathematical transfer function transformed object into wave storage and wave storage into image. The storage of wave patterns (the hologram) is thus reciprocally related to the imaging of objects. The wave functions are transforms of objects and their images.

Gabor named the wave pattern store a *hologram* because one of its most interesting characteristics is that information from the object becomes distributed over the surface of the photographic film, thus allowing the object to be reconstructed from each part. Each point of light diffracted from the object becomes blurred, spread over the entire surface of the film, as is each neighboring point of light. The equations that describe this blurring are called spread functions. The spread is not haphazard, however, as the blur would lead one to believe. Rather, ripples of waves move out from the point of light, much as ripples of waves are formed when a pebble strikes the smooth surface of a pond of water. Throw into the pond a handful of pebbles or sand and the ripples produced by each pebble or grain will crisscross with those produced by the other pebbles or grains setting up patterns of interfering wave fronts. The smooth mirror-like surface has become blurred but the blur has hidden within it an unsuspectedly orderly pattern. If the pond could suddenly be frozen at this moment, its surface would be a hologram. The photographic hologram is such a frozen record of interference patterns.

It seemed immediately plausible that the distributed memory store of the brain might resemble this holographic record. I developed a precisely formulated theory based on known neuroanatomy and known neurophysiology that could account for the brain's distributed memory store in holographic terms. In the dozen or so years since, many laboratories, including my own, have provided evidence in support of parts of this theory. Other data have sharpened the theory and made it even more precise and fitting to the known facts.

Essentially, the theory reads that the brain at one stage of processing performs its analyses in the frequency domain. This is accomplished at the junctions *between* neurons, not within neurons. Thus graded local waxings and wanings of neural potentials (waves) rather than nerve impulses are responsible. Nerve impulses are generated within neurons and are used to propagate the signals that constitute information over long distances via long nerve fibers. Graded local potential changes, waves, are constituted at the ends of these nerve fibers where they adjoin shorter branches that form a feltwork of interconnections among neurons. Some neurons, now called local circuit neurons, have no long fibers and display no nerve impulses. They function in the graded wave mode primarily and are especially responsible for horizontal connectivities in sheets of neural tissue, connectivities in which holographic-like interference patterns can become constructed.

Aside from these anatomical and physiological specifications, a solid body of evidence has accumulated that the auditory, somatosensory, motor and visual systems of the brain do in fact process, at one or several stages, input from the senses in the frequency domain. This distributed input must then in some form, perhaps as changes in the conformation of proteins at membrane surfaces, become encoded into distributed memory traces. The protein molecules would serve the neural hologram in the same way as oxidized silver grains in the photographic hologram.

The explanation of the fact that specific memory traces are resistant to brain damage (remembering demands only that a small part of the distributed store remain intact, in the same way that images can be reconstructed from small parts of a photographic hologram) has been only one of the contributions of holographic theory. Characteristics of the experience of imaging have been explained in an equally powerful manner. The projection of images away from their sources of origin has been demonstrated to result from processing phase relations (just as in the stereophonic audio systems). Simulations of image processing by computer have found no technique other than the holographic to provide the rich texture of scenes such as those that compose our experiences. And the complicated computations that go into three dimensional x-ray imaging by computerized tomography have relied heavily on the fact that such computations (mostly correlations) are performed readily in the frequency (holographic) domain.

The Evidence

The evidence regarding a brain holographic process developed from studies on the brain mechanisms involved in memory and perception. Only a little over 25 years ago Lashley uttered his famous remark that, on the basis of his lifetime of research on brain function, it was clear that "learning just could not take place." Lashley's despair was produced by his repeated findings of equivalence of function of parts of brain systems. Not only was he unable to excise any specific memory, but was unable to account for the facts of sensory and motor equivalence: "These three lines of evidence indicate that certain coordinated activities, known to be dependent upon definite cortical areas, can be carried out by any part (within undefined limits) of the whole area. Such a condition might arise from the presence of many duplicate reflex pathways through the areas and such an explanation will perhaps account for all of the reported cases of survival of functions after partial destruction of their special areas, but it is inadequate for the facts of sensory and motor equivalence. These facts establish the principle that once an associated reaction has been established (e.g., a positive reaction to a visual pattern), the same reaction will be elicited by the excitation of sensory cells which were never stimulated in that way during the course of training. Similarly, motor acts (e.g., opening a latch box), once acquired, may be executed immediately with motor organs which were not associated with the act during training." (Lashley, 1960, p. 240)

What sort of brain mechanism could be imagined which would account for the principle that "once an associated reaction has been established, the same reaction will be elicited by the excitation of sensory cells which were never stimulated in that way during the course of training"? And what mechanism could be devised to deal with the fact that "motor acts, once acquired, may be executed immediately with motor organs which were not associated with the act during training"? What sort of mechanism of association could be taking place during learning so that its residual would, as it were, act at a distance?

The difficulties of conceptualization may be summarized as follows: during acquisition associative processes must be operative. However, these associative processes must result in a distributed store. On the basis of Lashley's analysis, input must become dismembered before it becomes re-membered. Association and distribution are in some fundamental fashion inexorably linked.

During the mid nineteen-sixties it became apparent that image processing through holography could provide the model for a mechanism with such "distribution by association" properties. As in the case of every novel approach, there were, of course, earlier formulations, including those of Lashley, that attempted to explain these aspects of brain function in terms that today we would call holographic.

Historically, the ideas can be traced to problems posed during neurogenesis when the activity of relatively remote circuits of the developing nervous system must become integrated to account for such simple behaviors as swimming. Among others, the principle of chemical "resonances" that "tune" these circuits has had a long and influential life (see, e.g. Loeb, 1907; Weiss, 1939). More specifically, however, Goldscheider (1906) and Horton (1925) proposed that the establishment of tuned resonances in the form of interference patterns in the adult brain could account for a variety of perceptual phenomena. More recently, Lashley (1942) spelled out a mechanism of neural interference patterns to explain stimulus equivalence and Beurle (1956) developed a mathematically rigorous formulation of the origin of such patterns of plane wave interferences in neural tissue. But it was not until the advent of holography, with its powerful damage-resistant image storage and reconstructive capabilities, that the promise of an interference pattern mechanism of brain function became fully appreciated. As the properties of physical holograms became known (see Stroke, 1966; Goodman, 1968; Collier, Burckhardt and Lin, 1971), a number of scientists saw the relevance of holography to the problems of brain function, memory, and perception (e.g., van Heerden, 1963; Julesz and Pennington, 1965; Kabrisky, 1966; Pribram, 1966; Westlake, 1968; Baron, 1970; Cavanagh, 1972).

The advent of these explanations came with the development of physical holography (e.g. Stroke, 1966) from the mathematical principles enunciated by Gabor (1948). Equally important, however, was the failure of computer science to simulate perception and learning in any adequate fashion. The problem lies in the fact that computer based "perceptions" (e.g. Rosenblatt, 1962) were constructed on the basis of an assumed random connectivity in neural networks, when the actual anatomical situation is essentially otherwise. In the visual system, for instance, the retina and cortex are connected by a system of fibers that run to a great extent in parallel. Only two modifications of this parallelity occur: 1) The optic tracts and radiations that carry signals between the retina and cortex constitute a sheaf within which the retinal events converge to some extent onto the lateral geniculate nucleus of the thalamus from where they diverge to the cortex. The final effect of this parallel network is that each fiber in the system connects ten retinal outputs to about 5,000 cortical receiving cells. 2) In the process of termination of the fibers at various locations in the pathway, an effective overlap develops (to about 5° of visual angle) between neighboring branches of the conducting fibers.

Equally striking, and perhaps more important than these exceptions, however, is the interpolation at every cell station of a sheet of horizontally connected neurons in a plane perpendicular to the parallel fiber system. These horizontal cells are characterized by short or absent axons, but spreading dendrites. It has been shown in the retina (Werblin and Dowling, 1969) and to some extent also in the cortex (Creutzfeldt, 1961), that such spreading dendritic networks may not generate nerve impulses; in fact, they usually may not even polarize. Their activity is characterized by hyperpolarization that tends to organize the functions of the system by inhibitory rather than excitatory processes. In the retina, for instance, no nerve impulses are generated prior to the amacrine and the ganglion cells from which the optic nerve fibers originate. Thus, practically all of the complexity manifest in the optic nerve is a reflection of the organizing properties of depolarizing and hyperpolarizing events, not of interactions among nerve impulses.

Two mechanisms are, therefore, available to account for the distribution of signals within the neural system. One relies on the convergence and divergence of nerve impulses onto and from a neuronal pool. The other relies on the presence of lateral (mostly inhibitory) interactions taking place in sheets of horizontal dendritic networks situated at every cell station perpendicular to the essentially parallel system of input fibers. Let us explore the possible role of both of these mechanisms in explaining the results of the lesion studies.

Evidence is supplied by experiments in which conditions of anesthesia are used that suppress the functions of small nerve fibers, thus leaving intact and clearly discernible the connectivity by way of major nerve impulse pathways. These experiments have shown that localized retinal stimulation evokes a receptive field at the cortex over an area no greater than a few degrees in diameter (e.g. Talbot and Marshall, 1941), Yet, the data that must be explained indicate that some 80 percent or more of the visual cortex, including the foveal region, can be extirpated without marked impairment of the recognition of a previously learned visual pattern. Thus, whatever the mechanisms, distribution of input cannot be due to the major pathways, but must involve the fine fibered connectivity in the visual system, either via the divergence of nerve impulses and/or via the interactions taking place in the horizontal cell dendritic networks.

Both are probably to some extent responsible. It must be remembered that nerve impulses occurring in the fine fibers tend to decrement in amplitude and speed of conduction, thus becoming slow graded potentials. Further, these graded slow potentials or minispikes usually occur in the same anatomical location as the horizontal dendritic inhibitory hyperpolarizations and thus interact with them. In fact, the resulting micro-organization of junctional neural activity (synaptic and ephaptic) could be regarded as a simple summation of graded excitatory (depolarizing) and inhibitory (hyperpolarizing) slow potential processes.

These structural arrangements of slow potentials are especially evident in sheets of neural tissue such as in the retina and cortex. The cerebral cortex, for instance, may be thought of as consisting of columnar units that can be considered more or less independent basic computational elements, each of which is capable of performing a similar computation (Mountcastle, 1957; Hubel and Wiesel, 1968). Inputs to the basic computational elements are processed in a direction essentially perpendicular to the sheet of the cortex and, therefore, cortical processing occurs in stages, each stage transforming the activation pattern of the cells in one of the cortical layers to the cells of another cortical layer. Analyses by Kabrisky (1966) and by Werner (1970) show that processing by one basic computational element remains essentially within that element and, therefore, the cortex can be considered to consist of a large number of essentially similar parallel processing elements. Furthermore, the processing done by any one of the basic computational elements is itself a parallel process (see, for example, Spinelli, 1970a), each layer transforming the pattern of activity that arrived from the previous layer by the process of temporal and spatial summation, the summation of slow hyper and depolarizations in the dendritic microstructure of the cortex. Analyses by Ratliff

(1965) and Rodieck (1965) have shown that processing (at least at the sensory level) that occurs through successive stages in such a layered neural network can be described by linear equations. Each computational element is thus capable of transforming its inputs through a succession of stages, and each stage produces a linear transformation of the pattern of activity at the previous stage.

Let us trace in detail the evidence regarding these stages in the visual system. Quantitative descriptions of the interactions that occur in the retina are inferred from the output of ganglion cells, from which receptive field configurations are recorded by making extracellular microelectrode recordings from the optic nerve. The retinal interactions *per se* take place initially by virtue of local graded slow wave potentials—hyperpolarizations and depolarizations that linearly sum within the networks of receptors, bipolar and horizontal cells, from which nerve impulses are never recorded. The receptive fields generated by these graded potential changes display a more or less circular center surrounded by a ring of activity of sign opposite that of the center. This configuration has been interpreted to mean that the activity of a receptive neuron generates inhibition in neighboring neurons through lateral connectivities (e.g. Hartline, Wagner and Ratliff, 1956; Bekesy, 1967; Kuffler, 1953) perpendicular to the input channels. In view of the fact that no nerve impulses can be recorded from the cells (e.g. horizontal) that mediate the lateral inhibition, the inference can be made that the interactions among graded potentials, wave forms, are responsible (Pribram, 1971; Pribram, Nuwer and Baron, 1974). Such wave forms need not be thought of as existing in an unstructured homogeneous medium. The dendritic arborizations in which the graded potential changes occur can act as structural wave guides. However, as Beurle (1956) has shown, such a structural medium can still give rise to a geometry of plane waves provided the structure is reasonably symmetrical. The mathematical descriptions of receptive field configurations bear out Beurle's model. Such descriptions have been given by Ratliff (1965) and Rodieck (1965). Mathematically, they involve a convolution of luminance change of the retinal input with the inferred inhibitory characteristics of the network to compose the observed ganglion cell receptive field properties.

The gist of these experimental analyses is that the retinal mosaic becomes decomposed into an opponent process by depolarizing and hyperpolarizing slow potentials and transforms into more or less concentric receptive fields in which center and surround are of opposite sign. Sets of convolutional integrals fully describe this transformation.

The next cell station in the visual pathway is the lateral geniculate nucleus of the thalamus. The receptive field characteristics of the output from neurons of this nucleus are in some respects similar to the more or less concentric organization obtained at the ganglion cell level. Now, however, the concentric organization is more symmetrical, the surround usually has more clear-cut boundaries and is somewhat more extensive (e.g., Spinelli and Pribram, 1967). Furthermore, a second penumbra of the same sign as the center can be shown to be present, though its intensity (number of nerve impulses generated) is not nearly so great as that of the center. Occasionally, a third penumbra, again of opposite sign, can be made out beyond the second (Hammond, 1972).

Again, a transformation has occurred between the output of the retina and the output of the lateral geniculate nucleus. This transformation apparatus appears to act as a rectification process. Each geniculate cell thus acts as a peephole "viewing" a part of the retinal image mosaic. This is due to the fact that each geniculate cell has converging upon it some 10,000 ganglion cell fibers. This receptive field peephole of each geniculate cell is made of concentric rings of opposing sign, whose amplitudes fall off sharply with distance from the center of the field. In these ways the transformation accomplished is like very near-field optics that describes a Fresnel Hologram.

Pollen, Lee and Taylor (1971), though supportive of the suggestion that the visual mechanism as a whole may function in a holographic-like manner, emphasize that the geniculate output is essentially topographic and punctate, is not frequency specific and does not show translational invariance—i.e. every illuminated point within the receptive field does not produce the same effect. Further, the opponent properties noted at the retinal level of organization are maintained and enhanced at the cost of overall translational invariance. Yet a step toward a discrete transform domain has been taken since the output of an individual element of the retinal mosaic—a rod or cone receptor—is the origin of the signal transformed at the lateral geniculate level.

When the output of lateral geniculate cells reaches the cerebral cortex, further transformations take place. One set of cortical cells, christened "simple" by their discoverers (Hubel and Wiesel, 1968), has been suggested to be characterized by a receptive field organization composed by a literally linelike arrangement of the outputs of lateral geniculate cells. This proposal is supported by the fact that the simple-cell receptive field is accompanied by side bands of opposite sign and occasionally by a second side band of the same sign as the central field. Hubel and Wiesel proposed that these simple cells thus serve as line detectors in the first stage of a hierarchical arrangement of pattern detectors. Pollen et al. (1971) have countered this proposal on the basis that the output from simple cells varies with contrast luminance as well as orientation and that the receptive field is too narrow to show translational invariance. They argue, therefore, that an ensemble of simple cells would be needed to detect orientation. They suggest that such an ensemble would act much as the strip integrator used by astronomers (Bracewell, 1965) to cull data from a wide area with instruments of limited topographic capacity (as is found to be the case in lateral geniculate cells).

Another class of cortical cells has generated great interest. These cells were christened "complex" by their discoverers, Hubel and Wiesel, and thought by them (as well as by Pollen) to be the next step in the images processing hierarchy. Some doubt has been raised (Hoffman and Stone, 1971), because of their relatively short latency of response, as to whether all complex cells receive their input from simple cells. Whether their input comes directly from the geniculate or by way of simple cell processing, however, the output from complex cells of the visual cortex displays transformations of the retinal input, characteristics of the holographic domain.

A series of elegant experiments by Fergus Campbell and his group (1974) have suggested that these complex cortical cells are spatial-frequency sensitive elements. Initially, Campbell showed that the response of the potential evoked in man and cat by repeated flashed exposure to a variety of gratings of certain spacing (spatial frequency), adapted not only to that fundamental frequency, but also to any component harmonics present. He concluded, therefore, that the visual system must be encoding spatial frequency (perhaps in Fourier terms) rather than the intensity values of the grating. He further showed that when a square wave grating was used, adaptation was limited to the fundamental and its third harmonic as would be predicted by Fourier theory. Finally, he found neural units in the cat's cortex that behaved as did the gross potential recordings.

Pollen (1973) has evidence that suggests that these spatial-frequency sensitive units are Hubel and Wiesel's complex cells, although both his work and that of Maffei and Fiorentini (1973) have found that simple cells also have the properties of spatial frequency fibers, in that they are sensitive to a selective band of spatial frequencies. In addition, the latter investigators have found that the simple cells can transmit contrast and spatial phase information in terms of two different parameters of their response: contrast is coded in terms of impulses per second and spatial phase in terms of firing pattern.

The receptive field of complex cells is characterized by the broad extent (when compared with simple cells) over which a line of relatively indeterminate length, but a certain orientation, will elicit a response. Pollen demonstrated that the output of complex cells was not invariant to orientation alone—number of lines and their spacing appeared also to influence response. He concluded, therefore, as had Fergus Campbell, that these cells were spatial frequency sensitive and that the spatial frequency domain was fully achieved at this level of visual processing. Additional corroborating evidence has recently been presented from the Pavlov Institute of Physiology in Leningrad by Glezer, Ivanoff and Tscherbach (1973), who relate their findings on complex receptive fields as Fourier analyzers to the dendritic microstructure of the visual cortex much as we have done here.

Even more recently, a series of studies from the Cambridge laboratories, from MIT, Berkeley and our own at Stanford University, have substantiated the earlier reports. Pribram, Lassonde and Ptito (submitted to *J. Neurophysiology*) have confirmed that both simple and complex cells are selective to restricted band widths of spatial frequencies, but that simple cells encode spatial phase while complex cells do not. Thus, simple cells may be involved in the perception of spatial location while complex cells are more truly "holographic" in that they are responsible for translational invariance. Schiller, Finlay and Volman (1976a, b, c, d) have performed a comprehensive coverage of receptive field properties, including spatial frequency selectivity. Movshen, Thompson and Tolhurst (1978a, b, c) in another set of experiments showed that receptive fields could be thought of as spatial filters (much as van Heerden, 1963, originally proposed) whose Fourier transform precisely mapped the cell's response characteristics. De Valois, Albrecht and Thorell (1978) have taken this work even a step further by showing that, whereas these cells are tuned to from ½ to 1½ octaves of band width of the spatial frequency spectrum, they are not tuned at all to changes in bar width. Finally, De Valois has tested whether the cells are selective of edges making up patterns or their Fourier transforms. The main components of the transforms of checkerboards and plaids lie at different orientations from those of the edges making up the patterns. In every case the orientation selectivity of the cells was shifted when gratings were changed to checkerboards or plaids and the shift was to the exact amount in degrees and minutes of arc predicted by the Fourier transform.

The results of these experiments go a long way toward validating the holographic hypothesis of brain function. However, as I have noted previously (Pribram, Nuwer and Baron, 1974), a major problem remains even after these data are incorporated in the construction of a precise model. Each receptive field, even though it encodes in the frequency domain, does so over a relatively restricted portion of the total visual field. Robson (1975) has thus suggested that only a "patch" of the field becomes represented. However, this major problem has now been resolved and the solution has brought unexpected dividends. Ross (see review by Leith, 1976) has constructed holograms on the principles proposed by Bracewell (1965) and espoused by Pollen (see Pollen and Taylor, 1974). Such multiplex or strip integral holograms are now commercially available (Multiplex Co., San Francisco, California). Not only do they display all the properties of ordinary holograms, but can be used to encode movement as well. Thus, by combining frequency encoding with a spatial "patch" or "slit" representation, a lifelike three-dimensional moving image can be constructed.

Although detailed specification has been given for the visual system only, the foregoing analysis is in large part also relevant to the auditory system, the tactile system and the motor system (see Pribram, 1971, for review). The recently accumulated facts concerning the visual system are the most striking because it was not suspected that spatial pattern perception would be found to be based on a stage that involves frequency analysis. The finding of the ubiquity of frequency analysis by brain tissue has made accessible explanations of hitherto inexplicable observations, such as the distributed nature of the memory trace and the projection of images away from the surface in which their representation has become encoded. The model has had considerable explanatory power.

The Nature of Reality

I want now to address some consequences to psychology (and perhaps to philosophy) of the holographic process of brain function. The theory, as we have seen, 1) stems from the metaphors of machine and optical information processing systems; 2) has developed by analogy to those systems, spelling out some similarities and some differences; until 3) a testable holonomic model of brain function could be proposed. One way of understanding the model better is to compare it to another and to observe its relative explanatory power.

An apparent alternative to the holographic process is presented by James Gibson's comprehensive "ecological" model of perception (1966). Gibson's model proposes that the "information" perceived is inherent in the physical universe and that the perceiver is sensitive to whatever information remains invariant across transformations produced by changes in the environment, by organism-environment displacements and by the organism's processing apparatus. The key concept in the ecological theory is "direct perception"—the environment is directly apprehended by the perceiver.

By contrast, the holographic process is constructional. Images are constructed when input from the inferior temporal cortex (or its analogue in other perceptual systems—see Pribram, 1974a) activates and organizes the distributed holographic store. Images are produced and are therefore as much a *product of* the "information residing in" the organism, as they are of "information" contained in the environment. Philosophically speaking, the holonomic model is Kantian and Piagetian, the ecological model partakes of a naive realism.

Clinical neurological experience wholly supports the holographic view. Patients are seen who complain of macropsia and micropsia and other bizarre distortions of visual space. For instance, I once had a patient who, after a blow on the head, experienced episodes of vertigo during which the visual world went spinning. His major complaint was that every so often when his perceptions again stabilized, they left him with the world upside down until the next vertigo which might right things once again. He had developed a sense of humor about these experiences, which were becoming less frequent and of shorter duration: his major annoyance he stated to be the fact that girls' skirts stayed up despite the upside-down position!

Further "clinical" evidence in support of the holographic process comes from the experimental laboratory. Resections of the primate inferior temporal cortex markedly impair size constancy—the transformations across various distances over which environmental information must remain invariant in order to be "directly" perceived as of the same size.

Yet Gibson (1966; 1968) and others who share his views (e.g., Johansson, 1973; and more recently Hebb, in press), make a good case that, in normal adult humans, perception is direct. A series of ingenious experiments has shown that by appropriate manipulations of "information," illusions indistinguishable from the "real" can be created on a screen. The demonstrations are convincing and make it implausible to maintain a solopsistic or purely idealistic position with respect to the physical universe—that nothing but a buzzing blooming confusion characterizes external reality. With respect to the experiments he has devised, Gibson is correct.

Furthermore, if perception is direct, a dilemma for the holographic process would be resolved. When an optical hologram produces an image, a human observer is there to see it. When a neural hologram constructs an image, who is the observer? Where is the "little man" who views the "little man"? Direct perception needs no little men inside the head. Gibson, in fact, (1966) deplores the term image because it calls up the indirectness of the representational process. However, if what we "directly perceive" is a constructed *image* and not the true organization of the external world—and we mistake this perception as veridical—perception would be both direct and constructional.

The question to be answered therefore is by what mechanism can perception be both direct and constructional? A clue to the resolution of this dilemma comes from the Gibson (and Johansson) experiments themselves. Their displays produce the *illusion* of reality. When we know the entire experiment we can label the percept as an illusion, even though we directly experience it. In a similar fashion, the sound coming from the speakers of a stereophonic system is experienced directly. When we manipulate the dials of the system (changing the phase of the interacting, interfering sound waves) so that all of the sound comes from one of the speakers, we say the speaker is the source of the perception. When we manipulate the dials so that the sound emanates from somewhere (e.g. the fireplace) between the speakers, we say that an illusion has been produced—the sound has been projected to the space between the speakers. Perception continues to be direct, but considerable computation is involved in determining the conditions over which the "information" contained in the sound remains invariant. We do not naively assume that the fireplace generates the sound. Despite the directness of the perception, it can be superficially misleading as to the actual characteristics of the physical universe.

The issues appear to be these. Gibson abhors the concept "image." As already noted, he emphasizes the "information" which the environment "affords" the organism. As an ecological theorist, however, Gibson recognizes the importance of the organism in determining what is afforded. He details especially the role of movement and the temporal organization of the organism-environment relationship that results. Still, that organization does *not* consist of the construction of percepts from their elements; rather, the process is one of responding to the invariances in that relationship. Thus, perceptual learning involves progressive differentiation of such invariances, not the association of sensory elements.

The problem for me has been that I agree with all of the positive contributions to conceptualization which Gibson has made, yet find myself in disagreement with his negative views (such as on "images") and his ultimate philosophical position. If, indeed, the organism plays such a major role in the theory of ecological perception, does not this entail a constructional position? Gibson's answer is no, but perhaps this is due to the fact that he (in company with so many psychologists) is basically uninterested in what goes on inside the organism.

What, then, does go on in the perceptual systems that is relevant to this argument? I believe that to answer this question we need to analyze what is ordinarily meant by "image." Different disciplines have very different definitions of this term.

The situation is similar to that which obtained in neurology for almost a century with regard to the representation we call "motor." In that instance, the issue was stated in terms of whether the representation in the motor cortex was punctile or whether in fact movements were represented. A great number of experiments were done. Many of them, using anatomical and discrete electrical stimulation techniques, showed an exquisitely detailed anatomical mapping between cortical points and muscles and even parts of muscles (Chang, Ruch and Ward, 1947). The well known homunculus issued from such studies on man (Penfield and Boldrey, 1937).

But other, more physiologically oriented experiments, provided different results. In these, it was shown that the same electrical stimulation at the same cortical locus would produce *different* movements depending on such other factors as position of the limb, the density of stimulation and the state of the organism (e.g. his respiratory rate). For the most part, one could conceptualize the results as showing that the cortical representation consisted of movements centered on one or another joint (e.g. Phillips, 1965). The controversy was thus engaged — proponents of punctate muscle representation vis à vis the proponents of the representation of movement.

I decided to repeat some of the classical experiments in order to see for myself which view to espouse (reviewed in Pribram, 1971, Chapters 12 and 13). Among the experiments performed was one in which the motor cortex was removed (unilaterally and bilaterally) in monkeys who had been trained to open a rather complex latch box to obtain a peanut reward (Pribram, Kruger, Robinson and Berman, 1955–56). My results in this experiment were, as in all others, the replication of the findings of my predecessors. The latch box was opened, but with considerable clumsiness, thus prolonging the time taken some two- to three-fold.

But the interesting part of the study consisted in taking cinemato-graphic pictures of the monkeys' hands while performing the latch-box task and in their daily movements about the cage. Showing these films in slow motion we were able to establish to our satisfaction that no movement or even sequence of movements was specifically impaired by the motor cortex resections! The deficit appeared to be *task* specific, not muscle or movement specific.

My conclusion was, therefore, that depending on the *level of analysis*, one could speak of the motor representation in the cortex in three ways. Anatomically, the representation was punctate and of *muscles*. Physiologically, the representation consisted of mapping the muscle representation into *movements*, most likely around joints as anchor points. But behavioral analysis showed that these views of the representation were incomplete. No muscles were paralyzed, no movements precluded by total resection of the representation. *Action*, defined as the environmental consequence of movements, was what suffered when motor cortex was removed.

The realization that acts, not just movements of muscles, were represented in the motor systems of the brain accounted for the persistent puzzle of motor equivalences. We all know that we can, though perhaps clumsily, write with our left hands, our teeth or, if necessary, our toes. These muscle systems may never have been exercised to perform such tasks, yet, immediately and without practice, can accomplish at least the rudiment required. In a similar fashion, birds will build nests from a variety of materials and the resulting structure is always a habitable facsimile of a nest.

The problem immediately arose, of course, as to the precise nature of a representation of an act. Obviously there is no "image" of an action to be found in the brain, if by "image" one means specific words or the recognizable configuration of nests. Yet some sort of representation appears to be engaged that allows the generation of words and nests—an image of what is to be achieved, as it were.

The precise composition of images-of-achievement remained a puzzle for many years. The resolution of the problem came from experiments by Bernstein (1967), who made cinematographic records of people hammering nails and performing similar more or less repetitive acts. The films were taken against black backgrounds with the subjects dressed in black leotards. Only joints were made visible by placing white dots over them. The resulting record was a continuous wave form. Bernstein performed a Fourier analysis on these wave forms and was invariably able to predict within a few centimeters the amplitude of the next in the series of movements.

The suggestion from Bernstein's analysis is that a Fourier analysis of the invariant components of motor patterns (and their change over time) is computable and that an image-of-achievement may consist of such computation. Electrophysiological data from unit recordings obtained from the motor cortex have provided preliminary evidence that, in fact, such computations are performed (Evarts, 1967, 1968).

By "motor image," therefore, we mean a punctate muscle-brain connectivity that is mapped into movements over joints in order to process environmental invariants generated by or resulting from those movements. This three-level definition of the motor representation can be helpful in resolving the problems that have become associated with the term "image" in perceptual systems.

In vision, audition and somesthesis (and perhaps, to some extent, in the chemical senses as well) there is a punctate connectivity between receptor surface and cortical representation. This anatomical relationship serves as an *array* over which sensory signals are relayed. At a physiological level of analysis, however, a mapping of the punctate elements of the array into functions occurs. This is accomplished in part by convergences and divergences of pathways, but even more powerfully by networks of lateral interconnectivities, most of which operate by way of slow graded dendritic potentials rather than by nerve impulses propagated in long axons. Thus, in the retina, for instance, no nerve impulses can be recorded from receptors, bipolar or horizontal cells. It is only in the ganglion cell layer, the last stage of retinal processing, that nerve impulses are generated to be conducted in the optic nerve to the brain (reviewed in Pribram, 1971, Chapters 1, 6 and 8). These lateral networks of neurons operating by means of slow graded potentials thus map the punctate receptor-brain connectivities into functional *ambiences*.

By analogy to the motor system, this characterization of the perceptual process is incomplete. Behavioral analysis discerns perceptual constancies, just as this level had to account for motor equivalences. In short, *invariances* are processed over time and these invariances constitute the behaviorally derived aspects of the representation (see e.g. Pribram, 1974b). Ordinarily, an organism's representational processes are called *images* and there is no good reason not to use this term. But it must be clearly kept in mind that the perceptual image, just as the motor image, is more akin to a computation than to a photograph.

I have already presented the evidence that for the visual system at least, this computation (just as in the motor system) is most readily accomplished in the Fourier or some similar domain. The evidence that pattern perception depends on the processing of spatial frequencies has been reviewed. It is, after all, this evidence more than any other that has suggested the holonomic hypothesis of perception.

The perceptual image, so defined, is therefore a representation, a mechanism based on the precise anatomical punctate receptor-cortical connectivity that composes an *array*. This array is operated upon by lateral interconnections that provide the *ambiences* which process the *invariances* in the organism's input. The cortical representations of the percepts go, therefore, beyond the anatomical representations of the receptor surfaces, just as the cortical representation of actions goes beyond the mere anatomical representations of muscles.

It is, of course, a well known tenet of Gestalt psychology that the percept is not the equivalent of the retinal (or other receptor) image. This tenet is based on the facts of constancy (e.g. size) and the observations of illusions. Neurophysiologists, however, have only recently begun to seriously investigate this problem. Thus Horn (Horn, Stechler and Hill, 1972) showed that certain cells in the brainstem (superior colliculus) maintained their firing pattern to an environmental stimulus despite changes in body orientation; and in my laboratory Spinelli (1970b) and also Bridgeman (1972), using somewhat different techniques, demonstrated constancy in the firing pattern of cortical neurons over a range of body and environmental manipulations. Further, neurobehavioral studies have shown that size constancy is impaired when the perivisual and inferior temporal cortex is removed (Humphrey and Weiskrantz, 1969; Ungerleider, 1975).

The fact that the cortex becomes tuned to environmental invariances, rather than just to the retinal image, is borne out dramatically by a hitherto unexplained discrepancy in the results of two experiments. In both experiments, a successful attempt was made to modify the orientation selectivity of the cortical neurons of cats by raising them from birth in environments restricted to either horizontal or vertical stripes. In one experiment (Blakemore, 1974) the kittens were raised in a large cylinder appropriately striped. A collar prevented the animals from seeing parts of their bodies—so they were exposed to only the stripes. However, and this turns out to be critical, the kittens could observe the stripes from a variety of head and eye positions. By contrast, in the other experiment, which was performed in my laboratory (Hirsch and Spinelli, 1970), head and eye turning was prevented from influencing the experiment by tightly fitting goggles onto which the stripes were painted. In both experiments cortical neurons were found to be predominantly tuned to the horizontal or vertical depending on the kitten's environment, although the tuning in Blakemore's experiments appeared to be somewhat more effective. The discrepancy arose when behavioral testing was instituted. Blakemore's kittens were consistently and completely deficient in their ability to follow a bar moving perpendicular to the orientation of the horizontally or vertically striped environment in which they had been raised. In our experiment, Hirsch, despite years of effort using a great number of quantitative tests, could never demonstrate *any* change in visual behavior! The tuning of the cortical cells to the environmental situation which remained invariant across transformations of head and eye turning was behaviorally effective; the tuning of cortical cells to consistent retinal stimulation had no behavioral consequences.

These results are consonant with others obtained in other sensory modes and also help to provide some understanding of how brain processing achieves our perception of an objective world, separated from the receptor surfaces which interface the organism with his environment.

Von Bekesy (1967) has performed a large series of experiments on both auditory and somatosensory perceptions to clarify the conditions that produce projection and other perceptual effects. For example, he has shown that a series of vibrators placed on the forearm will produce a point perception when the phases of the vibrations are appropriately adjusted. Once again, in our laboratory we found that the cortical response to the type of somatosensory stimulation used by Bekesy was consonant with the perception, not with the pattern of physical stimulation of the receptor surface (Dewson, 1964; Lynch, 1971). Further, Bekesy showed that when such vibrators are applied to both forearms, and the subject wears them for awhile, the point perception suddenly leaps into the space between the arms. Other evidence for projection comes from the clinic. An amputated leg can still be perceived as a phantom for years after it has been severed and pickled in a pathologist's jar. A more ordinary experience comes daily to artisans and surgeons who "feel" the environment at the ends of their tools and instruments.

These observations suggest that direct perception is a special case of a more universal experience. When what we perceive is validated through other senses or other knowledge (accumulated over time in a variety of ways, e.g. through linguistic communication—see Gregory, 1966), we claim that perception to be veridical. When validation is lacking or incomplete, we tend to call the perception an illusion and pursue a search for what physical events may be responsible for the illusion. Gibson and his followers are correct, perception is direct. They are wrong if and when they think that this means that a constructional brain process is ruled out or that the percept invariably and directly gives evidence of the physical organization that gives rise to perception.

As noted, there is altogether too much evidence in support of a brain constructional theory of perception. The holonomic model, because of its inclusion of parallel processing and wave interference characteristics, readily handles the data of projection and illusion that make up the evidence for direct perception. The holonomic model also accounts for the "directness" of the perception: holographic images are not located at the holographic plane, but in front or beyond it, away from the construction apparatus and more into the apparently "real," consensually validatable external world.

In the concluding part of this paper, I want, therefore, to explore some questions as to the organization of this external "real" physical world. Unless we know something of consensually validatable "information" that remains invariant across transformations of the input to the brain—and, as we have seen, we cannot rely only on the directness of our perceptual experience for this knowledge—how can we think clearly about what is being perceived? Questions as to the nature of the physical universe lie in the domain of the theoretical physicist. Physics has enjoyed unprecedented successes not only in this century, but in the several preceding ones. Physics ought to know something, therefore, about the universe we perceive. And, of course, it does. However, as we shall shortly see, the structure-distribution problem is as pervasive here as it is in brain function.

The special theory of relativity made it clear that physical laws as conceived in classical mechanics hold only in certain circumscribed contexts. Perceptions of the Brownian "random" movements of small suspended particles, or of the paths of light coming from distances beyond the solar system, strained the classical conceptions to the point where additional concepts applying to a wider range of contexts had to be brought in. As in the case of direct perception, the laws of physics must take into account not only what is perceived but the more extended domain in which the perception occurs. The apparent flatness of the earth we now know as an illusion.

The limitations of classical physics were underscored by research into the microcosm of the atom. The very instruments of perception and even scientific observation itself became suspect as providing only limited, situation related information. Discrepancies appeared, such as an electron being in two places (orbits) at once or at best moving from one place to another faster than the speed of light—the agreed upon maximum velocity of any event. And within the nucleus of the atom matters are worse—a nuclear particle appears to arrive in one location before it has left another. Most of these discrepancies result from the assumption that these particles occupy only a point in space—thus when the equations that relate location to mass or velocity are solved, they lead to infinities. Furthermore, in the atomic universe, happenings take place in jumps—they appear to be quantized, i.e., particulate. Yet, when a small particle such as an electron or a photon of light, passes through a grating and another particle passes through a neighboring grating, the two particles appear to interact as if they were waves, since interference patterns can be recorded on the far side of the gratings. It all depends on the situation in which measurements are made whether the "wavicle" shows its particle or its wave characteristics.

Several approaches to this dilemma of situational specificity have been forwarded. The most popular, known as the Copenhagen solution, suggests that the wave equations (e.g., those of Schroedinger, 1935 and deBroglie, 1964) describe the average probabilities of chance occurrences of particulate events. An earlier solution by Niels Bohr (the "father" of the Copenhagen group, 1966) suggested that particle and wave were irreconcilable complementary aspects of the whole. Heisenberg (1959) extended this suggestion by pointing out that the whole cannot in fact be known because our knowledge is always dependent on the experimental situation in which the observations are made. Von Neumann (1932) added that, given a positivistic operational framework, the whole reality becomes, therefore, not only unknown, but unknowable. Thus, the whole becomes indeterminable because we cannot in any specific situation be certain that what we are observing and measuring reflects "reality." In this sense, as well as from the viewpoint of brain processes, we are always constructing physical reality. The arguments of the quantum physicist and those of the neurophysiologist and psychologist of perception are in this respect identical.

But several theoretical physicists are not satisfied with these solutions or lack of solutions. Feynman (1965), for instance, notes that though we have available most precise and quantitative mathematical descriptions in quantum mechanics, we lack good images of what is taking place. (His own famous diagrams show time flowing backwards in some segments!) DeBroglie, who first proposed wavelike characteristics for the electron, fails to find solace in a probabilistic explanation of the experimental results that led him to make the proposal (1964). And DeBroglie is joined by Schroedinger (1935), who formulated the wave equation in question and especially by Einstein, whose insights led him to remain unconvinced that an unknowable universe, macro- and micro-, was built on the principle of the roulette wheel or the throw of dice.

I share this discomfort with attributing too much to chance because of an experience of my own. In the Museum of Science and Industry in

Chicago, there is a display which demonstrates the composition of a Gaussian probability distribution. Large lead balls are let fall from a tube into an open maze made of a lattice of shelves. The written and auditory explanations of the display emphasize the indeterminate nature of the path of each of the falling balls and provide an excellent introduction to elementary statistics. However, nowhere is mention made of the symmetrical maze through which the balls must fall in order to achieve their probabilistic ending. Having just completed *Plans and the Structure of Behavior* (Miller, Galanter and Pribram, 1960), I was struck by the omission. In fact, students of biology routinely use statistics to discover the orderliness in the processes they are studying. For example, when a measurable entity shows a Gaussian distribution in a population, we immediately look for its heritability. Perhaps the gas laws from which statistics emerged have misled us. A Gaussian distribution reflects symmetrical *structure* and not just the random banging about of particles. Again, the physical reality behind the direct perception may contain surprises.

Moreover, when we obtain a probabilistic curve, we often refer to a distribution of events across a population of such events—e.g. a Gaussian distribution. Could it be that for the physical universe, just as in the case of brain function, structure and distribution mutually interact? After all, the brain is part of the physical universe. For brain function, we found structure to be in the form of program and distribution in the form of holograms. Is the rest of the physical universe built along these lines as well?

David Bohm (1957), initially working with Einstein, has, among others, made some substantial contributions to theoretical physics compatible with this line of reasoning. Bohm points out, as noted above, that the oddities of quantum mechanics derive almost exclusively from the assumption that the particles in question occupy only a point in space. He assumes instead that the "wavicle" occupies a finite space which is structured by subquantal forces akin to electromagnetic and gravitational interactions. These interacting forces display fluctuations—some are linear and account for the wave form characteristics of the space or field. Other interactions are nonlinear (similar to turbulence in fluid systems) and on occasion produce quantal events. In biology, Thom (1972) has developed a mathematics to deal with such occurrences in the morphogenetic field and this mathematics has been applied to perception by Bruter (1974). Thom calls the emergence of quasi-stable structures from turbulent processes "catastrophes." In physics, the quantal structures that result from such catastrophic processes may, therefore, be only partially stable. Thus, they can disappear and reappear nearby in a seemingly random fashion; on the average, however, they would be subject to the more regular oscillations of the subquantal forces. In biology, observations pertaining to the entrainment of oscillatory processes by clocks or temporary dominant foci parallel these concepts. Bohm goes on to point out where in the subquantal domain these events will become manifest: the interactions of high frequency and high energy particles in nuclear reactions, in black bodies, etc. An article in *Scientific American* reviews the contemporary scene in these attempts at a Unified Field Theory in the subquantal domain (Weinberg, 1974).

Bohm (1971, 1973) has reviewed the conceptual development of physics from Aristotelian through Galilean and Newtonian times to modern developments in the quantum mechanics. He points out how much of our image of the physical universe results from the fact that, since Galileo, the opening of new worlds of inquiry in physics has depended on the use of lenses. Lenses have shaped our images and lenses objectify. Thus, we tend to assess external space in terms of objects, things and particulars.

Bohm goes on to suggest that image formation is only one result of optical information processing and proposes that we seriously consider the hologram as providing an additional model for viewing the organization of physical processes. He and his group are now engaged in detailed application of this basic insight to see whether, in fact, a holographic approach can be helpful in solving the problems of high energy nuclear physics. Initial developments have shown promise.

As noted above, the subquantal domain shows striking similarities to holographic organization. Just as in the case for brain processes presented here, Bohm's theoretical formulations retain classical and quantum processes as well as adding the holographic. The holographic state described by wave equations and the particle state described quantally, are part of a more encompassing whole. The parallel holds because the holographic models describe only the deeper levels of the theory which is thus holonomic, rather than holographic, as we found it to be for the special case of brain function (where the deeper level is constituted of pre- and post-synaptic and dendritic potentials and the quantal level, of the nerve impulses generated by these slow potentials).

Bohm relates structural and holographic processes by specifying the differences in their organization. He terms classical and particle organization *explicate* and holographic organization *implicate*. Elsewhere (Pribram, 1976), I have made a parallel distinction for perceptual processes: following Bertrand Russell (1959), I proposed that scientific analysis as we practice it today, begets knowledge of the extrinsic properties (the rules, structures, etc.) of the physical world. My proposal departs from Russell, however, in suggesting that intrinsic properties (which he defines as the stoneness of stones, e.g.) are also knowable—that in fact they are the "ground" in which the extrinsic properties are embedded in order to become realized. Thus artists, artisans and engineers spend most of their time realizing the extrinsic programs, laws and rules of the arts and sciences by grounding them in an appropriate medium. For example, a Brahms symphony can be realized by an orchestra, on sheet music, on a long-playing record or on tape. Each of these realizations comes about after long hours of development of the medium in which the realization occurs. Russell was almost correct in his view that the intrinsic properties of the physical world are unknowable—they have apparently little to do with the more enduring extrinsic properties, show no resemblances amongst themselves and demand considerable know-*how* to replicate.

The sum of these ideas leads to the proposal that the intrinsic properties of the physical universe, their implicate organization, the field, ground or medium in which explicit organizations, extrinsic properties become realized, are multiform. In the extreme, the intrinsic properties, the implicate organization, are holographic. As extrinsic properties become realized, they make the implicate organization become more explicit.

The consequence for this view is a revaluation of what we mean by probabilistic. Until now, the image, the model of statistics, has been indeterminacy. If the above line of reasoning is correct, an alternate view would hold that a random distribution is based on holographic principles and is therefore determined. The uncertainty of occurrence of events is only superficial and is the result of holographic "blurring" which reflects underlying symmetries (much as does the Gaussian distribution in our earlier example) and not just haphazard occurrences. This relation between appearance and reality in the subquantal domain of nuclear physics and its dependence on underlying symmetries (spin) is detailed in the review article in *Scientific American* already referred to (Weinberg, 1974).

A preliminary answer to the question posed at the outset of this section—what is it that we perceive—is, therefore, that we perceive a physical universe not much different in basic organization from that of the brain. This is comforting since the brain is part of the physical universe as well as the organ of perception. It is also comforting to find that the theoretical physicist working from his end and with his tools and data has come to the identical problem (which is, in Gibson's terms, the nature of the information which remains invariant across situations) faced by the neurophysiologist and psychologist interested in perception (Bohm, 1965, Appendix). Though surprising, the fact that at least one renowned theoretical physicist has made a proposal that addresses this common problem in terms similar to those set forth on the basis of an analysis of brain function, is most encouraging. For science is of a piece, and full understanding cannot be restricted to the developments made possible by one discipline alone. This is especially true for perception—where perceiver meets the perceived and the perceived meets the perceiver.

Conclusion

But perhaps the most profound insight gained from holography is the reciprocal relationship between the frequency domain and the image/object domain. A fundamental question that is raised by this duality is whether mind should be conceived only as an emergent property resulting from the interaction of an organism with its environment, or whether mind truly reflects *the* basic organization of the universe (including the organism's brain). Images are mental constructions. They result from processes involving the brain (object), the senses (objects) in their interactions with the environment (considered objectively, i.e., as objects, particles such as photons, electrons, atoms, molecules and the objects of the reality of appearances). Images (one aspect of mind) are thus emergents in any objective, object-i-fying philosophical formulation. But the process of image construction involves a reciprocal stage, a transformation into the frequency (holographic) domain. This domain is characteristic not only of brain processing, as we have seen, but of physical reality as well. Bohm refers to it as the implicate order in which points become enfolded and distributed throughout the domain.

In the implicate, holographic domain the distinction between points becomes blurred, information becomes distributed as in the example of the surface of a pond. What is organism (with its component organs) is no longer sharply distinguished from what lies outside the boundaries of the skin. In the holographic domain each organism represents in some manner the universe and each portion of the universe represents in some manner the organisms within it. Earlier in this paper this was expressed in the statements that the perceptions of an organism could not be understood without an understanding of the nature of the physical universe and that the nature of the physical universe could not be understood without an understanding of the observing perceptual process.

It is, thus, the fact that the holographic domain is reciprocally related to the image/object domain that implies that mental operations (such as mathematics) reflect the basic order of the universe. Of special additional interest is one characteristic of the holographic order. This domain deals with the density of occurrences only; time and space are collapsed in the frequency domain. Therefore, the ordinary boundaries of space and time, locations in space and in time become suspended and must be "read out" when transformations into the object/image domain are effected. In the absence of space-time coordinates, the usual causality upon which most scientific explanation depends must also be suspended. Complementarities, synchronicities, symmetries and dualities must be called upon as explanatory principles.

Scientists are, as yet, only barely acquainted with the implicate holographic order. I believe, however, that it is this order which is being explored experientially by mystics, psychics and others delving in paranormal phenomena. Perhaps if the rules for "tuning-in" on the holographic implicate domain could be made more explicit we could attain that scientific understanding of putative paranormal phenomena that we aim for in conferences such as this. As set out in the introduction, true scientific sharing depends on this base of understanding, not just on proving the reliability of experimental realities. I believe that the paradigm shift in science, occasioned by the insights obtained in quantum physics and carried forward by the holographic model of brain function, will, in fact, provide us with that base of understanding which makes it clear that the world of appearances is but a reciprocal of another reality, a reality that may already have been explored experientially for untold millennia.

BIBLIOGRAPHY

Baron, R. J., "A Model for cortical memory," *J. of Mathematical Psychology*, 1970, 7:37–59.

Bekesy, G. von., *Sensory Inhibition*, Princeton: Princeton University Press, 1967.

Bernstein, N., *The Co-ordination and Regulation of Movements*, New York: Pergamon Press, 1967.

Beurle, R. L., "Properties of a mass of cells capable of regenerating pulses," *Philosophical Transactions of the Royal Society of London*, Ser. B., 1956, 240, 55–94.

Blakemore, C., "Developmental factors in the formation of feature extracting neurons," in F. O. Schmitt and F. G. Worden (Eds.) *The Neurosciences Third Study Program*, Cambridge: The MIT Press, 1974, pp. 105–113.

Bohm, D., *Causality and Chance in Modern Physics*, Philadelphia: University of Pennsylvania Press, 1957.

Bohm, D., *The Special Theory of Relativity*, New York: W. A. Benjamin, 1965.

Bohm, D., "Quantum theory as an indication of a new order in physics. Part A. The development of new orders as shown through the history of physics," *Foundations of Physics*, 1(4): 359–381, 1971.

Bohm, D., "Quantum theory as an indication of a new order in physics. Part B. Implicate and explicate order in physical law," *Foundations of Physics*, 3(2): 139–168, 1973.

Bohr, N., *Atomic Physics and Human Knowledge*, New York: Vintage Press, 1966.

Bracewell, R., *The Fourier Transform and its Applications*, New York: McGraw-Hill, 1965.

Bridgeman, B., "Visual receptive fields sensitive to absolute and relative motion during tracking," *Science, 178*:1106–1108, 1972.

Bruter, C. P., *Topologie et Perception*, Paris: Doin-Maloine S. A., 1974.

Campbell, F. W., "The transmission of spatial information through the visual system," in F. O. Schmitt and F. G. Worden (Eds.) *The Neurosciences Third Study Progam*, Cambridge, Mass.: The MIT Press, 1974, pp. 95–103.

Cavanagh, J. P., "Holographic processes realizable in the neural realm: Prediction of short-term memory and performance," unpublished doctoral dissertation, Carnegie-Mellon University, 1972.

Chang, H. T., Ruch, T. C. and Ward, A. A., Jr., "Topographical representation of muscles in motor cortex in monkeys," *J. Neurophysiol., 10*: 39–56, 1947.

Collier, R. J., Burckhardt, C. B. and Lin, L. H., *Optical Holography*, New York: Academic Press, 1971.

Creutzfeldt, O. D., "General physiology of cortical neurons and neuronal information in the visual system," in M. B. A. Brazier (Ed.,) *Brain and Behavior*, Washington, D.C.: American Inst. of Biological Sciences, 1961.

de Broglie, L., *The Current Interpretation of Wave Mechanisms: A Critical Study*, Amsterdam: Elsevier, 1964.

De Valois, R. L., Albrecht, D. G. and Thorell, L. G., "Spatial tuning of LGN and cortical cells in monkey visual system," in H. Spekreijse (Ed.,) *Spatial Contrast*, Amsterdam: Monograph Series, Royal Netherlands Academy of Sciences, 1978.

De Valois, R. L., Albrecht, D. G. and Thorell, L. G., "Cortical cells: Line and edge detectors, or spatial frequency filters?" in S. Cool (Ed.,) *Frontiers of Visual Science*, New York: Springer-Verlag, 1978.

Dewson, J. H. III., "Cortical responses to patterns of two-point cutaneous stimulation," *J. Comp. Physiol. Psychol.*, 58:387–389, 1964.

Evarts, E. V., "Representation of movements and muscles by pyramidal tract neurons of the precentral motor cortex," in M. D. Yahr and D. P. Purpura (Eds.,) *Neurophysiological Basis of Normal and Abnormal Motor Activities*, New York: Raven Press, 1967, pp. 215–254.

Evarts, E. V., "Relation of pyramidal tract activity to force exerted during voluntary movement," *J. Neurophysiol.*, 31:14–27, 1968.

Feynman, R. P., Leighton, R. B. and Sands, M., (Eds.,) *The Feynman Lectures on Physics. Quantum Mechanics, Vol. III*, Reading, Massachusetts: Addison-Wesley Pub. Co., 1965.

Gabor, D., "A new microscopic principle," *Nature*, 1948, *161*, 777–778.

Gibson, J. J., *The Senses Considered as Perceptual Systems*, Boston: Houghton-Mifflin Co., 1966.

Gibson, J. J., "What gives rise to the perception of motion?" *Psychological Review*, 75(4):335–346, 1968.

Glezer, V. D., Ivanoff, V. A. and Tscherbach, T. A., "Investigation of complex and hypercomplex receptive fields of visual cortex of the cat as spatial frequency filters," *Vision Res.*, 1973, *13*, 1875–1904.

Goldscheider, A., "Uber die materiellen Veranderungen bei der Assoziationsbildung," *Neurol. Zentralblatt*, 1906, *25*, 146.

Goodman, J. W., *Introduction to Fourier Optics*, San Francisco: McGraw-Hill, 1968.

Gregory, R. L., *Eye and Brain*, New York: McGraw-Hill, 1966.

Hammond, P., "Spatial organization of receptive fields of LGN neurons," *J. Physiol.*, 1972, *222*, 53–54.

Hartline, H. K., Wagner, H. G. and Ratliff, F., "Inhibition in the eye of limulus," *J. Gen. Physiol.*, 1956, *39*, 651–673.

Hebb, D. O., "To know your own mind," in *Images, Perception and Knowledge Symposium*, The University of Western Ontario (in press, 1978).

Heisenberg, W., *Physics and Philosophy*, London: G. Allen and Unwin, 1959.

Hirsch, H. and Spinelli, D. N., "Distribution of receptive field orientation: modification contingent on conditions of visual experience," *Science*, *168*:869–871, 1970.

Hoffman, K. P. and Stone, J., "Conduction velocity of afferents to cat visual cortex: A correlation with cortical receptive field properties," *Brain, Res.*, 1971, *32*, 460–466.

Horn, G., Stechler, G. and Hill, R. M., "Receptive field units in the visual cortex of the cat in the presence and absence of bodily tilt," *Exp. Brain Res.*, *15*: 113–132, 1972.

Horton, L. H., *Dissertation on the Dream Problem*, Philadelphia: Cartesian Research Society of Philadelphia, 1925.

Humphrey, N. K. and Wesikrantz, L., "Size constancy in monkeys with inferotemporal lesions," *Quarterly J. Exp. Psychology*, *21*:225–238, 1969.

Hubel, D. H. and Wiesel, T. N., "Receptive fields and functional architecture of monkey striate cortex," *J. Physiol.*, 1968, *195*, 215–243.

Johansson, G., "Visual perception of biological motion and a model for its analysis," *Perception and Psychophysics*, 1973, *14*(2): 201–211.

Julesz, B. and Pennington, K. S., "Equidistributed information mapping: An analogy to holograms and memory," *J. Opt. Soc. Am.*, 1965, *55*, 605.

Kabrisky, M., *A Proposed Model for Visual Information Processing in the Human Brain*, Urbana: University of Illinois Press, 1966.

Kuffler, S. W., "Discharge patterns and functional organizations of mammalian retina," *J. Neurophysiol.*, 1953, *16*, 37–69.

Lashley, K. S., "The problem of cerebral organization in vision," in *Biological Symposia, Vol. 7. Visual Mechanisms*. Lancaster, Pa.: Jacques Catell Press, 1942.

Lashley, K. S., "Continuity theory of discriminative learning," in F. A. Beach, D. O. Hebb, C. T. Morgan and H. W. Nissen (Eds.,) *The Neuropsychology of Lashley*, New York: McGraw-Hill, 1960, pp. 421–431.

Leith, E. N., "White-light holograms," *Scientific American*, 1976, *235*(4), 80–81.

Leith, E. N. and Upatnicks, J., "Photography by laser," *Scientific American*, 1965, *212*(6), 24–35.

Loeb, J., *Comparative Physiology of the Brain and Comparative Psychology*, Science Series, New York: Putnam, 1907.

Lynch, J. C., "A single unit analysis of contour enhancement in the somesthetic system of the cat," Ph.D. thesis, Stanford University, Neurological Sciences, 1971.

Maffei, L. and Fiorentini, A., "The visual cortex as a spatial frequency analyzer," *Vision Res.*, 1973, *13*, 1255–1267.

Miller, G. A., Galanter, E. H. and Pribram, K. H., *Plans and the Structure of Behavior*, New York: Henry Holt & Co., 1960.

Mountcastle, V. B., "Modality and topographic properties of single neurons of cat's somatic sensory cortex," *J. Neurophysiol.*, 1957, *20*, 408–434.

Movshon, J. A., Thompson, I. D. and Tolhurst, D. J., "Spatial summation in the receptive field of simple cells in the cat's striate cortex," *J. of Physiology*, (in press).

Movshon, J. A., Thompson, I. D. and Tolhurst, D. J., "Receptive field organization of complex cells in the cat's striate cortex," *J. of Physiology*, (in press).

Movshon, J. A., Thompson, I. D. and Tolhurst, D.J., "Spatial and temporal contrast sensitivity of cells in the cat's areas 17 and 18," *J. of Physiology*, (in press).

Penfield, W. and Boldrey, E., "Somatic motor and sensory representation in the cerebral cortex of man as studied by electrical stimulation," *Brain*, *60*, 389–443, 1937.

Phillips, C. G., "Changing concepts of the precentral motor area," in J. C. Eccles (Ed.,) *Brain and Conscious Experience*, New York: Springer-Verlag, 1965, pp. 389–421.

Pollen, D. A., "Striate cortex and the reconstruction of visual space," in *The Neurosciences Study Program, III*, Cambridge, Mass.: MIT Press, 1973.

Pollen, D. A., Lee, J. R. and Taylor, J. H., "How does the striate cortex begin the reconstruction of the visual world?" *Science*, 1971, *173*, 74–77.

Pollen, D. A. and Taylor, J. H., "The striate cortex and the spatial analysis of visual space," in *The Neurosciences Study Program, III*, Cambridge, Mass.: The MIT Press, 1974, pp. 239–247.

Pribram, K. H., "Some dimensions of remembering: Steps toward a neuropsychological model of memory," in J. Gaito (Ed.) *Macromolecules and Behavior*, New York: Academic Press, 1966, pp. 165–187.

Pribram, K. H., *Languages of the Brain*, Englewood Cliffs, N.J.: Prentice-Hall, 1971.

Pribram, K. H., "How is it that sensing so much we can do so little?" in *The Neurosciences Study Program, III*, Cambridge, Mass.: The MIT Press, 1974, pp. 249–261. (a)

Pribram, K. H., "The isocortex," in D. A. Hamburg and H. K. H. Brodie (Eds.,)*American Handbook of Psychiatry, Vol. 6.* New York: Basic Books, 1974 (b).

Pribram, K. H., "Problems concerning the structure of consciousness," in G. Globus, G. Maxwell and I. Savodnick (Eds.,) *Consciousness and Brain: A Scientific and Philosophical Inquiry*, New York: Plenum Press, 1976, pp. 297–313.

Pribram, K. H., Kruger, L., Robinson, R. and Berman, A. J., "The effects of precentral lesions on the behavior of monkeys,"*Yale J. Biol. and Med.*, 28:428–443, 1955–56.

Pribram, K. H., Lassonde, M. C. and Ptito, M., "Intracerebral influences on the microstructure of visual cortex: I. Classification of receptive field properties" (in preparation).

Pribram, K. H., Nuwer, M. and Baron, R., "The holographic hypothesis of memory structure in brain function and perception," in R. C. Atkinson, D. H. Krantz, R. C. Luce and P. Suppes (Eds.,) *Contemporary Developments in Mathematical Psychology*, San Francisco: W. H. Freeman and Co., 1974, pp. 416–467.

Ratliff, F., *Mach. bands: Quantitative Studies in Neural Networks in the Retina*, San Francisco: Holden-Day, 1965.

Robson, J. G., "Receptive fields: Neural representation of the spatial and intensive attributes of the visual image," in E. C. Carterette (Ed.), *Handbook of Perception, Vol. V. Seeing*, New York: Academic Press, 1975.

Rodieck, R. W., "Quantitative analysis of cat retinal ganglion cell response to visual stimuli," *Vision Res.*, 1965, 5, 583–601.

Rosenblatt, F., *Principles of Neurodynamics: Perceptions and the Theory of Brain Mechanism*, Washington, D.C.: Spartan Books, 1962.

Russell, B., *My Philosophical Development*, New York: Simon and Schuster, 1959.

Schiller, P. H., Finlay, B. L. and Volman, S. F., "Quantitative studies of single-cell properties in monkey striate cortex. I. Spatiotemporal organization of receptive fields," *J. Neurophysiol.*, 1976, 39, 1288–1319.

Schiller, P. H., Finlay, B. L. and Volman, S. F., "Quantitative studies of single-cell properties in monkey striate cortex. II. Orientation specificity and ocular dominance," *J. Neurophysiol.*, 1976, 39, 1320–1333.

Schiller, P. H., Finlay, B. L. and Volman, S. F., "Quantitative studies of single-cell properties in monkey striate cortex. III. Spatial frequency," *J. Neurophysiol.*, 1976, 39, 1334–1351.

Schiller, P. H., Finlay, B. L. and Volman, S. F., "Quantitative studies of single-cell properties in monkey striate cortex. V. Multivariate statistical analyses and models," *J. Neurophysiol.*, 1976, 39, 1362–1374.

Schroedinger, E., "Discussion of probability relations between separated systems," *Proceedings of the Cambridge Philosophical Society*, 1935, 31:555–563.

Spinelli, D. N., "Occam, a content addressable memory model for the brain," in K. H. Pribram and D. Broadbent (Eds.,) *The Biology of Memory*, New York: Academic Press, 1970. (a)

Spinelli, D. N. and Pribram, K. H., "Changes in visual recovery function and unit activity produced by frontal and temporal cortex stimulation," *Electroenceph. Clin. Neurophysiol.*, 1967, 22, 143–149.

Stroke, G. W., *An Introduction to Coherent Optics and Holography*, New York: Academic Press, 1966.

Talbot, S. A. and Marshall, U. H., "Physiological studies on neural mechanisms of visual localization and discrimination," *Amer. J. Ophthal.*, 1941, 24, 1255–1264.

Thom, R., *Stabilité Structurelle et Morphogenese*, Reading, Mass.: W. A. Benjamin, Inc., 1972.

Ungerleider, L., "Deficits in size constancy discrimination: Further evidence for dissociation between monkeys with inferotemporal and prestriate lesions," Paper presented at the Eastern Psychological Association Convention, April, 1975.

van Heerden, P. J., "A new method for storing and retrieving information," *Applied Optics*, 1963, *2*, 387–392.

von Neumann, J. *Mathematische Grundlagen der Quantenmechanik*, Berlin: Springer-Verlag, 1932.

Weinberg, S., "Unified theories of elementary-particle interaction," *Scientific American*, 231(1):50–59, 1974.

Weiss, P., *Principles of Development*, New York: Holt, 1939.

Werblin, F. S. and Dowling, J. E., "Organization of the retina of the mud puppy Necturus maculosus, II. Intracellular recording," *J. Neurophysiol.*, 1969, *32*, 339–355.

Werner, G., "The topology of the body representation in the somatic afferent pathway," in *The Neurosciences Study Program, II*, New York: Rockefeller University Press, 1970.

Westlake, P. R., "Towards a theory of brain functioning: A detailed investigation of the possibilities of neural holographic processes," Unpublished doctoral dissertation, University of California, Los Angeles, 1968.

DISCUSSION

BELOFF: I'm going to start with a very simple point, because I get lost in anything more than just the simple parts of the exposition. You began by talking about the holographic theory of memory. As a psychologist, one point that has always worried me about this theory since I first came across it is that it's always been assumed by psychologists, certainly since the work of Frederic Bartlett, that memories are never a literal reproduction of past experiences. Yet, when I think about your hologram analogy, I can see how it would work very nicely for reconstructing an image exactly as it was originally presented. But I can't quite see how you are going to account for all the kinds of distortions and errors that human memory reveals.

PRIBRAM: I puzzled about this a great deal, because I don't know that the facts are. We know what Sir Frederic Bartlett came up with, but then there are also people who come up with veridical memories—Mimi Strohmeyer, for instance, is one person who was mentioned yesterday who has eidetic imagery and she, for instance, can tell the difference between ordinary memory and eidetic memory. The holographic store when tapped directly produces eidetic imagery. When retrieval mechanisms intervene, the dismembered holographic store becomes re-membered and distortions can take place.

McGUINNESS: Would you expand the philosophical point of view in connection with interference patterns and holograms? Are our brains responsible for space and time? Would space and time exist without brains?

PRIBRAM: That's an important question. First of all, we know that events are stored in a spaceless and timeless fashion in our brain. I've given this talk in a variety of ways; sometimes it takes two hours. Today I did it in half an hour. It's all in my head packed together, and how it comes out is a matter of programming it out. That's why the computer analogy of retrieval is so helpful, because it tells us about how we can sequence our behavior. If things are packed this way in our heads, what produces time and space? It is not the right and left hemispheres, as was suggested yesterday. We cannot take these two things apart in that way. If, in fact, storage is organized as a hologram, we then retrieve time and space by moving with respect to our input. According to evolutionary theory, we have pretty well adapted to an environment which is constituted much as it appears to be: there are organisms that are moving with respect to each other, etc. However, there is no way of knowing whether *we* are constructing the images of objects and their movement, because our brain organization has evolved to match such an environment, or whether we are simply constructed in this fashion. For instance, in our laboratory we have shown that the cells in the brain react to visual white noise exactly as they do to a line. Thus, we don't know whether what we see is the result of built in brain machinery and that therefore the world of appearances is simply an artifact of the way we're built, or whether the way we're built is the result of the way the world of appearances has shaped us. The same problem faces physicists at this point. Wigner noted that physicists are now dealing with relations among observations, and no longer with relations among observables. So we cannot tell whether it's our instrumentation that's producing the results, or whether they are "really there."

HONORTON: I don't see how you have a scientific explanation here. I don't see how you're solving the mind/brain problem any more than Popper and Eccles are. It seems to me that you're calling the mystery by another name and providing an "explanation," at this stage at least, that to me is not obvious in terms of what its scientific implications are for further research. By analogy with this, is mind the background film on which all this is displayed, or what?

PRIBRAM: What I'm saying is that we must transcend dualism *and* understand it. There are two positions that Popper and Eccles have confounded. One states that the brain is a generator, or, using the words that we used yesterday, mind is an emergent property of behaving organisms. The other is a pan-psychic notion of mind, an extended mind, if you will, which operates *on* the brain. Mystics see conscious mind as being everywhere. Similarly, in a holographic reality, there are no boundaries. I'm suggesting that, in fact, when people have mystical experiences they tune in on this particular aspect of the duality. Since we can easily go back and forth between these two realities mathematically, perhaps there are ways in which organisms also go back and forth between the two.

You want to know what kind of experiments are to be done. Obviously, there are experiments on paranormal phenomena. Other types of experiments could be done at the quantum level in physics to find out whether in fact quarks "exist." Are quarks nothing more than nodes in a holographic matrix? Physicists are aware of such a possibility—that's why they have colors and flavors for quarks to remind us of the subjective element in their definition.

RUDOLPH: I have a comment and a question. The comment concerns the work of Lawrence LeShan on the Clairvoyant Reality versus the Sensory Reality. I've considered the possibility that these realities might, in some sense, be Fourier transforms of one another and this point of view seems to work. Because of the relationship between holography and Fourier transforms, I think this may be related to your work. My question is this. If the left brain/right brain dichotomy doesn't correspond to time and space, and it seems reasonable to me that it doesn't, does it perhaps correspond to the two transform domains?

PRIBRAM: No. I think we're trying to make too much of the left and right brain dichotomy and simply impose it on every dichotomy that exists to see if it fits. If we must oversimplify let us say that the right brain essentially is a visual brain, it makes visual images. The left brain is an auditory one and make auditory images. Now, when the auditory system begins to pull in more sequential properties, the visual system pulls in more spatial relationships and so the two hemispheres get to have somewhat different properties. But one must have holographic memory on the left as well as on the right side. Else how could we remember what to say?

DIXON: Some people have espoused an RNA theory of memory, which is another "distributed" theory of memory. It seems to me, thinking about it now, that this is not inconsistent with your hologram. What do you feel about that?

PRIBRAM: It can't be RNA *per se*, because RNA doesn't last long enough, but it certainly can be RNA producing some change in a protein molecule. If we're going to have anything permanent, we must change the conformation of a protein, but the techniques are not far enough advanced as yet to study such conformational changes in the brain.

DIXON: So that could be the physical basis of the hologram, possibly?

PRIBRAM: Right. If I'm right that memory is holographically encoded, we need to find out whether storage is in terms of the square of the intensity of the input rather than just the intensity itself. That would be all that would be necessary—that, and to maintain the phase of neighboring relationships. Perhaps this sort of experiment can be done on invertebrates, but most likely it needs to be explored in a brain where there is some sort of cortex. Such experiments can be outlined right now, as suggestions of what we might do once the techniques in chemistry become available.

OLMEDO: You seem to imply that your hologram fits moment to moment, although that may not be the fact in reference to the reality we perceive—how I perceive you now, how I perceive my neighbors. How is it that I can perhaps have an experience over which I have no control of how my brain would perceive you at that moment?

PRIBRAM: One of the ways I like to express this is that the *Veda*, which was written anywhere from ten to eight thousand years ago, has many of the illuminations that we're only learning about now in modern physics and modern biology. How did these ancients get hold of all this knowledge? Perhaps they just tuned in on all of our findings and plagiarized them. We do all the work in the here and now and they tune in ten thousand years ago on what we're going to find out next year. That's a facetious way of putting it, but it gets across the point.

EHRENWALD: I'm overawed by the vistas opened up by this discussion and by Pribram's holographic image of the world. It seems to be a new revolutionary paradigm. But let me remind you that paradigms have changed over the millenia and so have theories about brain/mind relationships. There was the Greek pneumatic notion of the soul. It was replaced, let's say, by the hydraulic paradigm of Freud's metapsychology.

PRIBRAM: Freud did not have any hydraulic imagery whatsoever. It was electric. I published a book a year ago on Freud's "Project." There is no hydraulic imagery in it. He tries to come up with an Ohm's law of the nervous system. It's all electric. The English translations are so poor that they have made it sound as though Freud's model were a hydraulic, because the translators knew no neurology. We mustn't do Freud in. He was a great neurologist and knew that the nervous system did not work by way of water pumps.

EHRENWALD: Whether we call it hydraulic or electric, we have in any case a different paradigm proposed by psychoanalysts. It grew into Freud's metapsychology and it is a distinctly hydraulic metaphor. Freud's "Project" was later abandoned because it did not go far enough. It was replaced by the metaphor of the brain as a giant telephone switchboard and later transformed into the metaphor of the computerized brain. Today we have Dr. Pribram's holographic metaphor. It is certainly a revolutionary new paradigm, telling us that the individual—or the homunculus—who ultimately reads the computer printouts is no longer necessary, that he can be dismissed. Yet I submit that this is a kind of epistemological sleight of hand because the homunculus goes only into hiding if and when we go into nirvana, into an egoless mystical state of mind. But as soon as we return, it is he or I or the homunculus or the son of homunculus who sneaks in through the backdoor, as it were, and the individual, or Eccles' "self-conscious mind," is back and tries to be in control again. After dismissing Cartesian dualism we are back where we started. As a result of an existential shift, when we shift from the clairvoyant reality or the psi form of reality to the here and now reality, the ego is again back in command and this is how we are communicating with one another. I think that the holographic imagery is extremely helpful, but does not do away with the ultimate questions which you can formulate in different forms—religious, epistemological, or otherwise.

PRIBRAM: I would only point out that it is no longer a metaphor. I gave you a brief account for the evidence that the brain does, in fact, work like this. Freud's "Project" does contain passages which clearly suggest that the cortex is a frequency analyzer; he calls it an analyzer of periodicities. The model has not changed from 1895 till now. I think the insights given by the data that we have now must be appreciated as being really revolutionary, but not in any sense that these insights have not been had before. Leibnitz, the inventor of the mathematics that Gabor used to invent the hologram for which he received the Nobel Prize—Leibnitz had this insight several centuries earlier. But we've attained more and more precision in these insights, and what we used to talk about as mystical, paranormal, etc., now falls within the purview of science. We now have available a science to deal with these phenomena.

AN EMERGENT-INTERACTIONIST UNDERSTANDING OF HUMAN CONSCIOUSNESS

CHARLES T. TART

Throughout my career I have been interested in a range of phenomena I usually group under the heading of states of consciousness, phenomena dealing with the fascinating, multitudinous changes that can take place in people's mode of experience. While changes in the manifestations of consciousness can be studied without asking any fundamental questions about the nature of consciousness, so avoiding dilemmas that have puzzled philosophers through the ages, I have, nevertheless, always been curious as to the ultimate nature of consciousness, and I have found parapsychological phenomena to be of extreme value in pointing the direction of an answer to that question. What I shall share with you today is the beginnings of a scientific approach to understanding the basic nature of consciousness, an approach that I call *Emergent Interactionism*, an approach that would be classified philosophically as dualistic, and yet has empirical consequences and so can be classified as scientific. I do not lay any great claim to originality in this approach, as I have drawn on multitudinous sources for the basic ideas, but I hope the particular way I have put these ideas together will be useful in understanding human consciousness. I shall also apologize in advance for the crudeness and gaps in these formulations, for, while I have touched on these ideas for years, this is my first attempt to express them more systematically.

My observational base for trying to understand consciousness begins with my own experience, which is then expanded by my experiences of the world and others about me. Perhaps the most striking thing about my own experience is the obviously different nature of my consciousness from the physical world about me. Despite difficulties in knowing precisely how to think it or express it, it is simply a given that there is something fundamentally different about the experiences I call my mental processes from what I call the external world. This basic distinction has been drawn by multitudes of others, and in formal philosophy has been called a dualistic position, a formal postulation of some fundamentally different qualities of mind and matter, such that the nature of one cannot be adequately explained by or reduced to the other.

I have had no formal training in philosophy, but at times I have attempted to study philosophical literature on the nature of consciousness, and, I must admit, I have always come away baffled and disappointed. Once the basic distinction between mind and matter is postulated, I get the feeling that most philosophers restrict themselves to playing word games, dealing with purely semantic distinctions, and end up with a dualistic position that might or might not be true; but the truth or falsity of that dualism does not seem to have any useful experimental or experiential consequences that I can discern. I am not comfortable with making a distinction that has no consequences, and I am strongly committed to the kind of scientific pragmatism that says observable consequences (whether physical or experiential) have priority over intellectual formulations.

Monistic Views

In terms of acceptance by the intellectual and scientific community, monistic philosophies, which postulate that mind and matter are basically manifestations of the same thing, that they are *totally* reducible to one another, are the accepted philosophies. This is particularly so in orthodox science. Figure 1 for example, taken from my *States of Consciousness* book (Tart, 1975a), diagrams the widely accepted scientific view of consciousness, what I have called the "orthodox" or scientifically conservative view of the mind. The basic reality that is being dealt with in this diagram is physical reality, fixed physical reality, immutable laws. As a result of these laws a particular physical system comes into existence, the brain and its associated nervous system and body (which I shall just refer to as brain for short for the rest of this paper). Many aspects of this brain are fixed in their functioning: instructions for your kidneys to work, for example, are encoded in the physical structure of the brain and ordinarily never changed. This physical structure also has many programmable capacities, so our culture, our language, the various events of our personal history, and our interactions with physical reality teach us a language, a way of thinking, values, and mores, etc. This large computer-like physical structure then functions in a wide variety of complex ways. At any given moment we are aware of only a small fraction of the total functioning of it, and this tiny fraction of physical functioning that we are aware of is consciousness as we experience it.

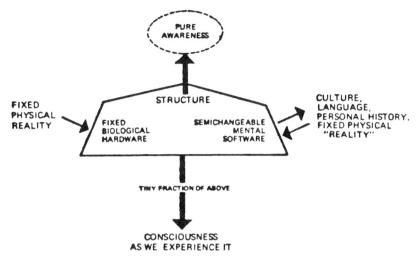

Figure 1. An orthodox, monistic representation of the nature of human consciousness. Reproduced from C. Tart, *States of Consciousness*, Dutton, 1975, by permission of the publisher.

In presenting this model I have added something called "pure awareness" in the upper part of it, which can refer in a general way for our context here to those feelings of mental activity which do not seem tied to obvious bodily functioning, such as certain meditative experiences or various altered states experiences. More formally, I have used the term pure awareness to mean that raw proto-experience of knowing that *something* is happening before that experience gets highly elaborated and articulated into semantic categories where it has obviously been influenced by brain structure. In the figure, I show pure awareness as "emerging" from the physical structure of the brain. That is, this is a representation of the monistic *psychoneural identity hypothesis*, which says that while we might find it convenient to distinguish certain types of mental activity for semantic purposes, all experience is, in principle, completely reducible to physical activity within the brain. In practice we are a long way from being able to carry out this reduction due to the sheer complexity of the brain, but in principle the orthodox scientific view believes this is possible.

The psychoneural identity approach is clearly a useful scientific approach, for it has observable consequences. It predicts, for example, that a physiological correlate of any and every kind of experience can ultimately be found. It further predicts that no experiences can occur in reality that violate the basic physical laws and system operation laws that govern the operation of the brain, although the brain may produce *illusory* experiences that seem to violate basic physical laws.

Complexity

In mentioning laws governing systems operation, I am reminded of the other disappointment I have always had with formal philosophical writings on the nature of consciousness. That is their typical obsession with an absolutistic understanding of simple mental events, when it has always been obvious to me that consciousness represents an *exceptionally* complex *system*, not a simple mechanism. Probably, my early experience in working with electronic systems, where alterations in one component can have many effects on the whole system operation, effects which are often not at all obviously predictable beforehand, sensitized me to this issue. Modern brain theory now recognizes the complexity of the brain and nervous system. Starting from a simplistic approach that likened each neural junction to a relay and thought the complexity of brain function could be handled by a simple additive operation of all these individual relay operations, modern understandings of the brain are increasingly looking to general systems theory to provide general laws about *emergent* properties of brain functioning, properties that are holistic outcomes of total system operation rather than simple linear additions of more basic subsystem elements. The Emergent Interactionism approach to understanding consciousness that I shall outline here tries to take this complexity, these emergent system properties of brain functioning (and, as we shall see, of mind functioning) into account, as well as dealing with the fundamental experience of a dualistic difference between experience and the physical world.

As a final introductory note, I should say that if I had to characterize my philosophical bias it is to be pragmatic. As a scientist, I am committed to the proposition that data, that experience, is primary, and our conceptualizations, our theories about the meaning of that data are secondary. If I cannot adequately or logically express my experience that is a shortcoming of my philosophy or grammar, not an invalidation of my experience. Theories must always be adjusted to account for the data, and theories must have consequences in terms of observable data. If my theory has no testable consequences, it may be intellectually interesting, but it is not scientifically worthwhile. I believe that the dualistic theory of consciousness I shall now present has such testable consequences and so forms the basis of a scientific set of theories about consciousness.

An aspect of this pragmatism is that I do not want to get into the kind of absolutism that marks philosophical discourse. I have no way to satisfactorily define concepts like mind versus matter or mind versus brain in any kind of absolute fashion. If I say that something is mental or nonmaterial, what I am saying is that that something seems to have observable or experiencable properties which cannot be adequately explained in terms of our current understanding of the physical world, or reasonable extrapolations of that understanding. It is quite possible that future advances at the cutting edge of physics will drastically change our conception of what is and is not "physical," and what can and cannot be handled within a physical explanatory system. Thus, in distinguishing mind and brain, I am doing no more than making distinctions which are pragmatically useful at present, regardless of their absolute validity.

Paraconceptual Phenomena

The basic support for my dualistic approach to understanding consciousness comes from the excellent scientific evidence for the existence of certain "paranormal" phenomena. Given our current understanding of the physical world, it is possible to talk about isolating or shielding one event from another so that no known, feasible form of information transfer channel exists between these two isolated events. If we now make physical observations, either the behaviors of people or the readings of physical instruments, which indicate that an information or energy transfer has nevertheless occurred between two isolated events, we have a paranormal or, more appropriately, a para*conceptual* event. We have an observation that cannot be satisfactorily explained by our theories. Since the majority of the population in America believe they have experienced some kinds of psi, (Greeley, 1975), these events are hardly para*normal*, beyond the norm, but they are certainly paraconceptual to the orthodox, current scientific view of how the physical universe works.

While there have been many types of observations reported on purported paraconceptual events, we have only had extensive experimental work on four kinds of experimental situations, leading us to postulate the existence of four basic types of paraconceptual events, namely telepathy, clairvoyance, precognition, and psychokinesis (PK), collectively referred to as psi events. There are dozens of experimental reports supporting the existence of each of these kinds of effects. Typically, we define telepathy as mind to mind communication, clairvoyance as matter to mind communication or sensing the physical state of affairs directly with the mind, precognition as predicting a future state of events (that we might further subdivide into precognitive telepathy or precognitive clairvoyance), and psychokinesis as directly effecting a state of physical events simply by wishing for it. These conventional types of definitions have an implicit dualism in them, so we could be more formal and distinguish the above four phenomena simply by the kinds of experimental operations by which they have been established. Thus, telepathy becomes a matter of a percipient making a behavioral response that is supposed to relate to what is in someone else's mind (as judged by his behavior), clairvoyance as perception of a physical event that is not in anyone's mind (as fixed by the experimental situation) at the time the percipient makes his responses, etc. We know, of course, that there has been no satisfactory way to absolutely demonstrate the existence of "pure" telepathy, for if you keep a physical record of the target in order to insure objectivity of scoring, then clairvoyance is always possible, even though we have a little evidence for pure telepathy (McMahan, 1946). Nevertheless, these common distinctions are useful.

The existence of these paraconceptual or psi phenomena provides a general basis for arguing that a dualistic view of mind and matter is a useful and *realistic* view; that is, that it reflects the nature of things rather than just being a semantically convenient distinction. The monistic view of mind and matter, the psychoneural identity hypothesis, so widely accepted in science, is one result of a world view that totally denies the existence of psi phenomena as we experimentally know them. The existence of psi phenomena is a clearcut scientific demonstration, however, that our understanding of the nature of a physical world is quite inadequate and will require major revisions. These paraconceptual events demonstrate the incompleteness of the overall conceptual system from which monism is derived. Thus, in a general sense, we can argue that a psychoneural identity position is far from proven, because it rests on an incomplete and, therefore, faulty conceptual system.

Emergent Interactionism

My psychological studies of consciousness and states of consciousness, as well as and especially my parapsychological studies, have forced me to go a step further than this and postulate that experience *and* high quality scientific data basically indicate that mind is of a fundamentally different nature than matter as we know it today, and, more specifically, postulate that certain psi functions are the mechanisms of mind-brain interaction. Consciousness, as we experience it, is an emergent property of this mind-brain interaction. This theory is represented in simplified form in Figure 2.

The physical structure of the brain is represented on the left hand side of Figure 2. We shall not be concerned with its internal structure

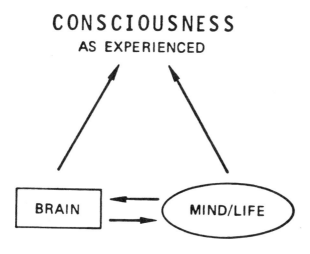

Figure 2. Simplified representation of the Emergent Interactionist position, in which consciousness, as experienced, is an emergent, system property of two basically different component systems interacting via psi.

or inherent system properties for the moment. The dualistic factor I shall begin calling mind/life is represented on the right hand side of the figure. I add the "life" designation to this side of the figure to point out that the "nonphysical" aspect of consciousness is not always a matter of mental *experience*, it includes a general "vitalistic" effect of mind/life that is more basic than conscious experience.

Consciousness, as we ordinarily experience it, is the higher level emergent of the psi interaction of brain and mind/life. To put it more formally, experienced consciousness is a system property, an *emergent*, of the complex interaction of the subsystems of brain on the one hand and the mind/life factor on the other.

The brain is, of course, the link between consciousness and the world about us. Environmental factors are detected through the sense organs and end up as electrical/chemical patterns within the brain. Actions begin as electrical/chemical patterns within the brain and end up as specific impulses to motor apparatus that create our overt behavior. The brain is an ultra-complex and especially interesting structure, however, for while many aspects of brain functioning seem completely determined, such as basic reflexes, many other important aspects seem to be under the control of quasi-random or fully random processes, that is, they are controlled by neurons or neural ensembles that are often almost but-not-quite, ready to fire. My Emergent Interactionism approach postulates that the mind/life factor cognizes important aspects of the state of the brain by means of clairvoyance, that is, that mind/life uses clairvoyance to "read" the brain and thus the state of the body and the body's immediate sensory world. Further, the action of the brain is influenced at critical junctures by PK from mind/life: that is, in addition to self-organizational system properties of its own, there are control functions exerted over the brain by mind/life through psychokinetic modification of brain firing. The holistic emergent of this interaction, the mutual interaction and mutual patterning of brain and mind/life on each other via clairvoyance and PK, leads to an overall pattern of functioning and experience that is consciousness as we experience it. Ordinarily, when we consult our own experience, we do not experience what brain alone is like, or experience what mind alone is like; we experience the emergent from their interaction, for which I use the term consciousness.

Having sketched the basic postulates of Emergent Interactionism in terms of "brain," "consciousness," and "mind/life," I must now face the semantic problem that others have used these terms in wider and overlapping ways, as I myself have done in the past. While I could request that you listen to these terms in just the way I define them, it is not that easy to drop lifetime associative patterns, so I shall try to avoid semantic problems by adopting more neutral abbreviations for the remainder of this paper. I shall use the term "B system" to refer to those physical functions of the brain, body, and nervous system that we already understand in physical concepts or expect to understand with straightforward extensions of current physical concepts. I shall use the term "M/L system" for those non-physical (by current and straightforward extensions of current physical concepts) aspects I have been calling mind/life. I shall retain "consciousness," with a reminder that I restrict it to our usual experience of ourselves, not to more exotic experiences. As for the psi interactions, I shall add the prefix auto- to designate psi in general or clairvoyance or PK in particular that is concerned with a person's M/L system interacting with his own B system: thus auto-psi, auto-clairvoyance (auto-CL in later diagrams), and auto-PK. For those cases where psi reaches outside the bounds of the normal B

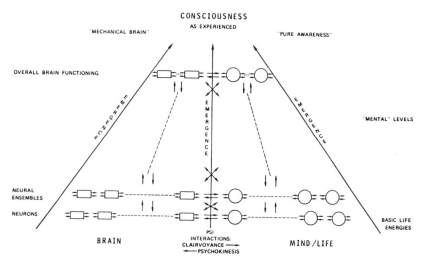

Figure 3. The Emergent Interactionist representation of consciousness.

system and M/L system interrelationship, as when we ask a percipient to tell us, e.g., what the order of a sealed deck of cards is, I shall add the prefix allo-: thus allo-psi in general, or more specifically allo-clairvoyance, allo-PK, allo-telepathy, etc.

Figure 2 was a very general schematic of B system and M/L system interaction and their emergent properties. A more realistic schematic, using just present knowledge, would be of the sort shown in Figure 3. This figure brings in a number of further considerations. First, there are various hierarchical levels of organization in the B system alone, without even beginning to bring the M/L system into the picture. The lowest level shown on the left hand side of the figure would be individual neurons, and while these have properties we are beginning to understand fairly well, they are organized into basic neural ensembles at the next level, so this next systems level has emergent properties. That is, simple neuron ensembles can have properties which are not clearly predicted from those of neurons alone. These level two neuron ensembles are influenced by the lower level properties of neurons, and these level two properties in turn influence level one functioning, thus the arrows representing interaction. Similarly, neuron ensembles are organized into more complex ensembles, etc., up to very high levels of complexity. System, emergent properties occur at all these various levels, as do numerous and complex interactions. It will not be an easy job to understand the B system, especially since the brain alone, without even bringing in the M/L system, is so many orders of magnitude more complex than any well understood present day system, such as computers.

Although we know far more about the B system than the M/L system, I have assumed, on the basis of the symmetry principle (Tart, 1975a, chapter 18) that the M/L system itself is probably a system of many hierarchical levels, and have diagrammed it accordingly on the right. I have avoided putting any labeling on that part of the scheme other than distinguishing the most basic life "energies" at the lowest levels versus more "mental" levels higher up in the system hierarchy. This is a matter of being cautious and not pretending to know more than we do know, but it seems very likely that there are fundamental aspects of the M/L system that interact with each other, produce more complex, emergent system properties, and so on, as with B system processes. All interaction within the M/L system is mediated by some kind of auto-psi, which might or might not be the same kind of psi auto-mediating M/L system and B system interactions. Thus we have an emergence of system properties on the M/L side of the diagram as well as the B system side.

I have shown auto-clairvoyance and auto-PK interactions between the B and M/L systems as potentially occurring between similar hierarchical levels of B and M/L subsystems, as well as potential cross level auto-psi interactions. There is probably no single locus of interaction of auto-clairvoyance and auto-PK between the B and M/L systems, but a variety of interactions occurring at different levels. Lower level auto-psi interactions between B and M/L systems, then, may change the isolated properties of both neural tissue and basic life energies at those lower levels, which in turn are reflected in further interactions and system property emergence in both the B and M/L system levels, further complicating interactions at higher levels.

I regret that this is not the simplistic kind of picture we seem to prefer, but real systems are complex! If one could separate out B system properties alone, one would observe an emergent that I have labeled as "mechanical brain" at the top of the left hand systems hierarchy. Similarly, if one could separate out M/L system properties and functionings without any interactions with brain ones, one would observe something I have called "pure awareness" at the top of the M/L side of the diagram. I suspect that we actually have some data on both of these relatively pure cases, but not in a form we can clearly recognize and make use of. Some meditative practices, for example, or variants of out-of-the-body experiences, lead to experiences which are usually described as "ineffable," that is, they cannot be expressed in terms of the emergent of language which deals with consciousness: these may be instances of isolated M/L system operation.

This has been a basic outline of the Emergent Interactionist position. Let us now consider a variety of topics from this point of view, starting with the psychological factor of automatization.

Automatization

A very important psychological consideration to now introduce into this Emergent Interactionism approach is that of *automatization*, the habitual, automatic way that consciousness seems to function a great deal of the time. Much of this results from the socialization process where various assumptions and habit patterns become implicit. That is, these processes lead to semi-permanent physical modifications in the B system which automatically tend to guide B system functioning (and M/L system interaction) along certain lines, lines which simply seem like the "natural" way of doing things, a process I have discussed at length elsewhere (Tart, 1975a). What this means in terms of the Emergent Interactionism position is that a great deal of information processing, decision making, perception and action may take place in the B system without there necessarily being any auto-psi interaction with the M/L system. The B system, as it were, can do a good many things "on automatic," without the M/L system being involved. We shall consider aspects of this in more detail later. For now, this point can be illustrated by considering this Emergent Interactionist point of view as analogous with the operation of a "smart" computer terminal.

An ordinary computer terminal consists essentially of a keyboard or other input device whose sole function is to transmit and receive data from a remote computer. The remote computer does some kind of processing of the information and sends back output, it sends "decisions" back to the ordinary computer terminal which simply prints them out unaltered. The smart computer terminal, on the other hand, actually has a small computer of its own built into the terminal. Certain kinds of data may be inputed to this terminal and, rather than simply transmitting it unaltered to the remote computer, the terminal will carry out some processing on the data right there. The resulting abstractions or transformations of the input data may then be sent to the remote computer when the remote computer is ready to accept them, and/or an output, a decision, may be made right there at the smart computer terminal and activate its output printer or control devices.

Let the B system be analogous with the smart computer terminal, and the M/L system be analogous to the remote computer. A good deal of information processing from both sensory input and internal, habitual concerns is carried on by the mechanical processes of the B system alone and outputs (behaviors) made. For much of this, there may be no auto-psi connection with the "remote" computer, the M/L system, at all. Sometimes, however, the remote computer is consulted and it modifies the action of the B system, the smart computer terminal, in ways which are not predictable from a knowledge of the smart computer terminal alone. The kinds of behaviors Stanford (1974a; 1974b) has described as psi-mediated instrumental responses (PMIRs) are excellent examples of this. Given the sensory and stored information available to the person and the processing capacities of the B system, he does not have the information necessary to reach a decision to carry out a certain kind of action which will be need relevant, yet he nevertheless behaves appropriately, for the M/L system has used allo-psi to gather the needed information and then influenced B system processes by auto-psi to modify the final emergent, the person's behavior, in ways which are need relevant. In the PMIR, the auto-psi process need not actually modify the emergent of conscious experience, however; the person just does the right thing without knowing why.

I believe the tremendous complexity of the B system and the automatization of much of its action in the course of ordinary socialization offers a partial explanation for why allo-psi about external events does not work very well in our ordinary state of consciousness. The information processing activity in the B system has become habitual and continuous, and it ties up most or all of the processing capacity of the B system. In terms of possible allo-psi messages being received or allo-psi outputs being initiated (via auto-psi intermediation), this produces a very high noise level that makes it unlikely that auto-psi will be able to influence the B system or vice versa. This view is congruent with various experimental data we have that indicate that allo-psi conducive states involve cutting down internal noise levels from irrelevant B system processes. In my extended presentation of my theory that immediate feedback will help learning (Tart, 1977c), I also stress that learning to discriminate the relevant psi signals from internal B system noise is a major requirement of success.

Altered States of Consciousness

In my systems approach to understanding altered states of consciousness (Lee et al., 1975; Tart, 1974; 1975a; 1976; 1977b; 1977d; in press a; in press b), I defined a discrete altered state of consciousness (d-ASC) as a radical pattern change in the functioning of consciousness, a combination both of particular subsystems or aspects of consciousness changing as well as the consequent emergent, system properties of consciousness changing. I was careful not to bring in serious dualistic considerations there, in order not to arouse possible prejudices in the psychologist audience the theory was primarily intended for. Thus while I talked about "awareness" as constituting a kind of activating energy for affecting the operation of subsystems of consciousness, I was careful to legitimatize this usage as primarily a matter of semantic convenience, if one adopted a monistic position. For the dualistic Emergent Interactionism position I am now proposing, however, some further distinctions about the nature of altered states of consciousness can be made.

Any discrete state of consciousness (d-SoC) consists of a particular *pattern* of functioning, a system functioning both within B system and M/L system levels. The d-SoC, the experienced consciousness, is the emergent from the interaction of both of these B and M/L levels of organization. A discrete *altered* state of consciousness, a radical pattern shift, can be induced by either (1) changing the organization of subsystems of the B system alone; (2) changing the organization of subsystems of the M/L system alone; and/or (3) changing the nature of the auto-psi interactions between B and M/L system levels. In terms of observable consequences of this Emergent Interactionist understanding, some d-ASC will turn out to be explainable strictly in terms of alterations of B system functioning, but others will not be reducible simply to alterations in B system functioning.

This view that some d-ASC are primarily functions of M/L system changes or auto-psi interaction changes has important implications for parapsychological research. We have a scattering of evidence to suggest that various altered states may be conducive to psi functioning. This may be partially due to the fact that well ingrained B system habits (automatisms) that create the noise that interferes with psi functioning in our ordinary state, are no longer functioning as strongly due to changes in B system operation. It may also mean that certain d-ASC have their balance of functioning shifted more toward the M/L system side, for which psi is a direct mode of expression. Thus we might expect some important breakthroughs for enhancing allo-psi by discovering which particular d-ASC are most favorable in this way.

Ordinary Psi and Non-Ordinary Psi

Given this Emergent Interactionist view of consciousness, it becomes clear that psi is being used a large amount of the time in everyone's life, but is being used, as it were, "internally." We frequently use auto-clairvoyance to read our own B system and auto-PK to affect our B systems. This is ordinary psi, auto-psi. What we observe in parapsychological experiments, however, is non-ordinary psi, it is taking a process ordinarily confined "within" a single organism and pushing it outside, making it allo-psi. I have tried to represent the general situation in an

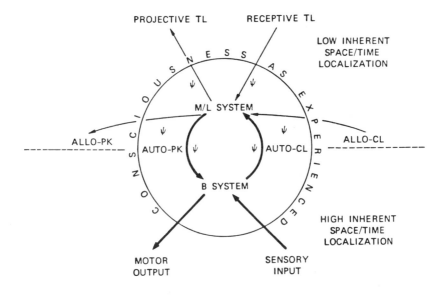

Figure 4. Psi processes within and external to the organism, from the
Emergent Interactionist point of view.

amplified model of consciousness in Figure 4. When the M/L system
reads the state of its own B system, we term this auto-clairvoyance
(auto-CL in the figure); when the M/L system influences B system
operation we term it auto-PK. The unusual use of psi outside of the
organism results in allo-clairvoyance (allo-CL) to obtain information
about the external environment, and allo-PK to affect the external
environment. This is non-B system matter to M/L system information
flow, and M/L system to non-B system information/energy flow. Communication from one distinct M/L system to another, telepathy, can be
subdivided into receptive telepathy, picking up information from
another M/L system, and projective telepathy, sending information
to another M/L system, a useful division for maintaining symmetry
with the clairvoyance and PK processes. Given our terminological
convention, telepathy is a form of allo-psi. Indeed, the fundamental
distinction seems to be with psi that deals with M/L system to M/L
system interaction, and psi that deals with matter and M/L system

interaction. There is, of course, a methodological problem in trying to observe "pure" allo-telepathy, for, if we want objective verification of it through the senses, we have to add in auto-PK to have a behavioral manifestation of the information.

On the B system side of consciousness, sensory input brings in information about the matter world around us, automatically abstracts this information along value lines and creates a continuous simulation of our environment (which we call perceiving the world). Motor output sends, though our various musculatures, information and energy back out into that matter world. I have shown the sensory input and motor output arrows, and the auto-CL and auto-PK arrows in heavy lines to represent the most prominent information flow channels ordinarily active in an organism. I have also drawn in consciousness as experienced as a circle around these other processes, to remind us that it is an emergent of B system and M/L system auto-psi interaction.

Earlier I listed precognition as one of the basic psi phenomena, but I am now inclined not to consider the temporal distinction as basic. In Figure 4 I have indicated that the M/L aspect of consciousness has a low inherent degree of localization in space and time (an idea developed further in my discussion of *trans-temporal inhibition* (Tart, 1977a; 1978)) while the B system aspect of consciousness is very highly localized in space and time. That is, the B system belongs to an order of reality in which you can specify with great confidence that a particular event is happening at a certain time, at a certain location in space and possesses highly specifiable and predictable matter and physical energy properties. The M/L system, on the other hand, is not so localized in terms of physical space/time measures. While it usually centers around the here and now of B system space and time, it is more widely spread than that (thus the need for trans-temporal inhibition in efficient ESP), and can volitionally focus at different spatial and temporal locations than the B system and its associated sensory and motor apparatus can. To be more speculative, I suspect the very diffuseness or non-localization of the M/L system has something to do with the reason that it is associated with a particular B system, for that B system acts as a stabilizing influence on the operation of the M/L system, it focuses and anchors that M/L system to a particular location and moment in space and time for evolutionary reasons. Indeed, as far as biological survival is concerned, events within the sensory range of the B system are almost always the most important ones for the organism to be concerned with, so the style of M/L system interaction with the B system would evolve toward maximizing the efficiency of the B system/consciousness for biological survival. To the extent to which this becomes habitual and automatized, this would be a reason why allo-psi seems relatively rare: the psi capacity is almost totally used up in auto-psi functioning which is geared to maximizing the functioning of the total organism in its physical environment.

Special Sensitivity of B System to Psi

The B system, from this Emergent Interactionism point of view, has two main properties. First are many self-organizing properties, independent of interaction with the M/L system, that are adaptive in dealing with the needs for maintaining homeostasis within the physical organism and dealing effectively with the physical environment. Second, it must have properties that not only make it receptive to M/L system influences via auto-PK, it should be *efficiently* receptive to these influences in order to maximize survival potential. This means semi-independent associative and decision making properties, "perceptual" properties, with respect to M/L system influences that compensate for inefficiencies and deficiencies in the interaction. The B system, for example, should automatically fill in a message from the M/L system that is a little incomplete and, in cases of doubt, fill it in along lines which are most relevant to biological survival. For example, if an ambiguous pattern seen in some bushes *could* be a tiger, it is highly adaptive for the simulation of the environment to make you perceive it as a tiger and take fast action, rather than ignore it because you aren't *sure* it's a tiger. The receptive function of the B system, then, for auto-PK, is likely to be elaborative as well as efficiently receptive, and, by being elaborative, it can be prone, like any similar communication system, to produce incorrect outputs.

This line of reasoning has two important consequences for parapsychological research. First, the B system must be especially sensitive to auto-PK, and, insofar as auto-PK and allo-PK are probably manifestations of the same fundamental process, investigation of what aspects of B system functioning make it especially sensitive to PK should be of great value in designing other physical processes which would be sensitive PK detectors. Second, not only does the M/L system need to use an appropriate allo-psi process to gather the relevant information about some distant target other than the percipient's own B system, this information must be then put into, or influence the B system of the percipient by auto-PK effects on B system functioning, in order to get relevant information into the emergent consciousness of the percipient, information which he can then express behaviorally so we can observe it. Auto-PK at least needs to affect relevant aspects of the

B system so we can observe a behavioral or physiological effect that manifests the psi information, even if it does not reach the percipient's consciousness. But, the B system is constantly producing an adaptive simulation of the percipient's immediate sensory environment (modified by his psychological concerns) in a way largely independent of current B and M/L system interactions, and this constitutes a high noise level that the auto-PK information carrying the allo-psi information must compete with. Further, the elaborative aspects of the B system's receptivity to auto-PK means that there is a strong probability that the psi message will tend to be elaborated/distorted in ways which fit the ongoing, survival-oriented simulation of the immediate physical environment being continuously constructed by the B system. The very "efficiency" and partial independence of the B system, then, automatically makes some distortion of allo-psi messages likely. Given this as a basic characteristic of the B system, practical measures to increase the incidence of psi in parapsychological experiments would need to involve some combination of B system noise reduction (as in, e.g. ganzfeld techniques), discrimination training (as in immediate feedback training), and enhanced discriminability of the allo-psi targets themselves (distinct remote locations, e.g. versus similar playing cards differing only in number).

Complexity of Psi Tasks

The B system is obviously an incredibly complex system, so auto-psi interaction with the M/L system must also be of a very complex nature. This leads to an interesting comparison: the kinds of allo-ESP and allo-PK tasks we have given percipients and agents in the laboratory have probably been enormously simple (and perhaps trivial) compared to what is routinely done by auto-clairvoyance and auto-PK. In an earlier modeling of PK along conventional lines (Tart, 1966; 1977c), for example, I argued that influencing a tumbling die by PK is quite complex, requiring continuous clairvoyant feedback about its three dimensional motion and mass-energy parameters and the surface characteristics of the surface it would bounce against, so just the right amount of PK force could be applied in just the right places and directions at just the right moments. This is, indeed, a formidable task from the viewpoint of physical mechanics as we currently conceive it, but from the point of view of an M/L system used to constantly reading and influencing enormous numbers of cells in a dynamically changing brain, the task may well be so trivial as to be hardly capable of attracting much attention! Similarly, the circuits of the electronic random number generators which have been influenced by allo-PK may also be trivially simple compared to the typical operations of auto-clairvoyance and auto-PK.

This leads me to an unusual prediction, namely, that allo-PK should work more successfully when directed toward super-complex systems, such as brains or huge computers, rather than when directed toward simple physical tasks: it's what the M/L system is used to doing, and habit is hard to break. Further, we probably can't reliably detect differences in PK efficacy for simple tasks that involve, say, influencing one versus ten decision-making elements. They are all ridiculously simple; we need to compare PK on single decision making RNGs versus those that employ millions or more of interacting decision-making elements leading to a random output.

A similar line of thinking might be applied to ESP tasks; perhaps ESP is more successful at detecting the overall *pattern* of complex elements than at picking out single elements.

Out-of-the-Body Experiences

Out-of-the-body experiences (OBEs) are especially interesting from a dualistic point of view. While there are both a wide variety of experiences and much looseness in the use of the term OBE, the basic, "classical" experience that we will consider here has two distinguishing elements. First, the experiencer finds himself located at some location other than where he knows his physical body is located. Second, and of crucial importance in definition, the experiencer knows *during* the experience that his consciousness is basically functioning in the pattern he recognizes as his ordinary state. He can call upon most or all of his ordinary cognitive abilities during the OBE, typically recognizing, e.g., the "impossibility" of his ongoing experience according to what he has been taught. As far as he can tell, he is perfectly "normal" in all mental ways that matter; it's just that he is obviously located somewhere other than where his physical body is.

Although some people manage to retrospectively talk themselves out of their experience, most people who have an OBE become confirmed dualists on an experiential basis. No matter what "logical" arguments one may make, they *know* that their consciousness is of a different nature than their physical body, because they've experienced them as separated.

As an outsider, listening to someone else's account of his OBE, we can dismiss the implications of his experience and remain convinced monists without much psychological effort. The OBE, as defined so far, can be seen as an interesting hallucination. It is like a dream in that a realistic, but hallucinatory environment is present, but obviously certain other parts of the B system responsible for ordinary consciousness are also activated. Indeed, if the experiencer would only call his experience a "lucid dream," instead of an OBE, that is, stop insisting that his experience was *real* and agree with our view that it was hallucinatory, even if it *seemed* real, he would not bother a confirmed monist. It is easy from a monistic point of view to model brain functioning that would create a lucid dream.

As defined so far, OBEs could easily be included within the domain of ordinary psychology (although they are not), for I haven't put any psi element into the definition. Indeed, it is useful to define them in purely psychological terms just to make them legitimate subjects for investigation by psychologists who might shy away from psi phenomena. But we know, of course, that in some OBEs the person accurately describes a distant location that he could not have known about except by psi, as when my Miss Z correctly read a five-digit random number on a shelf above her head (Tart, 1968).

Because of the strong psi component of some OBEs, I am inclined, from an Emergent Interactionist position, to take them as being pretty much what they seem to be, a temporary spatial/funtional separation of the M/L system from the B system. The separation is not only temporary (otherwise we wouldn't get any report!), it is probably only partial, with the M/L system still interacting with the B system to some extent. Several aspects of OBEs support this partial separation view.

First, in most OBEs the person experiences his consciousness as very like ordinary, yet ordinary consciousness arises as an emergent from B and M/L system interaction and mutual patterning. This suggests that a great deal of this interaction is still occurring, and/or that the force of habit, the lifetime practice of this patterning, is still fairly active in the M/L system alone.

Second, in cases of prolonged (more than a few minutes apparent duration) OBEs, or people who have had many OBEs, or OBEs associated with severe disruption of physical functioning as in near-death cases, consciousness as experienced tends to drift away from its ordinary patterning into various d-ASC. The OBE starts to become "ineffable," or more of a "mystical experience," even though it retains the basic feeling of separation of B and M/L systems. This is what we would expect for greatly reduced auto-psi interaction between these two systems; both the B system and the M/L system would start drifting toward unique patterns of functioning determined by their own inherent characteristics, now manifesting as they are freed from mutual, interactive patterning of each other. Indeed, it is these kinds of unusual OBEs that may give us valuable insights into what the M/L system in and of itself may be like, unpatterned by the B system.

Third, the sparse (and largely anecdotal) evidence we have on it suggests that there are few, if any, physiological changes of great consequence during *brief* OBEs. The B system functions pretty much as usual. But during temporarily prolonged OBEs, larger and potentially fatal physiological changes may begin to occur. Robert Monroe, for example, reports that his body has been quite chilled following prolonged OBEs (Monroe, 1971). I see this as showing that life and consciousness, as we know them, arise from the mutual interaction and patterning of the B and M/L systems, and when the patterning of the M/L system upon the B system begins to break down, the brain by itself cannot adequately run the complex system of the body, and small errors start to cumulate. In principle, this would eventually lead to death.

Survival

The Emergent Interactionist position allows for some kinds of potential survival of bodily death, but it would not necessarily be the kind of postmortem survival we usually conceive of. Our usual conceptions of survival mean survival of the basic pattern of our *consciousness*, our experience of our mental life, our feelings of personal identity. But consciousness, as we have seen, is an emergent of the auto-psi interactions of both the B and the M/L systems, an emergent of constant patterning of each system upon the other. If the B system ceases functioning in death, the patterning influence of the B system upon the M/L system will cease, so how is ordinary consciousness, as we know it, to survive? What is the emergent to emerge from?

One answer may be that personal identity, which is so intimately intertwined with ordinary consciousness (see my *States of Consciousness* for a discussion of this, Tart, 1975a), does not survive death, at least not for very long. The M/L system may survive, with the length of postmortem survival being determined by currently unknown characteristics of M/L systems in general, but this is survival of some *aspect* of a person, not the person. Indeed, we would expect this aspect to be quite different from the person.

This answer should be partially modified by referring back to our discussion of OBEs, where we noted that rather ordinary consciousness is frequently maintained for at least short periods in many OBEs. The customary patterning of the M/L system by the B system is thus capable, at least for short periods, of continuing to pattern the M/L system with reduced or perhaps temporarily eliminated auto-psi interaction. The patterning parameters may be stored in something analogous to ordinary "memory" in the M/L system, or the M/L system may be permanently or semi-permanently modified in its own stable pattern of functioning as a result of prolonged auto-psi interaction with the B system in its developmental history.

If B system patterning and consequent "ordinary" consciousness can manifest in the M/L system alone, at least temporarily in OBEs, then it is possible to conceive of survival of personal identity in at least some people. To the degree that a particular person's sense of identity was not strongly and permanently patterned in the M/L system *per se*, but was supported largely through environmental, bodily, and social constancies patterned in the B system, then we would expect the emergent of consciousness and personal identity to disintegrate rapidly once the B system ceased functioning. At the other extreme, if basic personal identity and consciousness patterns were strongly and permanently stored at the M/L level, for whatever reasons, such a person might withstand the loss of B system patterning influence and still maintain consciousness and personal identity patterning in the M/L system after death, thus achieving personal survival. Such intense patterning of the M/L system might arise for a variety of reasons, such as deliberate practice of meditative techniques or sheer psychological rigidity and fanaticism.

It would be premature to compare this Emergent Interactionist view with the data about mediumistic communications, as that is an area of complex phenomena strongly affected by social beliefs and experimenter/sitter biases.

What Can We Learn about the M/L System in Isolation?

As discussed earlier, we ordinarily know almost nothing about what the M/L system *per se* is like, the consciousness we experience is an emergent from the extensive interactions and mutual patternings of the B and M/L systems. Yet I believe we can learn at least some things about the properties of the M/L system in and of itself, when it is not patterned, or at least is patterned to a much lesser degree, by the B system.

The characteristics of allo-psi processes give us some clue to what the M/L system is like, so that we can generally say that the M/L system is probably capable of gathering information about and affecting at least some aspects of physical reality which are sensorily/energetically remote and shielded from the B system by either spatial shields or distances or temporal distances. That is, the M/L system can exercise allo-psi of the clairvoyant and psychokinetic type, either in real time or precognitively, and possibly postcognitively. Although there is little evidence for "pure" telepathy (where a clairvoyance interpretation of the data is completely excluded), I shall presume that the M/L system can also exercise allo-telepathy in both real time and pre- and post-cognitively.

As far as ordinary physical limits are concerned, our present knowledge of allo-psi indicates no obvious limits, but we have really only investigated a quite limited range of physical variables. There may well be limits inherent in the nature of psi that are perceptible from the point of view of the M/L system, even if not detectable from physical measures. This last point about the detectibility of limits or characteristics of psi being related to the perspective from which it is viewed, leads us to a specific proposal within a more general conceptual framework that I have written about elsewhere (Tart, 1972; 1975a; 1975b), namely the development of *state specific sciences* as a means of understanding psi.

The consciousness in which we ordinarily carry out scientific research is an emergent from auto-psi interaction between the B and M/L systems. It is not unlimited consciousness, but a specific kind of consciousness. Its characteristics and limitations are governed by the inherent properties of the B system, the inherent properties of the M/L system, the laws which govern auto-psi interaction, and the general laws of emergence which we hope to understand adequately some day through development of general systems theory. The part of all this to emphasize for our purposes is that ordinary consciousness has limitations, limitations in the way reality can be perceived, limitations in the kinds of concepts that can be generated about reality and limitations in the way such concepts can be tested.

While I believe that a great deal can be learned about psi from skillful scientific work in our ordinary state of consciousness, I suspect that important aspects of it will not be comprehensible, will remain *para*conceptual to ordinary consciousness because of these limitations. The little scientific and anecdotal knowledge we have about the range of functioning available in various d-ASC, however, suggests that there are alternative modes of consciousness, quite different emergents from B and M/L system interaction, that may yield more useful perceptions of, concepts about and tests of psi functioning. The paraconceptual aspect of psi is not saying something about any inherent perversity in the universe; it is saying something about the limitations of ordinary consciousness.

In discussing OBEs, I suggested that certain OBEs show more drastic alterations in consciousness because there is greatly reduced B and M/L interaction, so the consciousness experienced reflects M/L characteristics *per se* more than ordinary consciousness does. I have also suggested that in general some d-ASC may come about through reduced B and M/L system interaction. The state-specific sciences that could potentially be developed for these d-ASC then, including OBEs, could lead us to increased experiential and scientific knowledge about the M/L system under conditions of greatly reduced auto-psi interaction with the B system, from which we could make more accurate extrapolations to what the totally isolated M/L system would be like.

Our knowledge base is too small to warrant further speculation now about specific d-ASC and directions of development that will be useful for understanding psi, but this is the direction I ultimately see the field going in.

Summary

I have proposed the beginnings of a dualistic theory of consciousness, Emergent Interactionism, which is intended to be scientifically useful and has empirical, testable consequences. The existence of psi phenomena, which are paraconceptual for a physicalistic monism, is the basic evidence for a pragmatic dualism, a recognition of the need to understand consciousness in terms of two qualitatively different aspects of reality, what I have called the B system, the brain, body, and nervous system and the physical laws which govern it, and the M/L system, the mental and life aspects of reality. Consciousness is seen as a system property, an emergent, from the auto-psi interaction of the B and M/L systems. Ultimate understanding of consciousness, then, while it requires further and extensive development of conventional approaches in the study of brain functioning and physical law, also requires extensive development of our knowledge of psi, as well as development of general systems theory so principles of emergence in complex systems can be better understood. While this view is complex, it is more adequate to the reality of psi than a physicalistic monism, and exciting discoveries await us!

BIBLIOGRAPHY

Greeley, A., *The Sociology of the Paranormal*, Beverly Hills, CA.: Sage Publications, 1975.

Lee, P., Ornstein, R., Galin, D., Deikman, A., and Tart, C., *Symposium on Consciousness*, New York: Viking, 1975.

McMahan, E., "An experiment in pure telepathy," *Journal of Parapsychology*, 1946, *10*, 224–242.

Monroe, R., *Journeys out of the Body*, New York: Doubleday, 1971.

Stanford, R., "An experimentally testable model for spontaneous psi events. I. Extrasensory events," *Journal of the American Society for Psychical Research*, 1974, *68*, 34–57.

Stanford, R., "An experimentally testable model for spontaneous psi event. II. Psychokinetic events," *Journal of the American Society for Psychical Research*, 1974, *68*, 321–356.

Tart, C., "Models for the explanation of extrasensory perception," *International Journal of Neuropsychiatry*, 1966, *2*, 488–504.

Tart, C., "A psychophysiological study of out-of-the-body experiences in a selected subject," *Journal of the American Society for Psychical Research*, 1968, *62*, 3–27.

Tart, C., "States of consciousness and state-specific sciences," *Science*, 1972, *176*, 1203–1210.

Tart, C., "On the nature of altered states of consciousness, with special reference to parapsychological phenomena," in W. Roll, R. Morris, & J. Morris (Eds.,) *Research in Parapsychology 1973*, Metuchen, N.J.: Scarecrow Press, 1974. Pp. 163–218.

Tart, C., *States of Consciousness*, New York: Dutton, 1975. (a)

Tart, C. (Ed.,) *Transpersonal Psychologies*, New York: Harper & Row, 1975. (b)

Tart, C., "The basic nature of altered states of consciousness: A systems approach," *Journal of Transpersonal Psychology*, 1976, *8*, No. 1, 45–64.

Tart, C., "Improving real-time ESP by suppressing the future: trans-temporal inhibition," Paper, Institute of Electrical and Electronic Engineers Electro 77 meeting, New York City, 1977. (a)

Tart, C., "Drug-induced states of consciousness," in B. Wolman et al. (Eds.,) *Handbook of Parapsychology*, New York: Van Nostrand/Reinhold, 1977, Pp. 500–525. (b)

Tart, C., *Psi: Scientific Studies of the Psychic Realm*, New York: Dutton, 1977. (c)

Tart, C., "Putting the pieces together: A conceptual framework for understanding discrete states of consciousness," in N. Zinberg (Ed.,) *Alternate States of Consciousness*, New York: Free Press, 1977, Pp. 158–219. (d)

Tart, C., "Toward conscious control of psi through immediate feedback training: some considerations of internal processes," *Journal of the American Society for Psychical Research*, 1977, *71*, 375–408.

Tart, C., "Space, time, and mind," in W. Roll (Ed.,) *Research in Parapsychology 1977*, Metuchen, N.J.: Scarecrow Press, 1978, Pp. 197–249.

Tart, C., "Sex and drugs as altered states of consciousness," in K. Blum (Ed.,) *Social Meaning of Drugs: Principles of Social Pharmacology*, New York: Harper & Row, in press. (a)

Tart, C., "A systems approach to altered states of consciousness," in J. Davidson, R. Davidson, & G. Schwartz (Eds.,) *The Psychobiology of Consciousness*, New York: Plenum, in press. (b)

DISCUSSION

HONORTON: Please, Charlie, don't try to introduce another para-term. We've got too many of them already. Para-conceptual is not going to be any better than paranormal or parapsychology or any of the rest. Let's just stick with psi phenomena for the time being, until we have an adequate basis for descriptive terms.

If the natural function of psi phenomena is to provide the basis of communication back and forth between brain and mind, then we should see more consistent, more reliable evidence of psi phenomena if we're successfully able to monitor that interaction than we do in the allo-psi occurrences. It seems to me that in a series of experimental studies that are specifically designed to test the possibility that there are psi correlates of "normal functioning," if they were not to show a much more consistent and reliable level of psi functioning, then there would be something wrong with this formulation. Would you agree?

TART: I would say the possibility is there to achieve a much more reliable and consistent form of psi functioning, but I think in terms of practical aspects now. We have to consider two things, really. One is the social environment, which has a lot of pressures against psi functioning, and the other is the fact that the B system can carry out enormous amounts of activity, I think, with no reference to the M/L system. The M/L system has linked up with a kind of super-computer that can become self-programming in a lot of ways, that can run on automatic. I think we need to find training techniques to begin to cut down the noise level that comes from the automatic functioning of that B system. It's constant noise.

HONORTON: We have another point of evidence that favors this, and that is the very frequent finding in almost every area of psi research that novelty facilitates psi. If an experimenter comes up with a new idea, new stimuli, new tasks, the first result is usually quite good relative to what follows, and it may be that such initial exploratory activity is more likely to bring the M/L and B systems into contact, whereas after learning sets in, it may go on automatic, as you suggest.

TART: Yes, very much so. It's funny we've never learned the lesson never to repeat the same experiment.

BELOFF: I think that my position is very close to yours and I liked especially your whole idea of a pragmatic dualism. I think this is the kind of dualism at the moment we are all really looking for, but there are certain discrepancies between the kind of schema you adopt and the one that would be more congenial to my way of thinking. In particular, I notice that you couple together mind and life and you separate mind and consciousness. Now, of course, in traditional dualism, consciousness was always taken as the distinctive attribute of mind, and therefore I find this idea of consciousness as a sort of joint emergent property of mind and matter as something rather strange, and the idea of coupling mind and life—well, won't you sort of resuscitate vitalism? Are you going to say that the biochemical system, like the body, is somehow intrinsically different from other kinds of material structures? Or was this not part of what you mean?

TART: I'm definitely resuscitating vitalism as part of this. I've never thought of it as disreputable. Now let me make a comment on the specialized way I'm using "consciousness" here as an emergent, rather than as an inherent property, of the M/L system. The reason for this is that my work with altered states of consciousness as the basic reference for what mind must be like, is very misleading. Ordinary consciousness is a semi-arbitrary construction and can undergo enormous variations. It's just obvious to me that that is not the fundamental kind of thing that you should model the M/L system on, so I'm being very nonspecific at this point about what the characteristics of the M/L system are. But, clearly, whatever that basic thing is, it's not *simply* reflected in our ordinary consciousness.

MCGUINNESS: You're advocating a form of parallelism in which the vitalistic principle presumably is intact out there; it doesn't evolve. And then we have evolving brains and at some point these two begin to interact. Now, I'm assuming that the vitalism does not give rise to, does not generate the brain, and likewise the brain does not generate the other, so, therefore, they are independent and parallel.

TART: I don't known whether the M/L system in isolation, whatever it is, evolves or does not evolve. I'm simply saying it's qualitatively different and needs to be understood in terms of different kinds of principles. I don't want to say it's mysterious and non-understandable, but simply that the kind of principles that work so well on the B system don't account for all these aspects of the M/L system.

MCGUINNESS: Does a fly have a mind? Does a worm experience psi phenomena?

TART: I don't know, but I suspect we would find some low level psi phenomena occasionally, and of course, we have some experimental work indicating animal psi. It's a great methodological problem whether that's really animal psi or the experimenter influencing them; but I see no reason to assume that we're so incredibly special that only we have got it and other organisms haven't. There's probably a difference in amount and the kind of interactive system that's built up in its complexity.

PRIBRAM: Your M/L system, as you describe it, is no different in any way that I can imagine from what Whitehead or Wigner or David Bohm would call the "physical environment." In other words, the way they describe physics is exactly the way you have described your M/L system. To me, the M/L system is best described as holographic. In other words, your M/L system and my holographic universe are identical, if we go along with Bohm and Wigner and Whitehead.

TART: I think that's a very important point, because one assumption that's implicitly in my paper, which I now realize I didn't necessarily want to put in there, was that I've drawn an individual M/L system as totally discrete and associated with just one B system, and I'm not at all sure that we necessarily want to assume totally discrete M/L systems. They may very well be interacting in a holographic kind of way.

PRIBRAM: If that's so, the B system is the object/image universe. The way you describe it in Figure 4, for instance, the object/image has all the properties of space and time and all of that type of "objectivity." There is good evidence from neuroscience research that the M/L system also partakes of the brain system. Any time there is a sheet-like formation, as in the retina or in the cortex, there is a production of M/L properties, that is, holographic properties. I believe there is a duality between holographic and object/image reality, whereas you seem to be locked into a matter versus non-material framework. The paradigm shift that some of us are beginning to experience is a duality that's different from that between mind and matter. The physicists started it with the dematerialization of matter.

TART: Perhaps we're on a continuum here, but we're emphasizing different ends of the continuum. I'm deliberately emphasizing the part that seems less explainable. I'm saying, for instance, we will have communication events between people for which we will find no adequate explanation in terms of brain functioning.

KELLY: Well, not professing at this point to understand Dr. Pribram's theory in any detail, I certainly feel sympathy with the basic strategy of trying to assimilate the M/L system to other things that we know about. In short, I think my basic response to this is rather like my response to Eccles' theory—that it's an interesting story and it may, in fact, be something like correct, but I'm still quite dubious about the dualistic aspect of it.

I just recently started to read a book by Bergson, called *Matter and Memory*, which contains a number of things that are quite closely alike in spirit to what you are trying to do, and I think you might enjoy looking at that also. He's worked out ideas somewhat like yours in quite a detailed way, particularly with respect to memory, but to a lesser degree with respect to perception. Another thing I was struck by while listening to you was a paper given by Julian Isaacs at Utrecht. In mentioning this, I also want to underline another thing that's come out here repeatedly, that readers of these proceedings should take note of, and that is, I think we're all agreed that one very interesting and possibly productive line of work would be PK investigations using target systems that are relatively brain-like in their structure.

TART: I'm glad you're dubious, Ed, because dualistic systems usually come along with the implication that we can't understand consciousness by looking at the brain, and that is not at all the implication I would want here. If this dualism turns out to be more than just pragmatic at the moment, then its nature will be articulated much more precisely by extensive work on the brain, getting more and more precise about *exactly* what we can reduce to brain functioning, and *exactly* what we can't reduce to brain functioning.

KELLY: Yes, that was really one of the central messages.

PRIBRAM: One can have interactions between organisms and environments without being a dualist.

KELLY: I think Dr. Pribram's paper really raises in particularly acute form a question I'd like to raise. This may not be the right time, but just let me say that I, like John Beloff, found it very difficult to understand the ideas that were put forward. There are only a few places where I presently find a specific point to zero in on, and I think it raises the question whether we shouldn't try to get these papers available beforehand for the discussants. I had the same feeling about Charley's paper—there was so much to it, so complicated that I'd really like to digest it for awhile before discussing it.

SMALL: I have a question about reducing the noise in the B system in order to facilitate the psi action of the M/L system. We heard yesterday the question about a high degree of physiological arousal in conjunction with macro-PK, for example. How would you feel about that seemingly opposed finding? You did mention that this possibly has some implications for the question of survival, and since you say that you've now become an out-and-out dualist, do you see any kind of testable implications possibly emerging from this new formulation?

TART: As to the high level of activation in some macro-PK events, that's easily handled within this framework. High level of arousal, for instance, may be a convenient way of getting the B system so involved in its own processing that it gets out of the way, as it were. Or it may act as an induction technique for transition to an altered state of consciousness. There are a variety of ways you can handle that. It's not a simple thing.

Now as to the survival matter, I think the problem in most survival research so far is that the question has been put: Does consciousness survive transition to death intact? And when we have so much evidence that particular aspects of consciousness depend on B system functioning, you really wonder how in the world could it survive intact when there's no B system there. I'm not proposing simply that an M/L system patterns a B system and that's it. The B system is interacting with the M/L system and patterning it also, so that the emergent that we have for consciousness really depends on both. This makes it difficult for me to see how consciousness, as we ordinarily experience it, can survive for a prolonged period of time in the absence of a B system. The section of my paper about out-of-the-body experiences addresses this particularly. When people experience relatively brief out-of-the-body episodes, they usually indicate that their consciousness seems to be functioning in essentially the same way as it does ordinarily. This is the defining criteria I actually use for a classical out-of-the-body experience. But when these become prolonged out-of-the-body experiences, lasting an hour instead of minutes, or when they're associated with severe trauma to the B system as in near death cases, you begin to get shifts in the nature of functioning of consciousness that we, at this stage, vaguely talk about as "mystical experiences," or "ineffable" kinds of experiences. I think such experiences may well be telling us something about what the M/L system functions like when the degree of interaction with the B system is substantially reduced. The inherent pattern of the M/L system begins to show up rather than the modulated pattern ordinarily resulting from the extensive B and M/L interaction.

GRAD: On the interaction between the "L" part of your M/L system and brain, I believe that experimentally it should be possible to identify and establish relationships more easily by investigating those aspects that relate to the idea of a life energy as it effects biological processes. Some of these, such as wound healing, goiter inhibition, plant growth, enzyme action, etc., have already begun to be investigated, as have also some non-living systems, such as the infra-red spectra and surface tension of water, for example. I believe that by focusing efforts on such fundamental phenomena, a basis could then be built for a better understanding of the more complex ESP findings such as telepathy, clairvoyance, and precognition.

TART: Your work on healing is a primary reason that I emphasized the "L" part of that idea. We tend to think that vitalism was disproved long ago, but I think historically the case is more that it fell out of favor. People were told not to do the experiments and vitalistic results were ignored, and so there's been practically no experimental test.

SUBLIMINAL PERCEPTION AND PARAPSYCHOLOGY: POINTS OF CONTACT

Norman F. Dixon

While allowing that appearances may be deceptive, there do appear to be such remarkable similarities between certain parapsychological phenomena and those associated with subliminal perception that it would seem worth considering the possibility that the two sets of phenomena depend at least in part on some of the same underlying processes.

By way of examining this hypothesis, let us consider some ten paradigms which have, as their common denominator, the fact that a physical event, be it a word, a picture or the physiological substrate of a thought, occurring at a certain time and place can evoke a correlated happening, be it a gesture, a dream, a spoken word or some measurable physiological change, occurring at a different time and place, and all this without any awareness by the transmitter or the receiver, or indeed by any external observer, of the intermediate stages in this apparent communication. While all ten of these paradigms involve reception without awareness, culminating in some measurable behavioral or physiological response, nine of them have in common the fact that the causal link between the transmitting sources and the responding receiver is a definable physical stimulus. They also have in common that the overall signal/noise ratio for this stimulus is insufficient to activate cerebral processes which provide for awareness of an incoming stimulus.

The tenth paradigm is that which demonstrates what has, perhaps unjustifiably, been called extrasensory perception. It differs from the other nine in only one obvious respect—there is no known or definable physical stimulus to link events "A" outside the organism with apparently correlated events "B" inside the organism.

By way of trying to account for the data from this last paradigm let us look at the parameters of the other nine. Four of these are described at length in my book (Dixon, 1971). They may be summarized as follows:

Subliminal Determinants of Perceptual Experience

While it is axiomatic that all subjective perceptual phenomena, whether occurring in the waking or sleeping state, whether veridical or hallucinatory, must depend upon preceding preconscious processing by physiological mechanisms, a number of researches (Dixon, 1971; Somekh and Wilding, 1973; Henley and Dixon, 1974; Henley, 1975) have shown that visual or auditory stimuli, at such low energy levels as to prevent consciousness of their presence, may nevertheless influence the way in which a concurrent supraliminal stimulus is perceived. Adaptation level phenomena (e.g. the relative size of the different items in a sequence of stimulus presentations), the "happiness," "angriness," "sadness" etc., of neutral faces, visual illusions, the size/color/duration of After Images and After Effects (Anderson et al., 1970; Smith et al., 1974) visual imagery evoked by supraliminal music (Henley and Dixon, 1974), the meaning of supraliminal auditory homophones (Henley, 1976) and visual content of dreams occurring in REM sleep (Berger, 1966) have all been shown to be determined by the simultaneous presentation of visual or auditory stimuli of which the recipient remains wholly unaware.

Perhaps the most striking and extensively researched of all these effects is that embodied in the Defence Mechanism Test (DMT) developed by Kragh (1962), which, after 15 years of follow-up validation studies, is now part of the standard selection procedure for Swedish Airforce applicants. In this test, the applicants are required to reproduce (by drawing) a briefly exposed picture of a young man (the "Hero" figure). In carrying out this task, they remain unaware of the facts that, in addition to the centrally placed "hero figure," the stimulus card includes in its periphery a small picture of an "old ugly threatening male face." Though subliminal, this peripheral stimulus appears to interfere with their perception of the central figure, and this is a function of the percipient's underlying psychopathology. It is the nature of this interference which has prognostic value. To cut a long story short, those applicants who, in their drawings, demonstrate the operation of such defence mechanisms as "isolation," "denial," "condensation," etc., have been found to have significantly higher accident proneness when flying and also to be significantly more predisposed towards psychosomatic illness, than are those who remain relatively unaffected by the peripheral threatening face. Data from the DMT are, of course, closely akin to those of the Poetzl phenomena wherein unperceived parts of a perceptual display tend to emerge in subsequent dreams or associations.

One other finding from this group of studies which may have some significance for paranormal phenomena is the part played by laterality effects. In the experiment by Henley and Dixon (1974), successfully replicated by Mykel and Daves (1978), it was found that subliminal determination of auditory imagery only occurred when the supraliminal stimulus (orchestral music) was routed to the right hemisphere and the subliminal cue words to the left hemisphere.

Subliminal Determinants of Verbal Behavior

In all the foregoing experiments, subliminal effects were apparently mediated by ongoing conscious perceptual experience, as depicted in the figure.

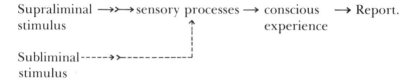

As many researchers have shown however, a conscious percept is *not* necessary for subliminal effects to occur. Words or pictures too brief, or too weak, to enter conscious experience have been found to influence verbal "guessing" behavior (Dixon 1956, 1958, 1971; Gordon, 1967; Spence and Holland, 1962), and retrieval from long term memory of previously learned material (Spence and Ehrenberg, 1964; Gordon and Spence, 1966).

In these various researches three main effects were found. First, if allowed only a limited ensemble of possible responses (as in a typical card guessing ESP experiment), subjects tend to respond with items conveyed by the subliminal stimulus (see Miller, 1939). If, however, the response ensemble is unlimited (i.e. "the first word that comes to mind"), or includes associations to the stimulus material, then subjects tend to respond with a semantic associate to the stimulus. Often this semantically related response appears to bear a symbolic relationship to the stimulus (e.g. the subliminal stimulus "Penis" evoked the response "Cheroot"). Here again, as with the first category of experiments, interesting laterality effects have been found. Thus, in a recent study, Fonagy (1977) has shown that if a subliminal word is presented to the right ear, the response tends to be a logical secondary process association (e.g. "Grass" → "green"). If, however, the same stimulus is presented to the left ear, the response tends to be of something which *looks like* the stimulus object (e.g. "Grass" → "hair" or "bed of nails," and "Arrow" → "hook" or "staple"). This implication of the right hemisphere, in evoking concrete visual symbolic responses, is interesting in the light of the widely held view that, whereas the left hemisphere is concerned with sequential logical linguistic processing, the right hemisphere involves mechanisms for parallel spatial primary processing of incoming information (Ornstein, 1977), whether this be sensory or extrasensory in origin.

Emotional Factors

Running through accounts of parapsychological phenomena is the suggestion that emotion and motivation appear to play a significant part in extrasensory perception. Here again, research on subliminal perception has produced comparable data, the most extensive being that from studies of perceptual defence (Brown, 1962; Dixon, 1971; Erdelyi, 1974). The main findings from this area of investigation may be summarized as follows:

(1) People have significantly longer (defence) or significantly shorter (vigilance) exposure duration thresholds for tachistoscopically exposed emotive material than they have for emotionally neutral stimulus items.

(2) The relationship between threshold and anxiety may be represented by an inverted "U" curve. Whereas low levels of anxiety evoked by the stimulus result in raised thresholds, high levels result in lowered thresholds.

(3) Data from several lines of research (Hardy and Legge, 1968; Broadbent and Gregory, 1967; Dorfman, 1967; Dixon and Lear, 1963; Emrich and Heineman, 1966; Worthington, 1969) suggest that perceptual defence is a sensory phenomenen and involves the following stages of pre-conscious processing: cortical registration and analysis of the input, followed by emotional classification leading to a cortico-reticular interaction whereby the cortex, in setting its own level of arousal, determines the conscious threshold for awareness of the incident stimulus.

The interaction between the motive state of the subject and the emotional connotations of the stimulus, at a completely unconscious level of cerebral processing, has been shown in various paradigms. In an experiment by Lazarus and McCleary (1951), subjects produced electrodermal responses to shock-associated nonsense syllables even when unable to report the critical stimuli. This so called subception effect has also been found in dichotic listening.

In studies of the latter phenomena (Corteen and Wood, 1972; Corteen and Dunn, 1974), subjects had to shadow (repeat back) prose on one ear while individual words, including city names that had pre-viously been associated with electric shock, were presented to the other ear. Though totally unaware of the words on the "unattended" ear, those which had been associated with shock, produced significant electrodermal responses from the subject's hand. Since the monitoring of and response to the words on the "unattended" ear did not inter-fere with the shadowing task, we must suppose that the brain is capable of simultaneously processing two independent streams of information, one above, the other below, consciousness.

Subliminal Perception and Memory

Yet another point of contact between paranormal and subliminal phenomena is in connection with memory. In both cases, it seems that ultimate responses are mediated by the brain's capacity to store in-formation. Somehow, both extrasensory transmissions *and* subliminal stimuli gain access to unconscious memory. But here again, emotion and motivation play a significant role. Researches by Spence and his colleagues (Spence and Ehrenburg, 1964; Spence and Gordon, 1967) illustrate this issue. In one study, subjects who had been food-deprived were required to learn and recall lists of words containing associates to the word "cheese." In a subsequent recall task, only those subjects who were (1) hungry, (2) had rated themselves for feelings of hunger and (3) had been presented with the subliminal word "cheese" retrieved significantly more "cheese associates" than those who had either not been hungry, or had not rated themselves for hunger, or had not re-ceived the subliminal stimulus "cheese."

In a second experiment (Spence and Gordon, 1967), involving a similar paradigm, only subjects who (1) had felt rejected by their peers, (2) were characteristically prone to indulge in oral behavior to reduce feelings of depression and (3) were presented with the subliminal word "milk," showed significantly greater recall for associates to "milk" in a memory task than did subjects who lacked any one of the preconditions for this improvement in retrieval from long term memory. A further significant and interesting result from this investigation was that the rejected, oral, "subliminal," group actually recalled associates to "milk" which had *not* figured in the memory task. Since these intrusions were of such early milk associates as "suck," "nipple," etc., Spence and Gordon concluded that the present state of need (to remove feelings of anxiety and depression) plus the subliminal stimulus "milk" served to activate a much older oral fantasy related to an early feeding situa-tion. The concatenation of factors responsible for the data from these experiments are depicted in the following flow diagram:

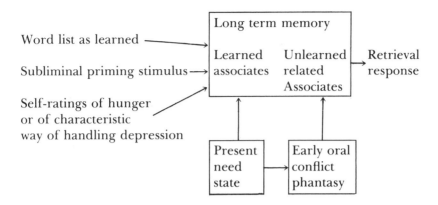

Physiological Bases of Perception without Awareness

A problem common to both sensory and extrasensory perception is the nature of those physiological processes which mediate between the external "stimulus" and the response whereby the organism indicates that he has been affected by this stimulus. In the case of telepathic communication, we simply do not know at what stage of cerebral processing the "stimulus" gains access to and hooks into the cerebral mechanisms of the recipient. A look at data from studies of subliminal perception might at least suggest some hypotheses regarding possible points of entry for the so-called extrasensory stimulus.

By way of a start, let's put together the data from three lines of research. First, there are studies by Libet et al. (1967) which involved using subdural electrodes, placed directly upon the somatosensory cortex, to record the cerebral effects of a tactile stimulus applied to the hand area of fully conscious patients who had been undergoing stereotaxic therapy for intractable pain. The principal finding from this paradigm was that a subliminal tactile stimulus applied to the hand evoked the early components of the compound evoked potential at the site of the cortical projection of the area stimulated. With increase in the peripheral stimulation two things happened, pari passu with the subject reporting consciousness of the stimulus the later components of the evoked potential appeared in the EEG record. This is probably the single most direct demonstration of the fact that consciousness of a previously subliminal stimulus depends upon coincident contribution from the ascending reticular activating system.

Other findings, pointing to the same conclusion, include Fuster's (1958) demonstration that a monkey's tachistoscopic recognition thresholds for a food-related stimulus may be modulated by concurrent stimulation of the mesencephalic reticular system. Finally, there are those studies of perceptual defence, mentioned earlier, which suggested that consciousness of a visual stimulus depends upon a preconscious semantic analysis and emotional classification at a cortical level leading to cortico-reticular interaction, which, in turn, increases or decreases cortical arousal via the fibers of the ascending reticular system.

Our second set of data having possible relevance to both subliminal and extrasensory phenomena comes from studies of neurologically caused "blind sight" (Weiskrantz and Warrington, 1974; Poppel, Held and Frost, 1973). The main conclusion from these studies is that, though cortically blind through structural damage to the CNS, these organic patients may, nevertheless, respond to visual stimuli presented in those areas of the visual field from which they receive no conscious impression. In the light of related findings by Ikeda and Wright (1974) it has been suggested that this "blind sight" is mediated by a secondary visual system involving the retina, the superior colliculus, the pulvinar and the association cortex. Whether this system, which appears to operate without giving rise to conscious experience and evidently provides for the orienting response, is implicated in other sorts of subliminal or extrasensory perception remains an interesting possibility.

Yet a third group of experiments which we need to consider are those involving unconscious registration of external stimuli in pattern-masking paradigms (Marcel and Paterson, 1976), in binocular rivalry (Walker, 1975), during fading of a stabilized image (Riggs and Whittle, 1967) and in the evoking of "K" complexes (in the EEG) by emotionally important auditory stimuli presented during sleep (Oswald, Taylor and Treisman, 1960). In all four of these paradigms not only does the brain continue to be affected by stimuli of which the mind remains unaware but, in at least two of them (pattern masking and stimulation during sleep), carries out a complex semantic analysis of the stimulus inflow. Given that the end result of subliminal perception is almost indistinguishable from extrasensory perception, namely, a purely statistical effect upon the probability matrix underlying the possible repertoire of behavioral and autonomic responses, it seems reasonable to ask at which processing stage extrasensory effects begin to occur— at the peripheral receptor, the midbrain, thalamic relays, cortex, or reticular system? If the results of extrasensory perception are likened to those of subliminal perception, then they must involve preconscious semantic analysis, emotional coding and access to long-term memory. Hence, we must assume that extrasensory effects lock into the nervous system at some stage prior to those responsible for these functions, yet capable of modulating the arousal systems of the brain. Sensory relays in the midbrain, thalamus, association cortex, or limbic system would all be possible candidates for this hypothetical mediating function. But let us look at some other factors which may be relevant to this problem, namely, those subject and situational variables which appear to be critical for subliminal perception. As to the former, the two most important appear to be arousal level and hemisphericity. Whereas numerous researches (see Dixon, 1971) have found that subliminal influences are maximal when the subject is in a relaxed state (presumably low arousal), a recent study by Sackiem (1977) has indicated that this relationship between arousal and subliminal influences is also greatest in people showing *right* hemisphericity. Subliminal effects are generally weaker in people showing left hemisphericity and in that case depend upon attentive readiness.

As to situational variables, the most striking finding to date from many researches (see Dixon, 1971) is that subliminal effects appear negatively correlated with stimulus energy. The further below threshold, the weaker or briefer the stimulus, the stronger its effect which, as we noted earlier, may be qualitatively quite different from that of a supraliminal stimulus.

Subliminal Perception, Psychosomatic Disorder and PK

There are grounds for believing (see Dixon, 1978) that the processes underlying subliminal perception phenomena in normals are closely kin to those responsible for psychosomatic conversion symptoms in those patients who quite involuntarily and unconsciously transform psychic conflict into a somatic outlet.

The following similarities between subliminal and psychosomatic phenomena are particularly relevant to this viewpoint:

(1) In both subliminal and psychosomatic phenomena the individual may remain totally unaware of cause/effect relationships, of the contingencies between stimulus and response.

(2) In both "syndromes" the stimulus makes contact with and activates complexes of emotionally charged ideas in unconscious long-term memory.

(3) In perceptual defence, as in psychosomatic disorder, the subject is prevented from experiencing negative affect. In both cases he, in a sense, trades negative affect for a somatic outlet.

(4) Both subliminal and psychosomatic disorders may involve the unconscious conversion of psychic material into a symbolic representation.

(5) In some psychosomatic disorders (e.g. asthma), a potentially threatening emotional stimulus may initiate a stress response involving the autonomic nervous system. The same holds true for subception

phenomena and in the subliminal effects demonstrated for dichotic listening (Corteen and Wood, 1972).

(6) The very close relationship between the two classes of phenomena is confirmed by the fact that subliminal stimulation has been successfully used to investigate and to ameliorate psychosomatic symptomatology (see Beech, 1959; C. Fisher, 1954; S. Fisher, 1968; Silverman, 1976; Tyrer, 1978), suggesting that identical processes may be involved in the two cases.

What possible relevance has all this to paranormal phenomena? Simply this. The psychosomatic process which seems to involve the same sort of mechanisms as underlie subliminal perception is a very special case of something that goes on in certain parapsychological demonstrations, namely, an influence of mind, of knowledge and feelings about knowledge upon matter.

Maybe a joint examination of the three sets of phenomena—the subliminal, the psychosomatic and the paranormal, may have a spin off for our comprehension of all three!

BIBLIOGRAPHY

Anderson, A., Fries, I. and Gudmund Smith, W., "Change in afterimage and spiral after-affect serials due to anxiety caused by subliminal threat," *Scan. J. Psychol.*, *11*, 7–16, 1970.

Beech, H. R., "An experimental investigation of sexual symbolism in anorexia nervosa employing a subliminal stimulation technique: preliminary report," *Psychosom. Med.*, *21*, 277–80, 1959.

Berger, R. J., "Experimental modification of dream content by meaningful verbal stimuli," *Brit. J. Psychiat.*, *109*, 722–40, 1963.

Broadbent, D. E. and Gregory, M., "Perception of emotionally toned words," *Nature*, *215*, No. 5101, 581–4, 1967.

Corteen, R. S. and Dunn, D., "Shock-associated words in a nonattended message: a test for momentary awareness," *J. Exp. Psychol.*, *102 (6)*, 1143–1144, 1974.

Corteen, R. S. and Wood, B., "Autonomic responses to shock associated words in an unattended channel," *J. Exp. Psychol.*, *94*, 308–313, 1972.

Dixon, N. F., "Symbolic associations following subliminal stimulation," *Int. J. Psychoanal.*, *37 (23)*, 159–70, 1956.

Dixon, N. F., "The effect of subliminal stimulation upon autonomic and verbal behaviour," *J. Abnorm. Soc. Psychol.*, *57 (1)*, 29–36, 1958.

Dixon, N. F., *Subliminal Perception: The Nature of a Controversy*. London: McGraw Hill, 1971.

Dixon, N. F., *Psychosomatic Disorder: A Special Case of Subliminal Perception?* John Wiley and Son (in press).

Dixon, N. F. and Lear, T. E., "Electroencephalograph correlates of threshold regulation," *Nature, London*, *198*, 870–2, 1963.

Dixon, N. F. and Lear, T. E., "Incidence of theta rhythm prior to awareness of a visual stimulus," *Nature*, *203*, 167–70, 1964.

Dorfman, D. D., "Recognition of taboo words as a function of *a priori* probability," *J. Person. and Soc. Psychol.*, *7 (1)*, 1–10, 1967.

Emrich, H. and Heinemann, L. G., "EEG bei unterschwelliger Wahrenhmung emotional bedeutsamer Wörter," *Psychol. Forsch*, *29*, 285–96, 1966.

Erdelyi, M., "A new look at the New Look," *Psych. Rev.*, *81 (1)*, 1–25, 1974.

Fisher, C., "Dreams and perception. The role of preconscious and primary modes of perception in dream formation," *J. Amer. Psychoanal. Ass.*, *2 (3)*, 389–445, 1954.

Fisher, S. "The effects of messages reported to be out of awareness upon the body boundary," *J. Nerv. Ment. Dis.*, *161 (2)*, 90–99, 1975.

Fisher, S., "Conditions affecting boundary response to messages out of awareness," *J. Nerv. Ment. Dis.*, *162 (5)*, 313–322, 1976.

Fonagy, P., "The use of subliminal stimuli in highlighting function differences between the two hemispheres," Paper given to December meeting of the Experimental Psychology Society at Birkbeck College, London, 1977.

Fuster, J. M., "Effects of stimulation of brain stem on tachistoscopic perception," *Science*, *127*, 150, 1958.

Gordon, G., "Semantic determination by subliminal verbal stimuli: A quantitative approach," Ph.D. Thesis, University of London, 1967.

Gordon, C. M. and Spence, D. P., "The facilitating effects of food set and food deprivation on responses to a subliminal food stimulus," *J. Person.*, *34*, 406–15, 1966.

Hardy, G. R. and Legge, D., "Cross-modal induction of changes in sensory thresholds," *Quart. J. Exp. Psychol.*, *20 (1)*, 20–9, 1958.

Henley, S. H. A., "Responses to homophones as a function of subliminal cues in the unattended channel," *Brit. J. Psychol.*, *67 (4)*, 559–67, 1976.

Henley, S. H. A., "Cross-modal effects of subliminal verbal stimuli," *Scand. J. Psychol.*, *16*, 30–36, 1975.

Henley, S. H. A. and Dixon, N. F., "Laterality differences in the effects of incidental stimuli upon evoked imagery," *Brit. J. Psychol.*, *65 (4)*, 529–536, 1974.

Ikeda, H. and Wright, M. J., "Is amblyopia due to inappropriate stimulation of the 'sustained' pathway during development?" *Brit. J. Opthal.*, *58*, 165–175, 1974.

Kragh, U., "Precognitive defensive organization with threatening and nonthreatening peripheral stimuli," *Scand. J. Psychol.*, *3*, 65–8, 1962.

Lazarus, R. S. and McCleary, R. A., "Autonomic discrimination without awareness: A study of subception," *Psychol. Rev.*, *58*, 113–23, 1951.

Libet, B., Alberts, W. W., Wright, E. W. and Feinstein, B., "Responses of human somato-sensory cortex to stimuli below the threshold for conscious sensation," *Science*, *158* (No. 3808) 1597–1600, 1967.

Miller, J. G., "The role of motivation in learning without awareness," *Amer. J. Psychol.*, *53*, 229–39, 1940.

Mykel, N. and Daves, W., "Emergence of unreported stimuli into imagery as a function of laterality of presentation," *Brit. J. Psychol.*, (in press), 1978.

Marcel, A. and Patterson, K., "Word recognition and production: reciprocity in clinical and normal studies," *Attention and Performance VII* J. Requin, (ed.) Lawrence Erlbaum, New Jersey, 1976.

Ornstein, R. E., *The Psychology of Consciousness*, Penguin Books, 1977.

Oswald, L., Taylor, A. M. and Treisman, M., "Discriminative responses to stimulation during human sleep," *Brain*, *83*, 440–53, 1960.

Poppel, E., Held, R. and Frost, D., "Residual visual function after brain wounds involving the central visual pathways in man," *Nature, London*, *243*, 295–296, 1973.

Riggs, L. A. and Whittle, P., "Human occipital and retinal potentials evoked by subjectively faded visual stimuli," *Vision Research*, 7, 441–51, 1967.

Sackeim, H. A., Packer, I. K. and Gur, R. C., "Hemisphericity, cognitive set and susceptibility to subliminal perception," *J. Abnorm. Psychol.*, *86(6)*, 624–630, 1977.

Silverman, L., "Psychoanalytic theory: The reports of my death are greatly exaggerated," *Amer. Psychologist.*, *31*, 621–637, 1976.

Smith, G. J. W., Sjoholm, L. and Nielzen, S., "Sensitive reactions and after-image variegation," *J. Person. Assess.*, *38 (1)*, 41–47, 1974.

Somekh, D. E. and Wilding, J. M., "Perception without awareness in a dichoptic viewing situation," *Brit. J. Psychol.*, *64 (3)*, 339–449, 1973.

Spence, D. P. and Ehrenberg, B., "Effects of oral deprivation on response to subliminal and supraliminal verbal food stimuli," *J. Abnorm. Soc. Psychol.*, *69*, 10–18, 1964.

Spence, D. P. and Gordon, C. M., "Activation and measurement of an early oral fantasy: an exploratory study," *J. Amer. Psychoanal. Ass.*, *15 (1)*, 99–129, 1967.

Spence, D. P. and Holland, B., "The restricting effects of awareness: A paradox and an explanation," *J. Abnorm. Soc. Psychol.*, *64*, 163–74, 1962.

Tyrer, P., Lee, I. and Horn, S., "Treatment of agoraphobia by subliminal and supraliminal exposure to phobic ciné film," *The Lancet*, Feb. 18th, 358–360, 1978.

Tyrer, P., Lewis, P. and Lee, I., "Effects of subliminal and supraliminal stress on symptoms of anxiety," *J. Nerv. Ment. Dis.*, *166 (2)*, 1978 (in press).

Walker, P., "The subliminal perception of movement and the 'suppression' in binocular rivalry," *Brit. J. Psychol.*, *66 (3)*, 347–356, 1975.

Weiskrantz, L., Warrington, E. K., Sanders, M. D. and Marshall, J., "Visual capacity in the hemianopic field following a restricted occipital ablation," *Brain*, *97*, 709–728, 1974.

Worthington, A. G., "Paired comparison scaling of brightness judgements: a method for the measurement of perceptual defence," *Brit. J. Psychol.*, *60 (3)*, 363–8, 1969.

DISCUSSION

BELOFF: In your talk, you cited the work on subliminal perception as raising doubts about any dualism. Now, it wasn't too clear, though, from the context, whether it was the dichotomy of conscious versus unconscious, or whether it was the dichotomy of mind versus brain, because one shouldn't automatically equate mind and consciousness. I mean, there are conceptions of mind which make it very much more comprehensive than just the aspect of consciousness that is often taken as the distinctive attribute of mind. It seems to me that if it weren't for the existence of such phenomena as ESP and PK, one would be very tempted to think of unconscious processing like subliminal perception, as the automatic physical workings of the brain and distinguish that from mentalistic processes which involve consciousness. But given that there are psi phenomena, one is faced with the very difficult problem as to what entity or source it is that produces these phenomena, and here it doesn't look very much as if brain processes, from what we know about them from brain physiology, etc., should give rise to such phenomena that they should be responsible for it, and, therefore, one looks elsewhere and one says that mind might be a source of psi phenomena as it is a source of consciousness and other things.

DIXON: I'm sorry if I misled you into thinking I'm taking an anti-dualism view. What I was trying to point out was that, if you change a purely physical relationship, the signal to noise ratio, discernible effects move from one realm into another—from cerebral to mental and conscious, and that the dichotomy that I was interested in was between purely cerebral processing (which can be explained in physiological terms) and conscious experience, which cannot. If I had only looked at subliminal perception studies and had heard of ESP, but had never studied it, I feel I could encompass parapsychological phenomena in terms of the dichotomy I'm talking about between conscious experience and unconscious processing. They share a final common path. The subject in an ESP experiment, whether he's guessing cards or describing what's going on in the mind of someone who is having a dream, is ultimately using the same physiological mechanisms as those involved in subliminal perception. Somehow, somewhere along the line psi transmission, or whatever it may be, is locking into the nervous system to produce effects comparable to those of subliminal perception. The interesting problem is, where does this occur? Is it at a sensory or motor level of processing? Preconscious or in consciousness?

BELOFF: I don't quite follow from your reply what you conceive of as responsible for this information transmission that takes place.

DIXON: The information transmission, do you mean, in telepathy?

BELOFF: Either in a PK transaction or ESP—I don't mind which, but what is it that interacts with the external world, when it doesn't seem to be the brain?

DIXON: Frankly, I don't know. You say it doesn't seem to be the brain, but I don't know any evidence to show it isn't the brain. We have an experiment now, being run by a student of mine. Neither she nor her subjects seem to be able to distinguish between effects occurring with the stimulus present or with the stimulus absent. Subliminal perception trials and ESP trials produce the same effects. As I point out in my paper, there are so many similarities between subliminal and psi effects—the laterality factor, the fact that state of relaxation appears to be a very important variable and that mild emotion and some volition appear to be common to both.

BELOFF: I entirely accept these analogies. I simply want you to admit that mind might be involved in subliminal perception as well.

PRIBRAM: The way you talk about things is reminiscent of Brentano. For him, unconscious processes were physiological and the province of brain physiologists. But consciousness is a psychological process that is separate from these physiological processes. However, Brentano has a cryptic footnote that says, "that's all true, unless Leibnitz is correct in his monadology." What I'm saying is that Leibnitz was correct in his monadology—that we have a *cortical* process which is responsible for consciousness, and this is the same position that Freud took in the "Project" where he said, "The part of the brain responsible for consciousness is cortex." All the rest of the brain, of course, deals with unconscious processes. And the Weiskrantz/Worthington experiments that you quoted bear this out. If one takes away the cortex, one no longer has self-reflective consciousness, but stimulus processing goes on reasonably well nonetheless.

DIXON: It seems to me that consciousness depends upon a relationship between the cortex and the arousal system. I find it very difficult to think that the consciousness system was physiologically or anatomically separate from the information transmission system.

BUDZYNSKI: The listening task which you mentioned reminded me of a paradigm that we're using now, which is to present very fast paced random numbers into the right ear (the speed is about two numbers per second) and have the individuals recite these numbers aloud, at the same time presenting other information in the left ear. This information is presented in such a form that it can be absorbed by the right hemisphere. In terms of what aphasics can absorb, the language is slow, redundant, concrete, lots of voice intonation. One of the things that we did with this type of paradigm is to present ten weight loss suggestions to people. Additionally there was a kind of a "hooker" which said "the back of your neck will itch." All this was presented below the conscious auditory threshold. It's loud enough to hear if you were to direct your attention to that other ear, but if you stick with the task of reciting the random numbers you're not aware consciously of that other material going in. Now, what we did when we presented this to a group of people was to count the number of scratches that people manifested and there were sixteen total scratches out of a group of twenty, twelve scratchers (some were repeaters). Afterwards I asked them how many heard a suggestion that had nothing to do with weight loss. Two people out of the twenty had, but neither one of those had scratched. Those who did scratch had not heard the suggestion and were not consciously aware of it, and yet carried out the simple task, as though they were hypnotized and had an amnesia for the suggestion. These kinds of studies are still continuing. We are now trying to affect other kinds of things, such as attitudes and belief systems, with this sort of paradigm. I was struck by the fact that it seems to me that a renewed interest in subliminal processes is very relevant at this stage.

DIXON: Well, it's nice to hear that. What's particularly intriguing about your paradigm is that the scratching response is not one people would particularly want to make.

TART: You said that you didn't see how subliminal perception could be reconciled by the dualistic view. I don't think it's reconcilable with classic dualistic views, which assume that the M/L system is involved in every conscious psychological process, but I think one of the chief points I didn't make in enough detail in my presentation was the enormous self-determination, the automatization of the B system. You don't need the M/L system involved for many psychological processes. It really is as your diagram showed, a parallel process in many instances; it's not necessarily involved. So I think they're quite reconcilable.

DIXON: They may well be, but having been reared in the tradition that one should always try and explain everything in terms of brain mechanisms, it's very difficult to accept these other views, but I'm moving in that direction particularly as we do get people who show psi results from time to time under subliminal conditions.

HONORTON: You refer to the study by Oswald, Taylor and Treisman on evoking "K" complexes. I believe there is a serious methodological flaw in that study. Several years ago, I attempted to do a parapsychological version of that experiment and ran into an article by LaVerne Johnson and Arnie Lubin in *Psychophysiology*, which clearly shows that "K" complexes cannot be considered independent. The statistical analysis that Oswald and his associates used assumed that each "K" complex was an independent event, so I think the question as to the significance of that work is somewhat in doubt.

DIXON: Yes, that's why I mentioned the Berger experiment, because there they have the third variable—the fact that the person actually reported a significant image and subsequently matched the stimulus with the accounts of the dream.

HONORTON: I think your description of the subliminal psi experiment was probably insufficient to get into the conscious recognition system of those who were not in St. Louis and heard the paper. Since you're talking about points of contact between subliminal perception and psi, I wonder if you might want to describe that study in a little more detail, for the benefit of those who were not at the St. Louis conference.

DIXON: I've been a subject in this study and I'd hoped I'd be able to bring some definitive data, but unfortunately the experimenter hasn't collected enough yet. What she does is to compare subliminal with extrasensory transmission. The subject sits in a dark room. The trial I was on also involved a ganzfeld condition, ping-pong balls over the eyes and while listening to white noise. During the trial, either a subliminal message or an ESP transmission from an experimenter in another part of the building is added to the white noise. Then a checklist is brought to the subject who has to check off what he thought were the stimuli. Neither the experimenter nor the subject knows which group the subject is in—whether he's in a subliminal group, or extrasensory group, or a control group, and obviously neither the experimenter nor the subject knows whether the particular stimulus is being presented at any one time. Half the subjects are run under the ganzfeld condition and half are run under the other condition. At the time I left London, she had significant effects under both subliminal and extrasensory conditions, but no difference between the two at all.

SMALL: I'd like to know if you can clarify this question of the threshold, because it seems to me that this is not something that is absolute, but something that is variable, adjustable according to the subject. It seems to me the only way to determine this would be statistically; that is, the threshold is that point at which the subject seems to identify a certain percentage of the stimuli correctly. If you have a point where the subject is identifying zero percent of those stimuli correctly, then how can we speak of perception in any sense? And yet if he is identifying in fact some percentage incorrectly, then how do we determine what percentage should determine what is subliminal and what is not? It seems there is bound to be some sense perception there, so how would you discriminate that? If there are parallels which seem to be emerging between paranormal processes and subliminal processes, then we should see some of the things that have been found in psi experiments, such as psi missing and decline effects, for example, emerging in subliminal experiments as well. The experiment that Dr. Budzynski was talking about seems relevant to this, but again, it seemed to be not quite really subliminal perception that we're talking about. If you can get the subject to show that he has been making use of that action in some way, that it is influencing his behavior, then you have clear evidence that he has incorporated it, otherwise it seems more like a statistical effect.

DIXON: Most studies of subliminal perception have not in fact taken the psychophysical threshold as their datum. Subliminal stimuli are usually presented two to five decibels below the lowest level at which the subject ever reported being conscious of the test stimulus. The more sophisticated studies using signal detection theory, look for changes in d' as opposed to changes in beta e.g. in perceptual defense experiments it has been shown that subliminal stimuli produce significant changes in d' rather than in β. The other criterion for the stimulus being subliminal is not in terms of measuring the threshold at all, but in terms of the fact that the person's response when he is unconscious of the stimulus is quite different (though causally related to the stimulus) from that given when the stimulus is supraliminal.

THE RIGHT HEMISPHERE:
PATHWAY TO PSI AND CREATIVITY

Jan Ehrenwald

The trail blazing split-brain researches of Sperry, Gazzaniga, Bogen, and their associates had an unexpected spin-off in the field of parapsychology. Experimental studies by Braud and Braud, Broughton and others, provided at least presumptive evidence of the part played by the right hemisphere in processing psi phenomena. On the other hand, clinical observations in patients with injuries in the left parieto-occipital region, including an older case of my own (1931), showed a striking similarity between the drawings of such patients, and the telepathic drawings obtained by Warcollier, Upton Sinclair and many others in normal subjects. The world of the patient suffering from optical agnosia and, one may add, from constructive apraxia, closely resembles the telepathic or clairvoyant percipient's impression of his target. Here, too, I stated, the impressions gained are distorted and disorganized, subject to displacement or "scatter" in the coordinates of both time and space. This apparently is the best the undamaged right hemisphere can do on its own. Thus clinical observations of this order lend added support to the conclusion that psi phenomena, lacking, as they do, the precise spatio-temporal ordering and organizing qualities characteristic of the dominant hemisphere, are processed in the "other", the right side of the brain.

Similar considerations apply to PK, the motor counterpart of telepathy, clairvoyance and related afferent psi functions. PK effects, even in the best of subjects, are not amenable to deliberate volition. They are poorly coordinated, like the associated movements of a newborn infant. On watching the films made of Nina Kulagina, Ted Serios or Uri Geller at work, one is struck by the similarity of their efforts with a paralyzed patient's attempts to move an afflicted limb. Here, too, it appears that the PK subject is lacking the fine-tuned motor controls provided by the left hemisphere, to say nothing of the modulating effects of the cerebellum and its corticothalamic and subcortical feedback loops.

However, there is another characteristic of right-hemispheric functioning that has been largely overlooked by modern neurophysiologists.
It is illustrated by the tendency of left-sided hemiplegics to develop
symptoms of *anosognosia* or Anton's syndrome, that is, imperception
of the defect involving the paralyzed or anesthetic side of the body.
In many cases the syndrome includes the loss of the sense of reality of
the patient's left side, a condition that I, somewhat loosely, described
as *hemi-depersonalization*.

Yet it should also be noted that hemi-depersonalization is, in effect,
the mirror image of the over-cathexis and exaggerated attention and
sense of reality attached to hallucinations or somatic delusions that are
associated with electric stimulation or other types of excitation of right-
hemispheric secondary projection areas. There is reason to believe that
it is the right side of the brain's poor ability at reality testing which
accounts for the apodictic certainty and unshakable conviction that is
usually attached to hallucinatory or delusional experiences. More recently, Julian Jaynes has gone so far as to attribute man's invention
of gods to the right side of the brain: "The language of men was involved with only one [the left] hemisphere in order to leave the other
free for the language of gods." On a more modest scale, Boyce Bennett
and myself suggested that the ecstatic experiences of the prophets of
the Old Testament were largely due to similar right-hemispheric
promptings and admonitions.

However, an important qualification has to be made at this point.
The arguments, both experimental and clinical, adduced so far in support of a right-hemispheric processing of psi, have one basic flaw.
As pointed out in earlier publications, they apply only to one category
of psi incidents: to spontaneous, macropsychological, emotionally
charged phenomena. Even the telepathic drawing tests mentioned
above are predicated on specific, psychodynamically meaningful inter-
personal configurations. This is still more true for psi incidents in
crises, dreams, trance conditions, in mother-child symbiosis, or in the
psychoanalytic situation, duplicating as it does the early symbiotic
relationship between parent and offspring. It is psi phenomena of this
order which Gardner Murphy referred to in his article "Extrasensory
Perception and Human Needs." The numinous quality of some such
incidents has been specifically emphasized by C. G. Jung. Broadly
speaking, most spontaneous phenomena can indeed be described as
need-determined.

This group has to be contrasted with the experimental, micropsycho-
logical card-calling tests of the Duke type. In their original form,
they were made to order in the parapsychological laboratory, using

such trivial, emotionally neutral target materials as a plus sign, a circle or a wavy line. They lacked any appreciable emotional charge or psychodynamic significance, to say nothing of Jung's numinous quality; nor do they have any apparent survival advantage.

Why, then, one may ask, should they attract the attention of a would-be participant? The fact is that, as a general rule, they do not. Our whole neurophysiological organization seems to be geared to excluding such irrelevant bits of information. And it does so for obvious reasons: the indiscriminate and unlimited influx into consciousness of impressions, both sensory and extrasensory, is wholly incompatible with the organisms' adaptation to its habitual environment. Our channels of communication would be clogged by such sensory as well as extrasensory overload; they would be deafened by noise; overwhelmed by the ceaseless barrage of inchoate messages from the past, present and future, from the here-and-now and from the far-away. F. W. H. Myers postulated the existence of a diaphragm separating the "supraliminal" from the "subliminal," designed to protect personality from what he called the "uprush from the subliminal"—including telepathy and related phenomena. In a similar vein, Henri Bergson, in an untitled Presidential Address to the English Society for Psychical Research, suggested that one of the foremost tasks of the organism is to prevent just such a contingency. Borrowing a term from modern information theory, the neural structures involved in this function have been described as the Bergsonian filter.

Today we can perhaps be more specific than were Myers or Bergson and point to four vertically organized lines of defense that are concerned with such screening functions: 1) the perceptual defenses described by such clinical psychologists as Bruner and Postman, R. W. Payne, Eysenck and many others. Payne suggests that "there is a filter mechanism which cuts out those stimuli, both internal and external, which are irrelevant to the task in hand, to allow the most efficient processing of incoming information." 2) Magoun's reticular formation in the brain stem, made up in part of efferent or descending tracts that exert a deactivating, inhibiting influence on afferent stimuli. Hernandez Peón found evidence that electric stimulation of these structures has "important inhibiting influences on incoming stimuli." 3) Békessy specifically hinted at the principle of lateral inhibition on the cortical level. More recently, Karl Pribram stressed the inhibitory potential of virtually every cortical neuron. Pribram, Dixon and others also suggested that limbic and callosal structures as well as the frontal and temporal lobes may likewise be involved in reducing excessive stimulation. 4) Sir John Eccles has noted, furthermore, that "efferent pathways from the sensory-motor cortex . . . relay and excite both post-synaptic and pre-synaptic inhibitory neurons in the cuneate nucleus" of the thalamus. Like Pribram, he too emphasized that clusters of cortical neurons in many modules of the sensory cortex are in themselves poised to inhibit the influx of stimuli which have passed the lower relay stations of the Myersian or Bergsonian filter.

I submit that it is random flaws or irregularities in the firing of such clusters of neurons which are responsible for the equally random, capricious intrusion into consciousness of ESP of the standard, card-calling type of experiments. If so, they are then processed in the right hemisphere only, but fail to be registered in the left hemisphere, the site of what Popper and Eccles dubbed that "self-conscious mind." This is why *flaw-determined* incidents usually pass unnoticed by the experimental subject. The same is true for the subliminal perceptions or sub-ceptions studied by Lazarus and MacLeary, Norman Dixon and others. By the same token, I hinted that need-determined phenomena that happen to pass through the filter show all the ambiguity and lack of precise structural organization characteristic of right-hemispheric functioning. Obviously, the left side of the brain is too busy with the serious business of adapting to the here-and-now of Euclidean or Newtonian reality to have "time" and "space" for psi.

Yet, I don't have to remind you at this point that the division of labor between the two hemispheres is by no means confined to the left brain ignoring, denying or repressing psi, while the right side is doing its best to register, process and decipher it. The left hemisphere also gives free reign to the right side to engage in dreaming, hallucinating, falling into trances and the making of myths and metaphors. We know today that it is also the source of creative expression and, above all, of musical ability, as shown by Sperry, Geschwind and Levitzky, Eccles, and their associates. The list is incomplete and still growing. It includes visuospatial analysis, holistic perception of objects, studies of prosody and gesture.

Reverting to parapsychological aspects, as early as 1903, F. W. H. Myers, and more recently, Gardner Murphy, Moriarti and Murphy, Osis and Krippner have pointed to the similarity between the predisposing and conditioning factors of psi phenomena on the one hand, and creativeness on the other. Both the artist and the psychic use the brain as an "open" system; both approach their task with positive motivation, relaxation and a tendency to mental dissociation or altered states of consciousness; and both seem to need the contributions of the left hemisphere to decode, organize or refine the material transmitted from the other side.

Indeed, creative artists have turned out to be poor card guessers. Ingo Swann, the gifted sensitive, expressionistic painter and science fiction writer, took to headlong flight from the dreary routine of statistical card-calling tests. He is credited with an IQ of 147 on the Stanford-Binet scale, but would have scored low on a Psi Q test, as it were. Mrs. Eileen Garrett submitted reluctantly to Rhine's ESP experiments. Compared with her spectacular performance as a psychic, author and all-around creative personality, her test scores were unimpressive. Moriarti and Murphy studied the relationship between creativity and ESP in normal children. Creativity ratings in those children showed no positive correlation with extrachance scores. There are more observations in the parapsychological literature pointing in the same direction.

In view of the flaw-determined origin of ESP responses of the card-calling type, such negative results can only be expected. This is also borne out by the fact that in the heroic days of the Duke experiments, Rhine's champion guessers, A. J. Linzmeyer and Hubert Pierce, showed no evidence of artistic or otherwise creative endowment. The same is true for Basil Shackleton, the champion guesser of the still controversial Soal-Goldney experiments.

On the other end of the scale are G. Schmeidler's ESP tests with brain-injured patients, or E. Shields' series with mongoloid or otherwise defective children who produced significantly higher scores than matching controls. Three mentally retarded children and adolescents to whom I called attention in previous publications belong in the same category. Little Bo and the Cambridge Boy were dyslectic, but could "read" when their mothers tried to function vicariously in their behalf. They combined a specific perceptual handicap with telepathic abilities. Ilga K., a retarded girl of nine, showed the same tendency under well-controlled experimental conditions. Though severely dyslectic, she could "read" any text which her mother was perusing while sitting in another room. Put in a capsule, in these cases, a low I.Q. was associated with a high Psi Q., as it were.

Cases of this order suggest once more that an intact right hemisphere is capable of making up, in a more or less specific way, for "minus functions" existing in corresponding areas of the left hemisphere. Idiot savants and certain child prodigies are extreme examples of the same principle.

Perhaps the most striking illustration of the right hemisphere's tendency to compensation—or to eclipsing its senior partner—is the case of Ludwig van Beethoven. On studying samples of his handwriting, I found occasional tendencies to scrambling, reversal, transposition and omission of letters or numerals, reminiscent of the writing and spelling mistakes seen in dyslectic children. He spelled *Heiglstadt* instead of *Heiligenstadt* in his celebrated *Heiligenstadt Testament*. He misspelled *mahoni* instead of *mahogony*, *alego* instead of *allegro*, and so on and so forth. The impression of dyslectic-agraphic disturbances was reinforced by the fact that the composer, one of the most creative minds of his century, was unable to do more than elementary additions and subtractions. He never learned to carry out simple divisions and multiplications. At the same time, we learn from his biographers that he was awkward and clumsy in his movements, had poor coordination and never learned to dance. He could not sharpen his pencils or cut his quills and had to call on friends to do it for him.

An irreverent neurologist may be tempted to diagnose this picture as a syndrome of subclinical dyslexia, acalculia and agraphia with a hint of constructive apraxia due to minimal brain damage in the left hemisphere. But he would be well-advised to realize that clinical appearances may be deceptive. Beethoven's functional deficits are more likely to be of developmental than neurological origin. I submit that they resulted from the rigorous training of the four- or five-year-old, grooming him to become a child prodigy, with an attending overdevelopment of the right cerebral hemisphere. Such a development testifies once more to its plasticity, its spectacular growth potential and virtually unlimited creative resources. By the same token, Beethoven's difficulties with the three R's and other shortcomings may have been due to a corresponding developmental block or arrest of the left parieto-occipital region. In short, the key toward a better understanding of his genius is not the paltry shortcomings of his left hemisphere, but the triumph of the right, conceivably aided by the intellectual discipline and the "unlimited capacity for taking pains" contributed by the left side. Eccles and Popper specifically stress the part played by the cooperation of the two hemispheres in musical expression and experience. Thus, while they concur that the primary foothold of musical ability is located in the right side of the brain, they suggest that "the left side" may be able to "sneak" over to the minor hemisphere and, with the aid of the corpus callosum, "have a look there, where the really subtle integrational, operational aspects" of musical ability are going on.

It would be tempting to speculate at this point to what extent the composer's personality problems, the cleavage between Beethoven the Hero and Beethoven the Antihero, were conditioned by the conflicting influences emanating from the two unequally endowed hemispheres. The fact is that his recurrent shifts from creativeness to dissipation; from the inspirations of genius to the fumblings of a social misfit, closely resemble what I described as *existential shifts*, associated with corresponding shifts from left hemispheric to right hemispheric functioning, and vice-versa. More recently, I also discussed the psychoanalytic aspects of Beethoven's apparent ego split; its wider implications for analytic ego psychology, for a presumed neural foothold of the autonomous Ego postulated by the Freudians, and its relation to the "self-conscious mind" by Popper and Eccles.

It would also be tempting to contrast Beethoven's right hemispheric genius with the wholly amusic, uncompromisingly pragmatic military genius of his erstwhile idol, Napoleon; or with what I described as the mediumistically inclined "mythophilic" temper of C. G. Jung, versus the distinctly "mythophobic," rationalistic temper of his great adversary, Sigmund Freud. The four could also bear comparison with the surpassing genius of Einstein, saddled as he reportedly was with relatively inferior mathematical and linguistic skills. One could point, furthermore, to Leonardo da Vinci, the Super-Jack of all trades and ambidextrous *uomo universale* of the Renaissance, who combined unmatched artistic and musical abilities with spectacular mathematical and scientific gifts. Yet while Jung went on record with detailed accounts of his mediumistic exploits and accomplishments as a charismatic healer; and while Freud made at least grudging concessions to his role as an involuntary telepathic agent, we know nothing about a genuine psi factor being involved in Beethoven's or Einstein's or Leonardo's psychohistory.

Reluctantly, one may also add to this list Adolf Hitler's evil genius, with his unmistakable psychic abilities and flashes of intuition. They, too, carry the imprints of an unusually endowed right hemisphere. But in Chapter 16 of my recent book, *The ESP Experience*, dealing with his personality, I emphasized the poor survival value, for both the individual and the group, of a mentality that has come under the exclusive sway of a right hemisphere gone berserk. The associated global breakdown of the Bergsonian filter may lead to an untrammeled "subliminal uprush" of the demonic forces in man, from trance states and ecstasies to possession and schizophrenia: "That way madness lies." It may be followed by suicide or mass suicide.

The right hemisphere, it could be stated, may well be the fount and origin of myths, dreams and metaphors; of poetry, artistic creativeness, of musical ability; it may serve as the pathway and processor of psi phenomena. But it is in dire need of the braking and balancing powers of the left side of the brain in order to keep their demonic counterparts under control. Indeed, contrary to the advocates of the esoteric, the faddist or the irrational, it is one of the paramount lessons taught by recent history that the survival of western civilization is dependent on the dispassionate reality testing and disciplined decision-making functions of the left hemisphere—and, preferably, on the harmonious cooperation between the two.

DISCUSSION

PRIBRAM: There are certain inconsistencies in this otherwise very delightful paper. The moment you say "left and right brain," everything seems to go to pieces in what you're saying. For instance, you said "left lesions of the parieto-occipital region give a psi-like picture, an optic agnosia." Well, the right hemisphere is supposed to be the hemisphere that gives us the really good spatial relationships not only two-dimensional, but three-dimensional. In other words, there is an agnosia of the picture kind with right-sided lesions whereas lesions of the left hemisphere usually give rise to alexia or some other verbal deficiency. Brenda Milner here in Montreal has documented this repeatedly with very careful testing. Her and my clinical experience and yours don't match in this one respect.

Now, you go to "paralyzed subjects act like PK subjects or patients" and try to say again that the left hemisphere lesioned patient is worse off than the right. Again, I don't know of anything in the literature or in my own experience that supports this. Left-side lesions produce right paralysis and vice versa, and there isn't much difference in the amount of skill remaining, except that of course people who are right-handed have much more skill in the right hand in the first place.

With regard to hemi-depersonalization: Norman Geschwind's recent studies show that if the parietal lesions are deep enough to invade the cingulate cortex, then depersonalization ensues. He has demonstrated the opposite to occur—a syndrome of "hyperpersonalization" from lesions of the medial structures of the temporal lobe. Now, those are lesions of limbic structures so this points to a dichotomy between the effects of lesions of the convexity and those of limbic structures.

EHRENWALD: There is a vast statistical amount of observations which show hemi-personalization—Anton's Syndrome. Imperception of defect is invariably more frequent in left-sided hemiplegia than right-sided hemiplegia. These are observations which go back forty or fifty years and include papers by my teacher, Pötzl, by French neurologists and others. More recently, some doubts have been expressed saying it is more a psychological or psychodynamic disturbance, but it is invariably associated with a physical defect, and the weight of evidence speaks in favor of a greater frequency of left-sided hemiplegia than right-sided hemiplegia.

PRIBRAM: You're saying that the sense of person is left-brained.

EHRENWALD: Yes, the left side of the brain is closer to the ego—that's my point, and I learned that from my personal, clinical experience. I also learned that recently from Eccles and Popper, who specifically look for the "self-conscious mind" in the left hemisphere.

PRIBRAM: I think we agree, then, on that point—that whatever is giving rise to this feeling of self comes at the same time as language. I'm convinced that what you're saying now is something different from what I was trying to say. The depersonalization that I was talking about has nothing to do with the self. When Geschwind says depersonalization, he means when you ignore an arm or a segment of the body, whereas what you're talking about is some kind of awareness of self as self. There's no question that the self-awareness is better articulated by the left hemisphere.

KELLY: In the first place, I'd like to underline the importance of something you mentioned earlier in your paper, and that is the importance of looking at systematic errors in these ESP processes. It's particularly in the case of errors that we gain the ability to see something of the mechanisms that underlie a performance. Beyond that, I would like to say that, in my opinion, the characteristics of errors in the case of free response situations, have not been clearly outlined. I think we've got to carry the thing beyond the level of looking at some ESP responses and looking at some brain injury drawings and perceiving similarities between them. I think we've got to do something more systematic than that, although I don't have any very concrete proposal right at the moment for how we might do it. And I would also like to point out that it is possible to do analogous things in a forced choice environment. For example, we succeeded in doing that with Bill Delmore, where we were able to show not only that he made systematic errors, but that they were like the systematic errors he made in an analogous visual task, where he was looking at slides of the target materials under bad viewing conditions. From that, we are inclined to infer that at least part of the mechanism underlying that performance was that the information was at some stage being encoded in the form of visual imagery which was rather degenerate in quality—fleeting, indistinct—so that he would make errors of identification at the secondary stage. That finding is also vaguely consistent with your left-right business. However, I also agree with Dr. Pribram that parapsychologists have so far been all too eager to jump on to this bandwagon. I think the work that we have done so far is very sketchy and indirect. One thing I think we could do to make a much more direct approach to the problem would be to do various kinds of psychophysiological studies and I think they may give us much more direct insight into these laterality matters.

The last point I'd like to make is that I don't quite understand why you make such a sharp dichotomy between the need-determined and flaw-determined. It seems to me that it would be very unlikely there would be two separate sets of mechanisms underlying these performances. I think I would be more interested in a version of your theory which would soften that distinction a good deal.

EHRENWALD: The reason why I made this distinction is in order to conceptualize two distinct possibilities, two extreme types, and, of course, in the experimental situation extreme types don't occur anymore. Originally, in the Duke experiments, there was nothing but a rigid Zener card set. But even there, it is not exclusively a merely random break through the Bergsonian filter because, even there, unbeknown to the experimenter and the subject, there was an emotional situation which caused the experimenter to get a result, even with so trivial a target as a wavy line or a cross. Even there, an emotional factor did sneak in, although originally that was not taken into account. I remember I made a few informal experiments when I let a child look at a plus sign and asked, "What do you see here?" She said, "Kisses in a letter." It shows that here, unbeknown to the experimenter, an emotional element was subliminally involved.

Nevertheless, I believe that the distinction is necessary because we have to realize that much in our mental organization is conducive to flaw-determined experiences. I don't agree, for instance, with the rigid Freudian position that in dreams every element in the manifest dream is psychodynamically determined. Some elements in a given dream cannot be resolved safely in psychodynamic terms. Some are flaw-determined due to random structure or functional inadequacies. An extreme example is an aphasic reaction. It is flaw-determined, due to an organic lesion. But at the same time, personality factors may likewise enter the clinical picture.

BELOFF: Regarding your interesting hypothesis that Beethoven's stunted development of his left hemisphere capacities might be due to his upbringing as a *Wunderkind*—I wondered whether you had found any confirmation of this in the careers of other such *Wunderkind*; particularly, one thinks of Mozart.

EHRENWALD: I wrote a paper about Mozart many years ago in which I focused on psychodynamic aspects. Yet I did not discover any indication of a specific role of the right hemisphere in his mental organization. What I found is that he had a lively correspondence with a girl cousin and that his letters to her were full of puns and scatological references. To me they seem to reflect his rebellion against his beloved, but rather straightlaced, father. Maybe musicologists could shed more light on this problem.

PRIBRAM: Scatological inhibition is usually conceived of as being frontal lobe rather than right or left hemisphere. Regarding musical ability, it is not necessarily a right hemisphere function. Composers and conductors use their left hemisphere for music as has been shown by EEG studies.

HONORTON: Your general conclusion that creativity ratings show no positive correlation with the card-guessing type of task is in conflict with the literature. The two most extensive studies of this type—one by Gertrude Schmeidler and one by myself which involved over three hundred subjects, showed significant positive relationships in card-calling tests.

EHRENWALD: Of course, I can use my argument both ways. If there is a very powerful motivation, a very successful experimenter such as you or Schmeidler, you may get emotional responses even with such trivial material as Zener cards.

HONORTON: I don't think you can have it both ways. I understand that you're a psychoanalyst, and that that is an occupational hazard.

EHRENWALD: Nature has it both ways invariably, because things are not cut and dried one way or another; as Emilio would say, "a little more and a little less of anything."

HONORTON: I think that you might want to modify that conclusion somewhat on that basis. Another point, briefly, when you refer to the work with Ilga K.—you may be more familiar with this than I am— my understanding is that she was completely unable to perform under conditions in which sensory cues were ruled out. Do you have a more complete description of those experiments?

EHRENWALD: Yes. Hans Bender repeated the experiments with Ilga K., a few years later, and found that she performed remarkably well with the mother sitting in another room or curtained off from the child, but what struck Bender was that the child seemed to perform this telepathic highwire act by mumbling the syllables synchronically, the same time that the mother was reading to herself.

HONORTON: But the curtain would not eliminate auditory cues.

EHRENWALD: The mother was not giving auditory cues. She was reading, and she moved her lips inaudibly. To my mind, this simultaneity only indicates that when the mother was reading to herself, she unconsciously pulled the strings, so to speak, telepathically or "telekinetically" in the child's mind. Thus, instead of invalidating or weakening the evidence, this is actually fortifying the statement that telepathy is ideally a simultaneous response. It is a co-sensory rather than extra-sensory response.

HONORTON: I just don't think that you should attempt to draw conclusions about psi from experiments that do not completely rule out the possibility of sensory leakage.

THE MIND-BODY PROBLEM, REALITY AND PSI

Emilio Servadio

The body is a largely alien entity even for a healthy normal person. A great many somatic processes take place, in fact, completely apart from man's immediate possibilities of control and orientation. One good example is the feeding process. Man can certainly control the quantity as well as the quality of what he eats. But once the food is ingested, the mechanisms of assimilation and digestion occur completely outside the control and the will of the conscious aspect of the mind, i.e., the Ego as immediate psychological experience. Excepting very particular cases, the Ego "submits" to them, and can only have recourse to external means and remedies if the digestive mechanisms stimulate the Ego beyond certain levels of acceptability.

The aforesaid "estrangeness" of the body vis-à-vis the Ego is, of course, sometimes total, sometimes limited, sometimes non-existent. If the average man cannot by any means accelerate or slow down his pulse-rate at will, he can have full command over some activities and innervations, such as e.g., lifting up his arms or closing his eyes. Other systems or modalities of somatic activities are, so to speak, at the limits of such possibilities; for example, the act of swallowing certain objects or rotating the arms in opposite ways simultaneously.

Up to now, I have mentioned the *conscious* Ego and its relation to the body. But there are Ego-mechanisms that are unconscious (the so-called "defense-mechanisms" for instance), and there are also unconscious processes of the mind that do not belong at all to the Ego, but to the Id. The idea that the body and its activities could be influenced by unconscious processes of the mind occurred to some people even before the inception of psychosomatic medicine. If the aforesaid influences are obnoxious or downright pathological (that is, if their outcome is a psychosomatic disorder), they can be affected and modified by purely psychological interventions, based on the main tenets of psychoanalysis. The psychoanalytic method, as it can be applied to psychosomatic disturbances, seeks first of all to obtain the emerging to the conscious level of what was before in the "dark depths" of the unconscious;

and next, the taking place of new and more convenient automatic mechanisms (e.g., digestive or respiratory), all to the subject's advantage. The aforesaid "emerging to the conscious level" is nevertheless something different from the voluntary control which one normally can exert over some bodily processes. This is why I have used the expression "new and more convenient automatic mechanisms." It would be absurd to believe that a person, submitted to psychoanalytic treatment because of some psychosomatic disorder, could thereby obtain conscious and complete control of the mind over his digestive processes or his pulse-rate!

Obviously, acknowledging that conscious or unconscious processes of the mind can influence the body, does not dispose of the problem of the Ego; not only because of the differences that exist between the Ego and the other, largely or totally unconscious, structures and dimensions of the mind, but also because we have to call upon the Ego whenever we try to throw some light upon the famous, mysterious "bridge" that links the mind to the body. Whatever the kind of psychoanalytic or psychotherapeutic treatment, the level we have to call upon and our constant point of reference is, in fact, the Ego. It is currently admitted that at least a part of the Ego of the analytic patient (i.e. the conscious and willing part of the mind) must be on the side of the therapist, and that only through the mediation of the patient's Ego is it possible to soften or to neutralize the unconscious springs whereby his organs and functions are continuously kept in a pathological condition.

Currently, it is also said that the Ego is the part of the mind that recuperates and integrates; the instrument whose mediation allows new and more convenient automatic processes to take place. But actually, this work is done—and to what extent—by *what*? For quite a long time, the Ego was thought of as a non-deductible, non-controversial, hardly definable "something." In the first era of psychoanalysis, the Ego was considered as a central and sufficiently stable point of reference—even in neurotic patients. Later on, research showed that things were different. Some investigators have continued to think, as Freud did, that the Ego is simply the result of certain modifications of the (previously totally unconscious) mind-structure, due to the impact of external stimuli. Others have gone back to the traditional concept of the Ego as an *a priori* entity. More recently, the very consistency of the Ego has been submitted to close scrutiny. Heinz Hartmann, for example, has purported that a conflict-free sphere of the Ego exists at birth. Another well-known psychoanalyst, Edward Glover, has contended that most likely the mature Ego is the result of a fusion of elements, which he calls "Ego-nuclei," that are typical of the mental structure of early infancy. But in whatever way we may consider it, can we ever say that the Ego is really and actually "autonomous"? Even admitting that Hartmann was right, could we say that a "lack of conflicts" is one and the same thing as "autonomy"? The answer must perforce be in the negative. Psychologically, it is well-known (and Freud knew it very well indeed) that in man generally, the Ego has a very limited "autonomy," so limited, that there have been and there are people who do not admit it in the least. It is also well-known that, according to Freud, the Ego is submitted to a threefold series of influences and constrictions. Two of them belong to the mind-structure: those of the Id and those of the Super-Ego. The third one is represented by external agencies. If this is true—and nowadays, nobody can seriously question such formulations on a scientific level—we are bound to ask ourselves what can be the extent of that Ego-autonomy, of which, openly or not, so many people seem to be proud.

The Ego of the average man appears, therefore, to say it bluntly, as a sort of appendix or as an underproduct of something else, if we think of its dependence on the Id, on the whole of the unconscious drives and processes of the mind, on the bodily needs, and on external reality. Looked at from a purely naturalistic view-point, the Ego reveals under scrutiny its flimsy consistency, and seems to justify the contentions of scientists like B. F. Skinner or Jacques Monod. Someone has maintained that man at large is just being presumptuous when he says "*I* love" or even "*I* am," not less than when he says "*I* am thirsty" or "*I* have dreamt." The pronoun "I," in such sentences, seems in fact to imply a "primacy" of the Ego, which simply does not exist. The maximum that can be achieved by the human Ego through natural means is a comparatively small amelioration of its dependence and subjection, such as can be obtained by a psychoanalytic treatment or other psychological or psychopharmacological or even external interventions. But loosing somewhat the chains of a prisoner is not the same thing as freeing him of his bonds!

At this point, however, we are confronted with an age-old query. Is the naturalistic approach the only valid one? Is the situation of the mind in the average man the only possible one? Several respectable traditions—philosophical, religious, or otherwise—have said and go on saying "no." In some of them, one can find teachings and technical prescriptions, which are aimed at a complete reversal of the situation, i.e. at the creation of a totally different Ego, which in the end would thereby achieve *real* autonomy and mastery in its relation with the dark side of the mind, with the body and, lastly, with reality. Such are, for instance, the indications of Yoga, of Zen, etc., in the East; of certain "spiritual exercises" or religiously-imbued practices in the West. Apart from any particular "system," let us now try to have a closer look at the main core of the aforesaid traditions.

According to the gist of many teachings, the organism with its processes, the unconscious with its drives and conflicts, etc., are the result of a "loan." They have "borrowed" their present "primacy" from an Ego that in its origin was—and potentially still is—free and unconditioned in its very essence. Such an original situation of man is reflected in all those myths that describe an earthly Paradise, a Golden Age, the "Halcyonic" days of the human kind—and, conversely, a downfall, a loss, a subsequent state of restriction and subjection (in the Christian tradition, a condemnation, due to an "original sin"; in other traditions, the inevitable consequence of an extremely slow, cosmic succession of eras or ages, of light and darkness).

The very idea of freeing the Ego from its bondages—i.e. from its submission to the body, to the unconscious part of the mind, or to reality—is felt at the same time as "dying" and as "being reborn." This is why, in many mystical and esoteric doctrines, a symbolic "passage through death" is described and prescribed. "To die," in a ritual sense, would mean to subtract from the elements of the non-Ego (body, unconscious, etc.) a "primacy" which they, in fact, have usurped: which means, "let them be extinguished, dissolved, let them die"!

If certain techniques are applied (according to a wide range of traditional doctrines), a new, positively "free" principle, comparable to the first grain of gold in the alchemist's crucible, comes into being. This principle is now called upon to proceed along a backward path. It must go through all the processes whereby the body was organized and "take back" all the powers that the body itself had "borrowed." An irradiation of the new mind-structure upon the different levels of bodily condition takes place—starting with the less "material" ones, such as preconscious or unconscious processes, up to the more material psychosomatic connections, so-called "functional" phenomena or disorders, and, lastly, the obscure and deep activity of the cells, of the tissues and of their molecular and atomic fixtures. In this way, what we called "body" becomes something quite different from the original and customary content of the term. Which means, empirically speaking, that certain premises are established vis-à-vis phenomena and manifestations, that to the man in the street (even if he were an academic scientist) would appear more or less "marvelous"—be they called parapsychological or paraphysiological occurrences, extra-normal performances, or otherwise. Ultimately, the "body" is controlled by a nonmaterial, radiant principle, and becomes its docile instrument. The reversal process is now over. The successor of the old body has been called by some the "magical body" or the "body of resurrection." An alchemist would say that the original lead has been totally transmuted into gold. If, in the common man, the mind was largely dependent on the body, in the perfect initiate the body depends on the mind, that can now mold it and use it in the same, "natural" way in which thought uses the word. Once more adopting the language of the alchemists, we might say that by now, the "dead stone" has become the "philosopher's stone."

Certain bodily or material conditions, to which the mind is usually submitted, can be diluted or dissolved, in particular cases and in some particular people, outside all control or participation of the Ego. In those cases, the forms and accompaniments of such dilutions or dissolutions have totally unpredictable duration, extension, and aspects. An external observer could only look at those aspects, describe them, find evidence for them, while the subject of the manifestation is usually their passive, often unconscious instrument. This, obviously enough, is the way (if we may call it a way) of the possessed, of the *shamans*, of our so-called mediums. The "observers" are the parapsychologists of our time. One can easily see the difference between the above mentioned, truly new, autonomous principle, and the Ego-disruptions that appear to be the premises of certain mediumistic phenomena. This difference could be metaphorically described as follows: in the first instance, we would have a person who controls a luminous energy; in the second, we would have a fellow in the dark, perceiving in a discontinuous way some flickering lights, without knowing where the light comes from, whether it is the light of the sun, or if a fire has started somewhere and is perhaps threatening to burn down his home.

I would now dare to go even further with my speculations. Up to this point, I have considered the relation between the mind and the body, and I have tried to show that, according to certain traditions, the relation itself can be completely changed and overturned. I wish now to extend my remarks to the relation between the mind and what we call reality, i.e. the "material" world.

An alchemist would probably say that, for the average man, the body is "lead," just as is any material object that his mind can perceive. In fact, such a body is itself submitted to the interplay of cells, molecules and atoms, and is unaware of the subtle laws and mechanisms of the same (laws of "chance and necessity" according to Monod). In other words, that entity which we call reality or material world is currently "external" to the mind, just as the "lead"—i.e. the body—of man-at-large. This body and the material world of reality, both belong to that "objectivity" that, according to some Eastern traditions (e.g. the *Advaita Vedanta* of India), is pure delusion or Maya. But if the newly-born Ego of the initiate can little by little modify the Maya of the body, and transform its delusional veil into a "robe of glory," one doesn't see why one could not extend this concept to the general connections between mind and matter, mind and phenomenal reality, mind and the cosmos. The reclaimed new mind is a truly autonomous, luminous center. As such, it should be capable of achieving mastery not only over the body, but also over the so-called "inert" matter, and finally, of obtaining a complete reversal of the relation between Ego and non-Ego, Ego and Reality, Principle and Phenomenon.

Such further, extreme possibilities seem to receive some evidence by certain manifestations that for many centuries have been ascribed to mystics, saints, yogis and men of power; also by the observations of modern parapsychology and paraphysics. The practical possibility of the mind exerting a direct influence over matter (the so-called PK effect) has been given innumerable demonstrations in parapsychological laboratories (not to mention the "physical phenomena" of the mediumistic seances of old). Only, as it is widely admitted, the ways and means of such "effects" are still largely unknown both to the performers and to the observers; and, needless to say, the "effects" themselves cannot be obtained at will, or according to any precise scheme or program, owing to the fact that with extremely rare exceptions, the mind of the performer has not undergone any modification or transformation whatsoever.

The aforesaid views seem to be in full accordance with Eastern as well as with Western traditions and wisdom. If one accepts them, one looks differently at phenomena such as, for instance, full control over all bodily functions (see, e.g., what some yogis can do in that respect), and, furthermore, levitation, telekinesis, walking on fire or water, modifying natural events—not to speak of certain controls over processes of the animal or of the vegetable worlds. Such phenomena cease to appear "marvels" or "miracles." They can be considered as perfectly logical consequences of a fact: the fact that the mind of the individual who produces or evokes such "marvels" is situated on and operates from, a plane completely different from what to other people—the vast majority—is the empirical, everyday reality. In a similar fashion, the customary operations of a tridimensional being would appear "marvelous" or "miraculous" to the inhabitants of a bidimensional world.

It appears quite obvious that the very concepts which we are using in our daily, scientific work, are bound to undergo a radical change if we adopt the aforesaid premises and accept their outcome. How could we talk in the same way of the mind, or of the body, or of the mind-body problem, with regard to the average man, and to somebody who would have achieved complete self-realization and enlightenment—a Buddha, a Lao-Tse, a Milarepa, a Jesus Christ?

In case these speculations may have seemed too bold for someone, I will just add a quotation from a reputed essayist and scholar, John White:

"Certain esoteric, occult and spiritual traditions claimed to have solved the mind-brain problem long ago, and parapsychology has rightly investigated them. If the rest of science will seriously investigate their general position then their further indications for research should contain useful guidelines to the nature of the cosmic interface—the meeting ground of inner and outer reality. With a new perspective, and with an acknowledgement by science that much of value to it can be learned from metaphysical domains, neuroscientists would probably learn in rapid fashion the details of how mind and brain are related. Then that very old question would be a question no longer."

BIBLIOGRAPHY

Freud, S., *The Ego and the Id*, 1922, Standard Edition of the Complete Psychological Works, Vol. XIII.
Glover, E., *The Birth of the Ego*, George Allen & Unwin Ltd., 1968.
Groddeck, G., *Das Buch vom Es*, Internationaler Psychoanalytischer Verlag, Wien, 1926.
Hartmann, H., *Ego Psychology and the Problem of Adaptation*, Imago Publishing Co., Ltd., London, 1958.
Skinner, B. F., *Science and Human Behavior*, MacMillan, New York, 1953.
Monod, J., *Le Hasard et la Nécéssité*, Editions du Seuil, Paris, 1970.
Servadio, E., *Passi sulla via iniziatica*, Edizioni Mediterranee, Roma, 1977.
White, J., "The mind-problem debate," *Psychic*, July–August, 1976.

DISCUSSION

PRIBRAM: If I had read this paper or heard it fifteen years ago, I wouldn't have had the slightest idea what you were talking about. I think that shows how powerful, to me at least, the holographic view is—that I now understand what someone like yourself is talking about. The fact that you start with Freud and can go on to this makes some good sense, if we go from Freud to Jung, for instance. Merton Gill and I wrote a book which was published in 1976 and it has been translated into Italian, so it's available in Italy. You might find it interesting to see that Freud thought of the Ego as a neurological mechanism. He built the ego of super-ego functions and Id functions—the Id functions coming from the inside of the body and super-ego being what the mother and the care-taking person adds. Ego structure is simply a network of neurons. Freud has a drawing which looks very much like a computer program with its connectivities. He spells out the conditions under which connections are made: a lowering of synaptic resistances.

SERVADIO: What is the title of the book?

PRIBRAM: *Freud's Project Reassessed.* In America, it's published by Basic Books, and in England by Hutchinson Press. I don't know who put it out in Italy.

SERVADIO: Of course, the Ego is a concept. It's not an entity, really; Freud used it conditionally.

PRIBRAM: But he gave it a very definite neuropsychological basis, so that one at least knows what he's talking about.

BELOFF: I am very interested in the conclusion you reached—that the path of enlightenment might also be the path to the production of various kinds of physical effects such as you mentioned, like meditation, etc. This is borne out to some extent by the general literature on the paranormal. I mean, there are some levitations, for example, that are associated with some persons of great spiritual training, and of course, there are numerous claims of the Indian mystics who, by no standards whatever, could be called spiritually elevated people. I'm interested to have your views on this because at the present time we have the Maharishi claiming that at the end of a few week's training you're going to be able to levitate. How far should we take seriously the idea that we should all be able to achieve this if we go through this training?

SERVADIO: Well, I hope I'm not offending anybody by saying that I don't take the Maharishi Mahesh very seriously. But I think that I pointed out in my paper that on certain occasions these phenomena occur independently of a real achievement, of a real progress. A real transformation of the Ego is part and parcel of the work of the initiate. I pointed out that the shaman or the medium sometimes can help obtain some psi phenomena. But, in my opinion, there is an enormous difference between these kind of occurrences which just come about without any particular preparation and what can happen to a true initiate. Usually, people like St. Theresa and all the yogis, maharishis, etc., in the East dislike these phenomena very much because they consider them obstacles in their path. They're not proud of them at all. Whereas, mediums are usually proud—that makes another difference between them and the other people.

SMALL: Yes, in relation to claims about levitation, it seems that something that hasn't come up and that would help us to see this in perspective, is the kind of physiological reactions that seem to go along with the transforming mystical experience you find in a lot of people— different religious conditions. You can look in the United States at the Shakers, for example, in the nineteenth century. That to me is along the same continuum. You can find it in Quakers, and revival meetings, and shamanistic healings, for example, where people will go into convulsive states. It seems to me that the Maharishi is making claims along those lines, and should be seen in the same perspective. Then, in relation to another point that I wanted to make, it seems to me that the Eastern tradition is often not fully appreciated because we tend to see a kind of introduction here of another principle. In other words, coming back to this homunculus, we spoke of something that radiates, and people, I think will feel that we're just going from one thing to another. I think that the point is, though, that in a lot of these Eastern traditions, such as Buddhist metaphysics, you can find a very clearly worked out system within which the very points you were making about the structure of the Ego, its relational quality, etc., are made. Now, we tend to see a continuum of progress, and I think this is one difference that should be pointed out between us and the Eastern tradition. The same kind of thing that LeShan points out, that we're rising upward and if we eventually attain this state, or some state, all these things are still in one continuum. In the East, there's a kind of dichotomy. So that, within our reality, these things function very well.

ROUND TABLE DISCUSSION

KELLY: I want to address a number of questions to Karl Pribram and I'd like to address them with a mildly lengthy preamble. Yesterday, I characterized my own position on the mind/body problem as being one that will, at the cost of considerable intellectual discomfort, stay as close as possible to the present majority doctrine. Therefore, unlike a number of other people here, who I think are quite prepared to make the leap to dualism, I feel greatly attracted to the *kind* of position Dr. Pribram offers apart from its specific contents, and I would love to be able to embrace it with open arms. At the same time, I must confess I feel considerable difficulty with it, which may well be due in substantial part to simple lack of understanding. I don't claim to have really grasped the theory in any depth, but I will certainly spend some time now looking into it further. I do, however, immediately feel certain kinds of discomfort.

First of all, as Dr. Pribram certainly knows and many of the rest of you probably know, there has been a history in psychology of too eager acceptance of certain kinds of technological metaphors and formal models from outside, some of which really haven't panned out very well. Things like Game Theory and Information Theory, for example, never really lived up to their advance billing in psychology. More specifically, I feel a kind of analogy here to Noam Chomsky's attitude toward Skinner's account of verbal behavior. Just to review that briefly—Chomsky argued that Skinner was attempting to analyze verbal behavior in terms of a certain kind of specific model derived from experimental work in operant conditioning. Chomsky argued that one of two things was taking place, neither of which was very satisfactory. Either on the one hand Skinner was using his experimental model literally, in which case Chomsky could show it failed to account for the relevant phenomena, or he was using it metaphorically, in which case—so what?

Now this, of course, is not a criticism of Dr. Pribram's theory. I'm merely expressing in a more particularized form the kind of general discomfort I feel. These are the questions I would like to see answered.

I certainly don't expect to have that happen in any detail here because there's just too much of it, but my general sort of vague discomfort over the last several hours has somehow mysteriously precipitated a small number of very specific doubts that I would like to address now to Dr. Pribram.

First of all, I wonder whether the theory would be extendable to handle PK-like phenomena. Secondly, I wonder if you could identify some feature of the theory that would seem to be required to account for the fact of great individual differences in ability to acquire paranormal information. It seems that something like the notion of an aperture, access to a greater or lesser portion of the holographic information, is required to account for that. I wonder if you would say something about that and whether it might be identifiable with some aspect of brain mechanism that we could look at.

And thirdly, I'd like to raise the question of the viability of this metaphor as an account of mechanisms of memory. Again, I know very little about holography, but the little I do know, derived from *Scientific American* articles and the like, suggests that it would be particularly apt as a model of storage and retrieval that would mimic, say, the properties of the laws of association. That is, retrieval of things that were physically or temporally contiguous would be rather easy to account for in this sort of model, but I think it's clear that our memory has to be much richer and stronger than that. We certainly can use stored information in a wide variety of contexts that are related in very indirect ways to the context in which they were learned, and I wondered whether the theory would be able to extend and handle things of that sort. Finally, I would just observe that the Bohm-style interpretation of physics (which means virtually nothing to me) though not *sufficient*, appears *necessary* for your interpretation of ESP events to have a chance of success.

PRIBRAM: Let me start with the less differentiated questions first. I don't think Game Theory and Information Theory were as bad for psychology as you may think. Ross Ashby once made the point that although Information Theory won't answer your questions, it allows the questions to be phrased in a much more precise way. I think originally we were very naive in the way we used Information Theory in our experiments. In one of mine, stimulus Sampling Theory turned out to be more useful than Information Theory. On the other hand, I've had some very good luck with Game Theory in a specific experiment. So I believe these theoretical approaches have not been as fruitless as all that. It's just that our expectations were too high. Just as in the brain hemisphere approach. I'm quite sure the hemispheres are very different in many of the respects that have been talked about here, but when one goes overboard and tries to prove that hemispheric differences explain everything, then the difficulties arise.

The same applies to holographic theory. When I started out, the holographic theory for me, was a metaphor. I turned that into an analogy very quickly by suggesting an experimental data base for it, and then over the years additional data have gradually made a precise model of it. The model deals with a network of graded potentials that I call a micro-structure in the brain. I'm now talking in mathematical specifics, which can be tested at the neural level, and no longer in terms of metaphor.

Now, as for your three specific questions. The first two I'm not going to be able to do very much with. PK phenomena I have thought about only in the context of this conference. As I've said, the closest thing that I've come to is that the motor cortex encodes a representation of the environment, and we, of course, act on the environment to make it a representation of us. The reason I can ride a bicycle is that it encodes something I can do, so there is some kind of reciprocity between motor cortical function and environmental function. Some of the things that were said at this conference, therefore, don't sound too wild if we once accept the fact that the skin is only an arbitrary boundary. Further, I think that the holographic hypothesis gets us into a ball park where one can conceive of the things that are being said here, but I have no specific mechanism to handle PK *per se*.

As I noted earlier—the holographic hypothesis or model is limited in its application. In many ways it's like the random access memory of a computer. The memory storage system of the computer doesn't help very much unless there are programs to address it. The only difference between a holographic brain store and a computer store is that the brain store is content addressable instead of location addressable. In a sense, the holographic store is what Chomsky calls "deep structure." Now we're dealing with a central memory process that has to be accessed by some kind of a program. Access is much more of parallel process than it is in our serial computers. Equations that produce holograms are called spread functions because information becomes distributed. The distributed, dismembered store has to be remembered. There is much more to brain function than just its holographic aspect.

For instance, you mentioned an aperture-kind of mechanism. This is intriguing. The limbic system and the basal ganglia might well control the band-width within which we process information. If we're operating in the frequency (holographic) domain, band-width would accomplish what you envision.

KELLY: The essential thing then is that the form of storage and the processing mechanisms that operate on that storage, you see as being separated, so that the capacities of the retrieval system would not be restricted to these relatively elementary properties of holograms.

PRIBRAM: Holograms don't have to be optical.

TART: I'd like to bring up for discussion a phenomenon which is either very difficult to reconcile in terms of brain functioning or which may fit very readily into Dr. Pribram's holographic model. I'm not sure which, but I'd like to get some comment on it. This is one aspect of what's frequently reported in "near death" experiences—the review of one's life; the feeling that all of one's life is remembered. For some people, judging from their reports, this is a metaphorical kind of statement about some important scenes flashing before them, but some of these people insist that in this near death experience, *all* of life is literally re-experienced.

One obvious way to deal with this is to say the experiencers are hallucinating, their brain is in a terrible shape and you don't have to believe a word of it, but I'd rather not throw out the experience. Now, if the experience is happening pretty much as described, it clearly is not happening in ordinary brain process time. Synapses cannot fire that fast, by many orders of magnitude. Moody gives a rather excellent example of someone "inducing" the near-death experience (if we can speak that way) by falling off a building and going "splatt" in a parking lot. He reported finding himself in the air, seeing people starting to run toward his body, then going into this near-death experience, re-experiencing his whole life, finding himself once again looking down on his body and observing that people have gotten only a couple of feet closer in the time during which he's reviewed his whole life!

Now, this is obviously incredibly fast—many orders of magnitude faster than ordinary processes. Does anyone have any light to throw on this?

PRIBRAM: Synapses don't fire, by the way. They operate only by way of graded potentials—the microstructure I was talking about—local circuit neurons don't fire at all—their potentials wax and wane.

With regard to your question: when a memory store is addressed simultaneously by a parallel process almost instantaneous correlations and other computations are achieved.

BELOFF: My reaction, very often, when I encounter some brand new theory of mind such as yours, is to ask myself, not so much, what does it explain, as what does it exclude? Searching around for one thing that it might perhaps exclude and which could therefore serve as a test of the theory, it occurs to me that survival in any form would come into this category. Once the brain is wiped out, the holograph is wiped out, and there can be no existing entity of any kind to survive. I wonder, therefore, whether, in the true spirit of science, you are a keen promoter of survival research, if only to see whether anything could come of it?

PRIBRAM: First of all, I do *not* have a general explanation for everything. *Let's get that very, very straight!* You're misinterpreting! I just got through saying that the holographic theory doesn't explain brain function without recourse to a computer analogy: programming is necessary for retrieval. With the holographic hypothesis I have provided a previously missing link, and *that is all*. Now, as far as survival is concerned, yes, the holographic theory does have something to do with this. I have said that in the frequency domain there is no time and space. To survive means something only in time. What then can be meant by survival? It is an inappropriate question for this domain.

BELOFF: I'm afraid I'm completely at sea here. I mean, one day you're going to die. Whether it's in time or in space or not, one day you're going to die. Now, can you conceive, the day after your funeral, of having any kind of experiences, trying to contact people, etc.?

PRIBRAM: I wish I were just at sea. I'm in a hologram. It's worse! It's so difficult for us to imagine what this kind of universe, this level of reality, is all about. There are no objects in it, there are only monads. We exist in terms of the whole. There isn't anything like "my dying," because there's no such thing as "me" in this domain. You have to get back to our ordinary domain to talk about me and dying. I've never understood what mystics were talking about until now. Now I realize they're talking about "nothing," but nothing is "no thing" not necessarily emptiness. It's an entirely different domain. It requires a metamorphosis in our thinking. The questions you're asking are about the ordinary domain, and they're very good questions, and I'd like to know the answers, but I don't know them. But in the holographic domain, these questions just don't make sense.

BUDZYNSKI: One thing in Dimond and Beaumont that I recall, reflecting on your comment, Charlie, was about the business of the near death experience and everything being read out all at once, as it were. They found that the right hemisphere apparently processes material in parallel much better than does the left, which likes to have things come in sequentially.

In another experiment they mention in that book, it was found that, if they give the left hemisphere and the right hemisphere vigilance tasks to perform separately, by flashing things in the left visual field or the right visual field, eventually the left hemisphere begins to fatigue. It begins to increase in errors. On the other hand, the right hemisphere does not seem to increase in its errors. It starts at a higher error rate and then continues through at the same rate. They ran the subjects for about eighty minutes, and they did not show a decrease in right hemisphere ability. What they concluded was that the right hemisphere acts as a backup computer in vigilance, so as the left drops off, the right is still there tracking along although at a lower vigilance level. Now, if a person is close to death, arousal level is decreasing in the cortex, and possibly the left hemisphere could lose its functioning ability at a faster rate than the right. The right is now released of its inhibition by the left. Perhaps there is some ability at that point to read out, in very fast time, the storage of a lot of visual imagery memories, since it does things parallel as opposed to sequentially.

EHRENWALD: What I have to say about out-of-the-body experiences, takes us very much up into the air. I think the problem has three aspects. The first aspect is the physiological correlate of the experience. That has been discussed before. I brought it up yesterday and tried to talk about it in purely clinical and neuro-pathological terms. Another aspect is the speeding up of the experiences during the moments preceding death. They, too, as Dr. Pribram explained, can very well be interpreted in neurophysiological terms. But there is a third aspect. It is the question of whether there is a veridical element involved in the out-of-the-body experience. Now, I submit that to the extent that there is a veridical experience involved it is much the same as that seen in various altered states of consciousness anywhere. It is in no way different from veridical experiences under trance conditions or under the influence of LSD, or some major traumatic or crisis experiences. But to my mind this has nothing to do with survival. It is true that some people who have gone through such experiences tend to misinterpret or embellish them and use them as evidence of survival. In order to understand such claims, we have to go beyond a purely physiological approach and look at psychodynamic aspects. Viewed in this light, the whole out-of-the-body experience appears as an heroic attempt at denying death. In fact, most cases that have come to my attention are subjects whose first experience along these lines occurred following a surgical operation or some other mental or physical stressful situation. For instance, Robert Monroe had his first out-of-the-body experience in the wake of an anxiety attack. He went into a panic when he had the fantasy that a "whiskered man" was lying next to him in bed. In the end he realized that it was in fact his alter ego or double.

Experiences of this order make people feel that they had a brush with death. But what actually happens is that they come back from a harrowing traumatic experience and may be elated to find themselves restored to life again. Some of you may have had similar feelings of elation following a migraine attack.

DIXON: I would like to take up the point you raised, regarding what appears to be a whole memory for past events in life that occurs in a crisis. I'm reminded of a recent paper by Weiskrantz on people who were suffering from organic memory disorders. I think an interesting point is not that these people can't retrieve, but that they suffer an intrusion of a whole lot of irrelevant material. He likens this to the same sort of thing that occurs in some cases of schizophrenia. But this raises another point—namely, the apparent exaltation of consciousness in the minds of many of us. It always seems to me (following the thinking of Spence and his colleagues in New York) that in fact in some ways consciousness is rather inefficient as reflected, for example, in what Spence has called the restricting effects of awareness. Now one consequence of this is the change in time sense with altered states of consciousness. Take, for example, the nitrous oxide experience which is rather like your "memory before death." You go to the dentist and are under for a few seconds while they remove teeth, yet during these few seconds you have a long dream which is full of material and almost your whole life passes before your eyes. I'd be interested to hear your comments on this.

TART: I'd like to make a brief reply to that. Time, as we ordinarily think of it, is a psychological *construction* which we have reified into an absolute concept that we think has to do with the world. But it's clear from the variations of experience that can occur in altered states that there's a lot of ways time can be constructed, and I'm very suspicious of ordinary physical time as the measure of any kind of absolute time. I've further been driven to that position by looking at the data on precognition and realizing that there are times when the mind can do what is para-temporal in terms of our ordinary conceptual systems. It makes no sense and yet it does happen.

As far as consciousness being a burden is concerned, I don't know. I've gotten more pessimistic lately, and I think consciousness is largely a trivial reflection of conditioned processes in a lot of cases. But I still have faith that consciousness can be an extremely important mediating variable when used as more than simply a trivial reflection of relatively automatic processes. Consciousness, in a sense, is almost a luxury. It's a rather passive mechanism for things that can be understood in a very behavioristic, neurophysiological kind of way ordinarily. But I see a more important role for it, one that gets back to seeing the more primary effects of the M/L system rather than strictly its emergence into consciousness. I don't really have time to go into this here.

UNIDENTIFIED VOICE: To put it very simply and crudely—and you're getting nearer to what I feel about it—I feel if there is some evolutionary purpose in consciousness, it is purely to provide us with a highly spurious and often deceiving form of positive reinforcement. There are conscious experiences that are pleasurable—humor is a very good example—and it makes us repeat that particular action, but so many complex, high level skills are not just ones that run off automatically, parts of your M/L system, but real creativity occurs in moments of unconsciousness. I mean, I'm sure you, in your work, must have experienced these, and I am sure Karl has had the same thing. His whole hologram theory might well have occurred during periods of total unconsciousness or in deep sleep, and this, you know, is a well-documented phenomenon.

TART: Well, to return that to a right-brain approach, if I offered you a drug right now that would obliterate your consciousness for the rest of your life but allow you to continue functioning, would you take it?

PRIBRAM: A clarification question here. Do you mean by "consciousness," "self-consciousness," or simply being able to respond? In other words, when I'm driving a car and stopping at lights, and talking to somebody about parapsychology, would you say driving the car is a conscious process? It could well be that when you're driving a car and talking to somebody next to you, it's your unconscious—not necessarily in the Freudian sense—which is doing all the work and all the thinking and being extremely creative. I believe there are descriptions of people who are just about to have a serious motor accident doing the right thing automatically. Afterwards they're amazed they were able to do it, and if they'd been self-conscious at the time, they'd probably have come unstuck. So what you are referring to is self-reflective consciousness.

TART: I'd make the distinction between simple and self conscious-ness also. But when I speak of consciousness as an emergent, I'm including both. Consciousness which is not very self-reflective as ordinarily experienced comes as an emergent of the B and M/L system.

Self-consciousness is a further development which may or may not be a handicap. As to your motor car accident cases, we have a biased sample from those who survived.

DIXON: Karl, could you please say more about the analogy you drew between a hologram and a Gestalt isomorphism.

PRIBRAM: What I said specifically was that if there is a hologram in the brain and if isomorphism is true, then we begin to look to see if there is one out there as well.

DIXON: But one of the implications that follows from this, surely, if I understand you rightly, is that there is a holographic correlate in the brain of the external world, which is very like the Gestalt we're talking about here. Now, what seems to me to be paradoxical here is that Lashley himself did experiments to show that this type of distribution within the brain did not occur. I've always assumed that this was a valid experiment. The question I wanted to ask you is, are there equivalent experiments that have been done or would be done to test your theory; are there particular perturbations that we would predict would destroy a hologram? This would seem to be a crucial test of your hypothesis.

HONORTON: I was slightly disturbed, Karl, by your reaction to John Beloff, because I think you set us up yesterday to expect more than you were able to deliver today and if you hadn't done that, we wouldn't have had such high expectations. It seems to me that your paper is more of a tutorial, perhaps, than a "progress report on a scientific understanding of paranormal phenomena." Whenever questions were given to you concerning the application of this to psi phenomena, you have had no comment in terms of how this theory specifically relates to what we here are primarily interested in, which is advancing an understanding of these phenomena in a way that allows for experimental study. At the present time, it seems to me that the kind of responses you're giving us are very similar to what we would get from a guru who is proposing what, I gather, you consider to be in some ways a similar type of proposition, but which at the present time, at least, seems not to have any clearly defined empirical consequences for parapsychology. If I'm wrong, I wish you'd correct me.

PRIBRAM: In reply, I would say you're wrong in the sense that by scientific understanding, I mean, not a statistical base, but a base of understanding of possibilities for a phenomenon to occur. That's what I mean by an understanding. As George Miller once said, "The reason we want a good theory is so that we *don't* have to do any more experiments."

HONORTON: Then how do you go about deciding whether you're going to accept or reject a particular theoretical proposition?

PRIBRAM: There's only one criterion. The same criterion you use when looking at a painting—elegance.

HONORTON: Well, then we should abandon this and call ourselves philosophers.

PRIBRAM: No, I don't agree with that. Elegance in *science* has to have some *practical* outcome. We do have to be able to test in science. George Miller's statement was made merely to point out that testing and data gathering *per se* is not *all* that science is about.

HONORTON: Then it has to have empirical consequences.

PRIBRAM: Of course; I gave you a large number of them with regard to the holographic theory.

HONORTON: Not in our area, though. Not in parapsychology.

PRIBRAM: You don't have an "area."

HONORTON: I beg your pardon?

PRIBRAM: You see, what you're trying to do is to hang on to a conceptual frame that separates an area which in another frame does not exist. I don't think paranormal phenomena are that different from any other phenomena that scientists address. I don't think there is an area called "paranormal." Mystics, humanists and scientists are all in the same boat studying *experiences*. No one is going to obtain scientific understanding of experience, normal or "paranormal," by simply trying to prove that it exists.

HONORTON: I agree, but I don't see that what you are proposing is helping me as a researcher right now. That's my only point.

PRIBRAM: I think that, if you can make that transformation into thinking in the holographic domain, certain questions will be asked in a very different way. It will sharpen the way questions are being asked. It's how you ask the question, as I said about information theory.

HONORTON: O.K. I wanted to ask Tom about the current status of the Miller/DiCara replication problem. Is there an explanation of that? Is it working again? Is it not working? What's the story?

BUDZYNSKI: The last I heard, it was working, but not as well as DiCara had presented it. The answer to your question, "Why doesn't it work as well?" is still a mystery. There are a number of variables that have not been able to be replicated, such as the exact kind of curare drug that was used. The company that made it went out of business. The early respirators were fairly poor. It's now known that the animals were probably in a state of hyper-arousal or sympathetic drive at the time that they were being respirated. So you were starting from a high arousal point, and in some cases asking the animals to decrease certain autonomic responses which they, of course, would find it easy to do, since, in a sense, they were already at a ceiling point and could easily drop down. They were probably in a state of acute discomfort with their stomachs being dilated in certain instances because the respirators didn't work the way they were supposed to. Barry Dworkin came over from Oxford, I believe, and succeeded in generating a better preparation—that is, a rat that will live for eleven days rather than four hours under repeated curare, but as I understand it (I haven't seen anything in print yet) though they did get some results, they still have never come back to the level of results that were reported by Miller and DiCara originally.

ANGOFF: The end is at hand. We have ranged far in the realms of psi and consciousness, and yet, to paraphrase a famous line, "Oh, that a man might know the end of the business of these two days." This we have not achieved, but surely we have here made important explorations. The accounts of these explorations, I again remind you, have been recorded and will appear in book form. After you have had an opportunity to review your contributions, and with your cooperation, a book will result within eight or ten months, and it will reach the larger audience of your colleagues, of scientists everywhere. The Parapsychology Foundation thanks you for your efforts, for your participation in the meetings of these two days.

Ladies and gentlemen, this concludes the Twenty-Seventh Annual International Conference of the Parapsychology Foundation.